Simon Majumdar

Eat My Globe

One Year to Go Everywhere and Eat Everything

Free Press
New York
London
Toronto
Sydney

*f*P

FREE PRESS
A Division of Simon & Schuster, Inc.
1230 Avenue of the Americas
New York, NY 10020

First Free Press hardcover edition May 2009

FREE PRESS and colophon are trademarks of Simon & Schuster, Inc.

For information about special discounts for bulk purchases, please contact Simon
& Schuster Special Sales at 1-800-456-6798 or business@simonandschuster.com

Designed by C. Linda Dingler

Manufactured in the United States of America

10 9 8 7 6 5 4 3 2 1

Library of Congress Cataloging-in-Publication Data

Majumdar, Simon.
Eat my globe : one year to go everywhere and eat everything / Simon
Majumdar. —1st ed.
p. cm.
1. Gastronomy—Anecdotes. 2. Tourism and gastronomy—Anecdotes.
3. Food habits—Anecdotes. 4. Cookery, International—Anecdotes. I.
Title.
TX631.M333 2009
641'.013—dc22
2008048708

ISBN-13: 978-1-4165-7602-0
ISBN-10:   1-4165-7602-9

To my father, Pratip Majumdar,
for his constancy
and to my mother, Gwen Majumdar,
for, well, just about everything. Her yogurt chicken is the one dish
I crave more than any other and know that I shall never eat again.

CONTENTS

PART III: UNITED STATES, MEXICO, ARGENTINA, BRAZIL, U.S. WEST COAST, SCOTLAND, MUNICH, AND ICELAND

PART IV: THAILAND, MALAYSIA, VIETNAM, PHILIPPINES, AND INDIA

PART V: SOUTH AFRICA, MOZAMBIQUE, SENEGAL, MOROCCO, SPAIN, TURKEY, AND ITALY

Eat My Globe

INTRODUCTION

Close your eyes and imagine that you are sitting in a small bar in Andalucia, Spain.

In front of you, a grumpy-looking man in a an ill-fitting white dinner jacket is wielding a long, sharp knife and taking small, thin slices from an Iberico ham that he has locked into a weathered stand. The legs of many pigs have given their all upon this stand.

As he slices, he places each piece of the deeply flavored meat onto a large plate in concentric circles, like the petals of a flower. Like yours, his attention is on the ham, and only the ham. It is as if nothing else on this earth matters and it doesn't. This is, after all, the greatest single item of food on the face of the planet. Forget your truffles and caviar. If you want proof of the existence of God that does not involve Natalie Portman doing something unsavory for your pleasure, this is it.

When, after what seems like an eternity, he has finished his cutting, he places a few fried almonds in the center of the plate and slides it towards you.

Next to the plate, he places a small glass, a copita, which he fills close to the brim with a buttery-colored Manzanilla sherry whose saltiness you know will be the perfect foil for the richness of the ham and its creamy fat flavored with the acorns upon which the pig has fed before giving up its life for your pleasure.

Your mouth salivates at the prospect. You reach towards the plate, your fingers aiming for the choicest morsel.

Suddenly, your hand is brushed aside and you are brought back to reality by the words "Oi, lardy, me first" as another hand, that of an older sibling, claims dibs on the prime piece.

Welcome to my world. A world where food is everything, but the right order of the family hierarchy comes first.

I was probably five years old, or even maybe a little younger, when I first learned the natural order of things.

There was nothing unusual in the fact that, when my parents went out for the evening, they put the oldest of their children, my brother Robin, in charge for the night. There was not even anything particularly out of the ordinary in the fact that he took the opportunity to make his fellow siblings' lives miserable that night by torturing us. That's what older brothers do.

He was very good at it. I have blocked much of the horror from my mind but I do recall many hours locked in the downstairs bathroom because I had transgressed some unwritten law that only Robin seemed to understand.

On this particular evening, however, Robin decided to declare himself a god, the Lord High Ruler of 20 Broom Lane, Rotherham, South Yorkshire, and took upon himself the title of—wait for it—the Great Salami. My older sister, Auriel, my younger brother, Jeremy, and I were forced to crawl along the floor on our bellies paying obeisance to him with the words "Oh, Salami."

Ah, the Great Salami. You see, even then, it was all about food.

To say that our family was obsessed with what we ate would be like saying that J. K. Rowling is comfortably off. Food was not just fuel to keep the plump bodies of the Majumdar clan going. It was the very essence of who we were and, indeed, are, and that passion has remained the focus of our every waking moment and every conversation.

At breakfast, we would sit and discuss what was for lunch, and at lunch, what was for supper, and at supper, what we had eaten for lunch and breakfast. There would be comparisons to previous breakfasts, lunches, and suppers, and fond and wistful remembrances of breakfasts, lunches, and suppers past. It was not uncommon for any one of the clan to be slumped on a sofa and suddenly cry out, unprompted, "Those sausages were nice," and the rest of us would nod in enthusiastic agreement, even if said sausages had formed part of a meal over a week ago. We would all understand.

In my student days, I was just the same. For some reason—still don't know why—I chose to study theology and headed down to London. The other choice was Lampeter St. David's in the middle of Wales where, research told me, the sun only came out for about thirty minutes every other June and the pubs were only open on Monday. Those were the heady days when governments paid students to go to college and, unlike the poor kids of today who will go to their graves still paying for their education, I got a grant—a nice, fat check for six hundred pounds or more at the beginning of each term. It was supposed to last ten weeks, and cover all sorts of important things, like buying books about doctrinal Christology and exegesis of the Lucan Gospel, but, in fact, lasted about ten days, as I spent it with gay abandon in the Indian restaurants and steak houses of South London and the Turkish Okabassi and Cypriot pastry shops of Green Lanes.

By this time, the Great Salami had also moved south and was making pots o' cash. He was more than happy to share the love and would take me out for meals. Not just any meals, though. Meals at places that I had read about in food guides. Meals at places that had dragged London kicking and screaming from the moribund food scene that had engulfed it since postwar rationing to become one of the best places to eat on earth. The Salami is a man of extraordinary generosity, even if that generosity comes at the cost of my never trying to usurp his primary position in the Majumdar hierarchy.

On my twenty-first birthday, my parents gave me one hundred pounds to spend only on one meal, which I duly did. A very fine meal it was, too, at an old-school trattoria called Gino's, at the bottom of Charing Cross Road. In the early eighties, one hundred pounds bought you a great deal, and I had no trouble finding two companions to help me spend five hours blowing the lot, with little thought of rent to be paid or books to be bought. When it comes to money, food was and is always my primary concern.

I can still recall what I ate: tortellini in a mushroom cream sauce; poussin flamed in cognac and served with rosemary and soft, melting chestnuts; followed by a frothy zabaglione made at the table by a waiter in a loud waistcoat who had a liberal hand with the Marsala. It was all washed down with any number of bottles of Valpolicella and my first tastes of a complimentary rough grappa, the burn of which I can also still remember.

You think it odd to recall what I ate at a meal twenty-three years ago? In fact, I can recall every meal I ever ate. It's true. If you meet me, you can give me a pop quiz. It is a Majumdar family trait. We signpost our lives by what we have eaten and when. If I were to ask any one of my family about a significant event, they would look at me blankly until I reminded them of what we had to eat on that occasion, then it would all become clear. A lengthy discussion about the dish in question would then follow, possibly even a heated debate about whether it was any good or not.

Heated debates about food are also fairly common in my life. There is nothing I hate more than bad food and, hard though it is to believe, I have also been known to be ever so slightly opinionated about it. I try not to be judgmental, but fail miserably, and a wife and any number of girlfriends have fallen by the wayside as they try to keep up with my fixation. This has included trailing round after me as I take the long route home so I can go from restaurant to restaurant just to see if there is something new on the menu, or sitting opposite me as I dissect a meal that they have lovingly prepared. "It's delicious, darling, but I guess the good butcher was closed today?" or "That was great, sweetheart. Couldn't you find the good lentils?"

At least one nascent relationship came to a screeching halt when I was being treated to a meal at a very grand place on my birthday. I tried to be generous, knowing that my girlfriend had put a great deal of effort into choosing the location and securing the booking, but this was such a lousy meal it abused the privilege. I grimaced my way through the first course, sent back the fish course with a complaint that it was overcooked, and the next course with a complaint that it was undercooked. By now, my friend was close to tears, although I was too engrossed in what was going wrong with this meal to notice. I think my description of the saucing as "jejune," a word that I had just gleaned from a Woody Allen film and was using at every opportunity, that finally sent her hurtling to the bathroom in floods of tears, only to emerge about thirty minutes later to ask for the bill and leave, never to be seen again by me or the restaurant. Such occurrences are not uncommon in my life.

If possible, I am even more passionate about food now than when I was younger. Certainly, I can afford to eat out more than I could when I was a student, but that is only part of it. My obsession has been fueled by access to any number of cookbooks in my past life as a book publisher, membership on Web sites and Internet forums on which people discuss and argue about the best food and restaurants and, more recently, the advent of television channels in the United Kingdom and United States dedicated entirely to food, even though some make me want to howl at the screen in derision.

Quite simply, I adore food. I also love people who are as passionate about growing, preparing, and talking about food as I am about eating it.

I love the glamour and glitz of the Michelin-starred restaurants in London, Paris, and New York. If I were to bump into Gary Rhodes, the chef known for reviving British classics, I would probably faint like a bobbysoxer at a Fabian concert. I love the skill, craft, and technique that the great chefs show in transforming the mundane into the utterly fabulous and delicious. I love being presented with the wine list and the plop of the cork when that first of many bottles arrives. I love the little cups of foaming soup that the chef sends out as a welcome and the homemade petit fours that arrive to accompany the tinkle of tea being poured in fine china at the end. And I love all points in between.

I don't just love the fancy-schmancy places, though. If I were asked to choose my last meal, it would be a plate of fish and chips, from northern England, where I grew up, of course. The crunch of bubbly crisp batter breaking under the slightest pressure to reveal glistening white haddock that had been allowed to steam inside its protective coating to a perfect flake. Alongside it, a mound of proper chips or French fries, crunchy on the outside and soft and yielding in the middle. All washed down with a mug of strong tea. Perfection.

A close second would come meat. I have to admit that I like meat a great deal. A journalist once described me as "The Great Majumdar, a man for whom many animals have died." It's true. If it once had eyes, and a face, and a mom and a pop, I want to eat it. A perfectly prepared steak, with a charred crust and rare and bloody in the middle is one of the true tests of any chef's art. Many try and most fail. Those who succeed are as worthy of note as any great artist.

I also think that if you eat meat, it is disingenuous not to eat all of the animal whence your choice cut may have come. So, I like my bits: entrails, hooves, noses, and lips—nether regions and innards that are so often thrown away in these days of packaged foods but are often the sources of the best flavors. Gnawing on meat from the roasted head of a suckling pig at London's legendary St. John restaurant or slurping up a bowl of tripe soup in Chinatown are a regular treat and, yes, before you ask, I have eaten testicles. Jolly good they were, too.

Food is the first thing I think of in the morning, while I ponder my day over a bowl of slow-cooked porridge with peanut butter and a nicely chopped-up black banana, sipping on that glorious first cuppa. And it is the last thing I think of at night, as I sit down with a bowl of macadamia nuts and a shot glass of peaty whisky from Islay.

Food is not just what I eat, it is what I am and what I do.

That realization, and the realization that I am not alone in my obsession, is what led to the book you have in your hands, and the blog that preceded it. It is what led to the whole notion of *Eat My Globe* and my desire to go everywhere, eat everything. It is what made me walk away from my old life of self-indulgent hedonism and head off around the world in search of the weird, the wonderful, and the downright tasty. It was what made me move from a comfort zone in which my idea of hardship was having only Chardonnay in the minibar to a trip that saw me endure over one hundred flights, the same number of different beds, and the unspeakable horror of Chinese toilets and trains.

Best of all, it was the realization that brought me into contact with hundreds of people all over the world who shared my passion for incredible things to eat and who opened up their lives and their hearts to let me share a meal with them or to be part of the process that brings these treasures to our tables.

I hope that by reading this book, you will not only get some vicarious pleasure from learning about the people, the places, and, of course, the food, but also rekindle your own desire to go to places far and wide because they do great noodles, or to spend time preparing a meal for someone special even if they can be, like me, an overcritical dolt.

Most of all, however, I hope it just makes you really, really hungry and want to put the book down (after buying it and taking it home first, of course) so that you can go to eat something incredible.

That is, of course, if an older brother does not steal it off you first.

PART 1:

UNITED KINGDOM AND AUSTRALIA

Chapter 1
"I HATE MY JOB"

Who has not, at some point, uttered the words, "I hate my job"? I had on numerous times and, although at the time I might have been having the day from hell, it was nothing compared to the real privations of people around the globe. In fact, I had loved my job. I worked in book publishing and got to travel to far-flung places where I could usually score a decent meal on my expense account. I led a life that some other people would consider charmed or, at least, enviable.

A few years before, the Great Salami and I had decided to buy a flat together on the edge of London's fashionable Hoxton, just north of the financial district. The burgeoning bar and food scene fed our cravings for decent cocktails and offered a pleasing variety of restaurants. Between us, we ate out about seven times a week. Neither of us was ever going to be mistaken for cool at any point, so our perambulations around the achingly trendy neighborhood often drew contemptuous stares from the young folk as we headed off for dinner or a martini. We were tempted to have T-shirts made that said on the front: "We May Not Be Hip Enough To Drink Here, But We Are Rich Enough To Live Here," and on the back in larger letters: "Fuck Off Back To Clapham." Like giving the finger to the bridge-and-tunnel crowd. But that was a small price to pay for being able to walk to work at my office in well-to-do Islington. In fact, as I mentioned, I enjoyed my job so much, I would practically run to work. I could not wait to get there, switch on my computer, and see what e-mails had flooded in from customers around the globe.

Of course, I had to have my breakfast first. Porridge. Now, porridge gets a bad rap from so many people who think back to the misshapen lumps of oaty mush they may have been forced to eat as children. For me, there is no other way to start the day. If I don't have a great deal of time, then a microwave will suffice, but if I am on a more leisurely schedule, I take the opportunity to slow cook my coarse ground oatmeal on the stove, in a combination of milk and water until it is rich and creamy. Then, I stir in a spoonful of thick, organic peanut butter before topping it off with a pile of berries, which will burst in the residual heat to release their juices, or slices of a blackening banana. If I am feeling particularly indulgent, I will treat myself to a large dollop of Greek yogurt, which will slowly amalgamate into the dish as I eat it. Try it; it will change your life.

So, there I was living a life that could hardly be described as uncomfortable, with a smart flat, a highly paid job, and well within my tolerance levels of never living more than fifteen minutes from the nearest source of Madagascan vanilla extract. Yet, one day, I sat at my desk and wrote forty-two e-mails to friends, all of which read, simply, "I HATE MY JOB."

Looking back, I see this was due to a combination of things. Certainly my job had changed, having gone from being an exciting, challenging opportunity to grow a business to a dreary procession of spreadsheets and arguments over budgets. But it ran much deeper than that. A couple of years before, I had turned forty. Now, lots of people turn forty without any great fanfare, but the occurrence hit me in the face like a slap with a wet haddock, an undyed, lightly smoked one of course, not one of those yellow monstrosities they sell on supermarket fish counters, but a haddock, nevertheless.

At a quiet supper, a few days after the event, a friend said to me, "Congratulations, you are now officially middle-aged."

As the words came out of her mouth, I could practically feel my prostate swelling inside me, and see the remaining years of my life filled with nighttime visits to the bathroom with only a pathetic little dribble to show for it.

There are any number of signs that you are hurtling towards the middle years. You become entirely invisible to attractive young women; that's a given. It takes three times as much effort to prevent getting on the talking scale in the morning and hear it sneer at you, "One at a time, please."

But, worst of all, you lose all ability to move urinal cakes around the bowl. Men may deny it, but we all do it. Once, I could move them around at a pace that would have given Michael Schumacher pause.

Now, after a few begrudging millimeters, they refuse to budge anymore, taunting me with their fluorescent unmovingness. Bastards.

It became increasingly obvious that I had more sand in the bottom of my egg timer than the top. A sobering thought.

That same year, my mother died. It happened quickly from that most pernicious of diseases, leukemia, and I was not there to see it, a fact that haunts me. Most people you meet will tell you that they love their mother, and that she is an incredible person. I am no different. Gwen Majumdar really was an incredible person, the biggest influence in my life and certainly the inspiration for my obsession with food.

Gwen John was one of three nursing sisters from South Wales. She first met my father in the mid 1950s when he came from India to complete his surgical exams at the Royal Gwent Hospital in Newport, Wales, which was a training center for many doctors from around the former empire. Despite the restrictions of the day, many liaisons happened between the exotic young men with dark skin from the former colonies and the hot-tempered young Welsh women with fiery red hair.

My father, Pratip, known as Pat, asked my mother out under the pretense of wanting to take pictures with a new camera in the local park. It is a ruse I used a few times myself in my teenage years, with considerably less success, probably because I didn't own a camera. Despite the fact she was, at first, going to send her identical twin sister, Ann, she went along. Yours truly and three other siblings are the result. To her credit, she never once looked at us in times of profound disappointment and said, "If only I had sent Ann."

Theirs was a fairly chaste courtship. These were more innocent days and my father, or Baba as he is known to his children, used to tell to our great glee and to my mum's great embarrassment that, on their wedding night in a small hotel in the Lake District, he asked the management if he could have a hot water bottle. Despite this, the marriage lasted for forty-odd years and my mum went from being Gwen John to Gwen Majumdar. A wonderful combination of names that I have had to explain to people over and over again. It was not uncommon for the Indian doctors and the Welsh nurses to marry and I suspect that the children of Mfannwy Bannerji and Blodwyn Patel have equally interesting stories to tell.

Soon after they were married, and not long after the Great Salami was born, they moved to India, where this young woman, who had never strayed too far from the Valleys, found herself in a high-caste Brahmin household in Calcutta with servants and drivers to wait on her, and with precious little to fill her time. Fortunately, households such as these also had cooks, and my mother spent her days peering in the kitchen and watching the various wives in the family work with the cooks to supply the constant dishes of food that Bengali men, possibly the most demanding people on earth, required.

Mother returned to the United Kingdom with my father in the early 1960s with an ability to cook Bengali food that she used to good effect feeding her brood. I grew up on the thin but deeply delicious Bengali dahl made with red lentils, stews of fish flavored with mustard oil and, best of all, a simple chicken dish with yogurt and a few spices that is one of the great tastes of my life, and to which I dedicate this book. Add to this the baking prowess that came with my mother's Welsh upbringing, and the smells from the kitchen made for a unique combination.

Her death shook me to the core and I miss her every day, not only for her intense loyalty to her family but for her fiery temper, which was often hilarious and aimed at the most quixotic of targets. Television personalities were a particular favorite and she developed an unexplained loathing of a certain female newscaster whom she denounced as "all fur coat and no knickers." Local dignitaries too got short shrift. For a time, she was a local magistrate and had soon acquired the well-earned nickname of "the Hanging Judge" for her conservative views, which would have meant transportation to the colonies, if we had still had any, for the most minor of crimes. Other magistrates were seen as too soft or lenient, which to her obviously meant they were Communists; ironic really, since my father's family had been leading members of the Communist Party of India, a fact that fazed my mother not one jot.

Most hated of all, however, was my father's secretary, for whom she dreamed up exquisite punishments for whatever imagined transgression crossed her mind. Usually, this meant buying expensive but appalling Christmas presents. I can still recall the delight in her voice as she announced, in the Welsh accent she never lost, that she had bought the victim a large bottle of "Elizabeth Taylor's Passion. It's really disgusting."

My mother was not, it has to be said, someone you would ever wish to cross. Ever.

Most of all, however, I miss her for her food, for the stupendous smells of cooking and groaning tables that used to greet me on my return from school and, in later years, fleeting visits to my hometown,

Rotherham, near Sheffield, from London. She had no concept of the word *ample,* and both the larder and the fridge were constantly filled to bursting with the fruits of her labors: pies and Welsh cakes, chutneys and pickled onions, curries and stews. It is little surprise that the fondest memories of friends who were lucky enough to visit are about the sheer volume of food she put in front of them and the clucks of disapproval if they turned down fourth helpings, and bemusement if they did not want to try all eight flavors of ice cream in the large family freezer.

So, there I was, forty and feeling it, in a job that I suddenly loathed and dealing with the loss of a parent, perhaps the hardest thing that anyone has to face. Any one of these problems could make a person unhappy with his lot. Put together, they made me feel as if I were rapidly heading towards the sort of breakdown with a newspaper story ending "and then he turned the gun on himself."

The night of my negative e-mail fest, I returned home and flopped down on my deep, comfortable sofa with a large glass of a favorite Spanish red wine in my hand and stared out the window at the glittering lights of London's financial district.

After a while, the whiff of onions frying, drifting up through a vent from the flat below brought me from my torpor and I realized that I had been sitting there, in the dark, wineglass in hand, for nearly two hours, and that I had not eaten a thing since lunchtime. So, I got up determined to lose myself in cooking for a while. It was one of the few things that I knew would stop me feeling quite so miserable.

Checking on what was in the cupboard, I saw that I had a bag of red lentils and decided upon a standby of Bengali dahl, a thin soup made with the lentils, ground mustard, ginger, and turmeric cooked slowly with quartered lemons to give it a gentle citrus flavor. For our family, this dish is like chicken soup. I call it LSD, "Life-Saving Dahl," the sort of dish you turn to when you need both emotional and physical nourishment.

After dry-toasting the lentils until they released a pleasing nuttiness, I added the dry spices and a little water, followed by the lemons. It began to bubble gently and I turned my attention back to my wine.

At this point, I noticed among my cookbooks an old notebook, one that I had bought when—don't you dare laugh—I had decided to follow a course by that rather scary, perma-grinned, self-help guru, Anthony Robbins. I can't recall the name of the course, which was probably something like "Awaken the Unleashed Giant Inside Your Inner Child for Extraordinary Success" or some such nonsense. I don't even recall if I ever listened to all twenty-four CDs that came with the course. Before I had gotten bored with the whole thing, however, I followed one piece of advice: I had written down a set of goals to achieve once I had turned forty.

As I absentmindedly stirred the lentils which were, by now, giving off a pleasingly familiar whiff of lemon and spices, I began to read.

1) Fix teeth.

I am British and of a generation when teeth were considered things of function rather than things of esthetic worth. Consequently, by the time I hit my fifth decade, I had choppers that were healthy but as crooked as Dick Nixon. No one else seemed to notice or care, but they bothered me a lot. So, I got myself fitted with braces.

I can't pretend that I enjoyed the next two years wandering around with a metal mouth like a teenaged girl, but, at least now that the offending appliances are off, I have teeth that are determinedly straight and pearly white. I am now officially gorgeous.

2) Have a suit made to measure.

In this generation of disposable everything, the made-to-measure suit must be every man's dream and ultimate clothing indulgence. The end result, delivered in 2004, was worth it, a striking suit of grey herringbone that garners admiring looks and comments every time I can find an occasion to wear it. The process, however, was not as much fun as I expected, particularly as the man taking my measurements made no attempt to spare my feelings.

At the first fitting, I offered up helpfully, having read about such things, "I dress to the left." The tailor looked at where my obviously less than John Holmes–like appendage was situated and sniffed, "I don't think it is really going to make a difference, do you, sir?"

Moving around to get a glimpse of my behind, he added, "Sir has got quite a wide seat, hasn't sir?" as he pulled the tape across my rear end.

I suppose, as a way of telling you that you have an arse like an old sofa, it is one of the nicest, but I have to admit that it did rather take the gleam off the whole occasion.

3) Run a marathon.

Despite my obsession with food, I have always been quite fit. I'm an early riser, and mornings often see me pounding the streets in running shoes wherever I happen to be, or lifting weights in the gym with all the requisite grunts. At the beginning of 2006, I decided that I should try to put all of this to good use and aim for that ultimate of challenges, running 26.2 miles in the company of about thirty thousand other people. Timing meant that the event to aim for was the ING New York Marathon in November, and the next months saw me running forty miles a week until the big day.

The race itself was the single hardest thing I have ever done, particularly when my hip gave a loud pop at the twenty-three-mile mark and I had to limp the rest of the way through Central Park while well-meaning Americans shouted encouragement through mouthfuls of bagel and muffin. There is no chance in hell that I will ever repeat the exercise, but I did it and have a medal to prove it.

I had listed a few other things on my goals list, most of which were either too stupid or implausible to worry about. For example, it is unlikely that I am going to live on an island with Kiera Knightley or own my hometown football team, Rotherham United, and take them to European glory.

However, at the bottom of the page, in large capital letters, were four words that brought me up short:

GO EVERYWHERE, EAT EVERYTHING

I could not recall exactly what I was thinking when I wrote down that particular goal, but, as I stood in the small galley kitchen of my flat, the seed was definitely planted.

I chopped a large bunch of spinach and scattered it into the pot to wilt among the lentils, then spooned my dahl into a large bowl in which I had placed a couple of peeled hard-boiled eggs. As far as comfort food goes, this is the perfect meal.

As I sat back on the sofa and placed my supper on the coffee table in front of me, I turned on the television, tuned as always to the Food Channel, and muted it so I could just look at the pictures, while writing in the same notebook what going everywhere and eating everything might entail. The more I wrote, the more excited I became.

A friend in the United States had been inviting me for years to be part of his team at the American Royal BBQ Competition in Kansas City. I adored sushi, yet had never been to Japan. I knew nothing about

Mexican food apart from the Tex-Mex garbage that London offered. I had always planned to go to Buenos Aires, arguably the home of the world's best beef. What would Beijing roast duck taste like in Beijing or phad Thai in Bangkok? What about Africa and, of course, my father's homeland, India?

By the time I had finished my second bowl of dahl—one is never enough—I had written down more than forty things. And, at the bottom of the list, I had written the words that you see on the cover of this book: EAT MY GLOBE.

I may not have gone anywhere beyond my living room, but the journey had definitely begun.

The next morning, as I pottered along in my usual stately fashion on the treadmill, my mind added to my list of the previous evening. People had told me that Melbourne, Australia, was one of the great eating cities on earth. What about that moldy shark in Iceland—was it really as vile as they say? Perhaps some unsuspecting dupe would let me work behind a bar to learn how to mix cocktails. Could I persuade myself that wines from California were not all like melted Life Savers? I loved both whisky and gin, but had not a clue how they were made. No longer just mildly curious, I began to feel I was on a mission.

One hour and six miles of sweat later, I'd made my decision.

I showered, shaved, dressed in a hurry, and headed off on the short walk to work. For the previous few months as I approached the office, I had begun to develop a heavy sinking feeling in the pit of my stomach. In more recent weeks, it had become closer to a panic attack as I forced myself towards a day that I knew would be filled with arguments and torturous meetings.

Today was different. I felt exhilarated. Not just from the great run, which had flown by with all my thoughts of food, but because the deed was about to be done, and I felt that a colossal weight had been lifted from my chest.

I was surprisingly well behaved, spending the morning smiling beatifically through a board meeting about budgets, which would normally have contributed a great deal to a future ulcer.

Meeting over, I returned to my desk, switched on my computer and began to write a short, standard letter of resignation. I printed it out, signed it, and placed it in a crisp white envelope, which I handed over to the owner of the company, my friend Zaro, who uttered words

I was to hear more than once on the trip, "Can I carry your bags?"

That afternoon, I wrote forty-two e-mails to the same people who had received the previous rather depressing e-mail. This one simply read: I DID IT.

I am not sure quite what I expected, but apart from a few return e-mails from people saying, "Ooh, that's brave," the world seemed to be fairly well attached to its normal axis. Inevitably, the word began to get around to colleagues and clients that I was leaving and I began to receive e-mails asking me what exactly it was I was going to do.

It was a good question. What the hell did "going everywhere, eating everything" actually mean? I had done the easy bit of handing in my notice and indulged in a few fanciful thoughts about jetting off; now I had to do the hard bit of figuring out where to go, whom to meet, and how to pay for it all.

Money was an issue, of course, but, for the previous five years I had been putting away a decent sum every month and promising myself that when I reached my set goal, I was going to do something different. I was fortunate to have no mortgage, and was pretty sure I could get by for a year on the road even if, at the end of it, I would be penniless, jobless, and could see myself standing on a street corner with a sign that read, "Will drop trou' for foie gras."

To answer the question "Who would I travel to meet?" I turned inevitably to the Internet. A few years before, I had discovered food discussion boards and, sad though it may seem, they changed my life. Until that point, I had felt as if I were the only person in the world—with the exception of my family—for whom food was the first thought in the morning and the last thought before heading to bed. The people with whom I worked wanted to have water-cooler conversations about music, TV shows from the night before, films, or even politics. I joined in, but I really wanted to talk about what to serve with hake (floury potatoes, just in case you were wondering) the latest restaurant openings, and what I had cooked the night before, why it was good or could have been better.

Then, one night, the Great Salami sent me a link to a Web site called Chowhound. I couldn't believe it. It was like discovering Narnia at the back of my refrigerator. There was this wonderland filled with people like me whom I could ask, "Where can I find a decent sausage in East London?" and for whom I could write a thousand words about a new restaurant without people thinking I was stark, raving bonkers.

I felt at home immediately and soon began to post lengthy accounts of dining experiences. I spent a lot of time on there, to the extent that it was even commented upon in an article in *The New Statesman*: "One name—Simon Majumdar—intrigued me. He featured comfortably more often than anyone else. Who was this Uber-chowhound, with his encyclopedic knowledge of London restaurants?"

As with all matters Internet, one Web site soon begat another, until I was, at one point, easily one of the most active contributors on four at the same time, clocking more than 10,000 posts on one site alone as I became embroiled in lengthy arguments about important matters such as "Best Sichuan Hot Pot in London" and "Lobsters Tastier Big or Small?"

I am happy to admit—now—that I spent far too much time on these sites. I would look at them as I ate breakfast and lunch and often sneak a peek during the day when I should have been doing something altogether more productive, but this was my world and these were my people, and I felt happy there with them.

By 2006, however, I had weaned myself from them, primarily because, being a cutting-edge kind of guy, I had started a blog with the Great Salami called Dos Hermanos, on which I was now posting extensive reports of every meal, home or away. When it came to planning *Eat My Globe*, however, the foodie sites were a godsend. During the years I had pored over these sites, I had met people I considered friends, first virtually and then, as my travels allowed, in person. In the United Kingdom, I had organized regular get-togethers where those as afflicted as I could sit around large plates of food and argue in person. Trips to New York saw me sitting with people I had never physically met before but knew everything about (often far too much about) and having astonishing meals in Queens or Brooklyn at restaurants or at the houses of people who were willing to feed like-minded souls.

Now, as I prepared to head off into the world, I decided to call in every offer that had ever been made of a bed for the night or a meal. I made a reappearance on one or two of the sites and posted about my planned trip. Almost immediately, I started to get replies and e-mails with offers. Did I want someone to guide me around Mexico? Had I ever experienced a proper Thanksgiving meal? Did I fancy a day on the barbecue trail in Texas or would I like someone to put me up for a whole week in Melbourne?

The response was astonishing, but one that I later found throughout my trip to nearly always be the case. Like nothing else I have ever encountered, food and the desire to share it brings out the generosity in people wherever they are in the world and whatever other problems they may have.

The suggestions did not just come over the Web, however. Friends from my real life were soon chipping in. A Finnish friend dangled the possibility of a hunting trip in the Nordic countryside with an eighty-year-old man who only knew two words of recognizable English, of which one was *vodka* and the other wasn't. Another suggested that I head up to spend a week with him at a Scotch whisky distillery. And, so it would not be a case of what to do to fill my year, but what I was going to have to leave out.

The answer to when to embark on my trip was pretty clear, too. I had agreed to leave work at the beginning of March 2007. That gave me a little over two and a half months to get my backside into gear and plan. I spent most evenings in the next weeks flopped on the sofa with my laptop open and a large mug of tea to keep me fortified while I fired off e-mails to everyone and anyone I could think of.

Slowly, things began to take shape and, by the end of the year and with a few key dates in place, I had my itinerary pretty much planned:

March and April: The United Kingdom and Ireland
May: Australia
June: More things in the United Kingdom
July: Japan
August: Hong Kong and China
September: Mongolia, Russia, and Finland
October: The United States of America
November: Mexico, Argentina, Brazil, and back to the United States for Thanksgiving
December: Home for Christmas and a little bit of a nap
January: Germany and Iceland
February: Thailand, Vietnam, Malaysia
March: The Philippines and India
April: South Africa, Mozambique, Senegal, and Morocco
May: Turkey, Italy, France, and Spain

Reading it now makes me breathless, and to want to go and have a bit of a lie-down. Nearly thirty countries in a little over twelve months. Two things made me determined to carry on.

The first was the fact that, now I had told everyone what I was about to do, I would look like a prize tool if I gave up at the first hurdle. The second was the fact that I was, as the Great Salami put it none too kindly, "an old git," and would never get this opportunity again. Circumstances, finances, and emotions had collided in a once-in-a-lifetime way, which truly meant it was now or never.

Well-underway plans were nonetheless the cause of many sleepless nights. Not used to being out of work, I developed a dread fear that once my office hours were up, I would turn into one of those people who spend all day in a dressing gown, slumped on the sofa watching episodes of *The Jerry Springer Show* while eating broken crackers or baked beans out of a can.

Actually, I like baked beans out of a can, particularly if they have those little sausages and burgers made out of reclaimed meat in them, but that is another story.

I made a very definite decision to treat what I was doing as work. I was not out of a job or on holiday. I was organizing a project. The fact that I was doing it at home and was never more than a five-second walk from a cookie was just an added bonus. I kept to my normal schedule: got up at five-thirty every morning, went to the gym, came home and showered, then walked to work. Admittedly, my walk had been shortened to about five seconds from bedroom to sofa, but I think the principle is what counts.

It is just as well that I adhered to this modus, since I had no idea what was involved in organizing such a global trip. Flights, accommodation, visas, currency—all required more than a nine-to-five job. Itinerary mapped out, I turned my attention to how to get to these far-flung places and what I was going to do when I actually arrived there.

One frustrating Saturday morning, I was busy screaming at my computer. None of the normal travel and airline Web sites seemed to be able to cope with my plans. Finally, resorting to Google, I came across a link for a company called Airtreks, based in San Francisco. While my trip may have been one of the more unusual they'd been faced with, it did not seem to phase them at all. Within twenty-four hours of my submitting my rather daunting schedule, I was contacted by a woman called Deborah Morales who, it turned out, had the patience of any number of saints, which is just as well, because I put it all to the test as I moved dates around, put in demands for aisle seats, and changed destinations enough times that I suspect that the good lord himself would have wanted to slap me.

She came through with the goods and, before I could say, "Although the bag will not inflate, oxygen will be flowing through the mask," I had already handed over the best part of two thousand pounds for my first set of flights to Australia and around Asia.

There was now, officially, no turning back.

Chapter 2
EATING BRITAIN AND IRELAND

My first long-haul jaunt would not be until May, for two reasons. First, obviously, was the amount of organization needed. The second, though, was much more important. Before I headed off around the world looking for good things to eat, I wanted to explore at least some places closer to home.

Britain and Ireland's relationship with their food is one of the most confused in the world. With the possible exception of the United States, we are probably the farthest removed from the sources of production of our food than any nation on earth. You could point at the huge sales of celebrity cookbooks and to the extraordinary popularity of cooking shows on television as proof of a renaissance in the United Kingdom's relationship with food. However, the truth is that the majority of British people are perfectly happy to eat crap as long as it is cheap crap. You can still see signs outside pubs that say, "Steak and Chips for £4.95," and few wonder why the meal is so cheap. The reason places like these can offer a meal at that price isn't down to altruism, but is because their suppliers use the cheapest industrial ingredients and their low-paid staff are not trained to prepare them carefully or skillfully. Because of this desire for low cost and large quantity, we also have beers with no discernable taste that require no more skill to brew than they require to serve with a push of a button. In the postwar years, people promulgated the view that cheap was good, and so the majority of Britons put up with food that borders on the inedible.

Good food does not have to be expensive. A plate of astonishingly good fish and chips from my hometown can come in at well under five pounds and be as delicious, in context, as any three-star meal I have ever eaten. Similarly, you can buy cuts of meat like brisket or lamb breast (ribs and forequarter) from a decent butcher for less than it costs to feed a cat for a day. Slow-roast the brisket or roll and stuff the lamb breast and you will have something delicious, nourishing, and afford-able.

To many people, of course, food is merely fuel and, while I may be bewildered by that view, it is no less valid than my own view that clothes are something I buy twice a year, when the seat of my jeans starts to shred. Nonetheless, it is hard not to view as schizophrenic a country in which untalented chefs can become megastars, sell millions of books and DVDs, but where you can still find the words "Thai Veg-etarian Schnitzel" scribbled on a pub's blackboard menu.

Britian and Ireland have some of the best raw materials in the world. Despite the farming problems of recent years, we still have fan-tastic beef, pork, and lamb; spectacular seafood from Scotland and Cornwall; hundreds of varieties of apples and pears; producers of as-tonishing breads and cheeses that I consider better than anything else in the world. Don't get me started on the wonders of English asparagus. Yet, it is still a rarity to see these beauties appearing on menus with any regularity, because much of what we produce is whisked across the Channel to more appreciative audiences in Europe.

Like an abused child, Britain has lost its confidence and sense of worth in what it produces and in its cooking after nearly a century of being the butt of the world's jokes about its food. Some of the fantastic foods Britain produces are made with ingredients of the highest quality, as good as anything you will taste anywhere in the world. If they were made in any other country, they would be national treasures.

I thought about this a lot as I was planning my trip and came up with a short list of foods that I adore but have a bad reputation in the United Kingdom, primarily because they are mass-produced and badly made. I decided to go in search of just three of my favorites: black pudding (blood sausage or *boudin noir* to Americans), pork pies, and cheese.

Few foods divide people quite as much as black pudding. Some people, me included, love it and become fanatical about it in all its forms. Oth-ers, usually those who have never tasted it, declare that they hate it. When asked why, they usually squeal, "You know it's made of blood, don't you?"

The first time I ate black pudding would have been at a Majumdar family breakfast. Our breakfasts, I am guessing, were very different from yours, primarily because everything on our plates was yellow. My father prepared breakfast, and always used the same pan that he had used to prepare Bengali food. The jaundice yellow of turmeric imbued everything else that ever crossed its less-than-nonstick surface. So, for breakfast, we had yellow fried eggs, yellow fried bread, and yellow bacon. I knew no different and thought this was perfectly natural.

I once made quite a show of myself at my friend Andrew Ross's house when his mum produced a tea that contained a perfectly cooked but glisteningly white egg. I announced in a loud scream to my fellow diners that it was "probably poisonous" and was sent the one hundred yards back to my house in tears of disgrace.

I was a critic even then.

At the yellow family breakfast, the only thing that had a chance to power through the turmeric shackles was the black pudding—thin round slices of it cooked in the fat of the yellow bacon. God, it was lovely. This was good black pudding from the local butcher, none of the mass-produced rubbish that littered the supermarkets then and now. I loved the crunch when I first bit into a black slice, its slight spiciness, and I loved finding a blob of hot fat. Those were special days, even if I am looking at them through glasses tinted with a very yellow hue of turmeric.

Most of my school friends thought I was a weirdo for liking black pudding, but then, they thought I was weird for many reasons, including, but not limited to, the fact that I was a fat Indian kid who brought poppadums to school.

Never one to follow the crowd, I continued in my love of by-products of the pork industry, and, as I got older and traveled more, I realized that not only was I not the only one who liked the stuff, but that just about every country had its own version. The French have *boudin* which is soft and silky smooth to the tongue. The Spanish have *morcilla*, which is appropriately spicy, laced with paprika, and plumped with rice. It is a party in your mouth, everybody is invited. The Germans, true to form, are not interested in any frills and have the simple *Blutwurst*. All of them are fine attempts and heaven knows I tried enough of them, but none can compare to our own black pudding.

By the time my food obsession was flowing unchecked in the early nineties, the pudding had undergone a bit of rehabilitation. No longer considered just the gross use-up of abattoir leftovers, it inspired a new wave of chefs and, along with other British ingredients, became hip. I chose them every time I saw them on a menu, and cooked them for myself and others, taking great delight in preparing meals that guests declared fabulous. Conversion by stealth.

So, we don't belabor the point, let's just agree, I am a fan of black pudding. I don't care what anyone says.

The best black pudding comes only from Bury, Lancashire, a small town that is rapidly becoming subsumed into a suburb of Manchester. Bury is best known for two things: One is that it was the birthplace of Robert Peel, founding father of the police force (nope, I didn't know this either, but they are inordinately proud of this fact and there is a large statue in his honor in the town square); the other is black pudding.

What Graceland is to Elvis, Bury is to black pudding, its spiritual home since the early part of the twentieth century, when the town had more than a dozen pork butchers and as many pig farms, and needed some way of using up all that blood. Every morning would be spent catching the blood, mixing it with local barley and blends of herbs that changed from shop to shop. By opening time, the puddings had been stuffed into skins, boiled, and hung in the shop windows. By lunchtime, they would be gone, the locals knowing a good thing when they see one.

My first call was to Debbie Pierce, the co-owner of the Bury Black Pudding Company, who agreed to let me come up north and spend half a day up to my elbows in blood and fat, making splendid sausages of boiled blood speckled with jewels of fat.

A three-hour drive from London found me in the raw room of the facility, resplendent in blue overalls, oversized blue Wellington boots, and a fetching hair net covering my smoothly shaved scalp. This was what it was about, meeting people who were as obsessed with food as I was. All summed up in one huge mixing bowl of blood, barley, spices, and back fat in a beef intestine. Fantastic.

In my slightly childish imaginings, I had hoped a black-pudding factory would have a conveyor belt from the outside where smiling, innocent little porkers would be loaded, oinking happily before entering a dark, satanic, foreboding building with at least three chimneys puffing out acrid, black smoke. Inside would be a nightmare version of a perpetual motion machine that would involve crushers, mincers, grinders, slicers, and an extra crusher just in case the first machine did not crush enough. There would be a few vain squeals from the porcine victims before they were dispatched, and out the other side would plop nicely packaged little puddings ready for the eating.

As a pleasing afterthought, there may be a side door where you could, perhaps, see a pie or two.

Instead, I got a tidy, bright building in a small industrial park, hardly the charnel house I was expecting and, I have to admit, slightly disappointing. But I pressed on and was soon sitting in the neat boardroom of The Bury Black Pudding Company with a cup of welcoming tea in one hand and my notepad in the other. I was introduced to Richard Morris, son of James Morris, a legend in the black pudding world. Richard gave me a history lesson, then Debbie gave me a tour. The raw ingredients room and cooked ingredients room are strictly separated and required a change from blue to red uniforms. I moved from storerooms of fat and dried blood to ones that housed the finished product hanging from lines like miniature clowns' trousers out to dry. Very interesting, but all I wanted was to taste the puddings. Debbie picked one particularly plump specimen off the rails and cut it expertly in half. She made me another cup of tea and took me back to the boardroom to sample the freshly made beauty. She left me alone, which is just as well, as the sounds I made were those that are normally only sanctioned for the marital bed.

It was everything I expected and more. The casing melted away to reveal a dense dark inside with the herbs and flavorings, particularly white pepper, giving a result that had length, almost like a fine wine. "Chateau Pudding, sir? It's the 2007. An exceptional year for blood." After the initial flavor comes the mouth feel, the creaminess of the fat with the slight bite of barley, followed by the final touch of herbs and spices. Make no mistake, this is a very special thing indeed and, if you have not tried one, you are missing out.

As I went to leave, Debbie filled a bag with samples of black pudding that lasted only about an hour after I arrived back home, once the Great Salami got involved.

The simple pork pie is another thing that people either love or hate. The main dissuasion is its few ingredients: ground pork, jelly made from the pig's trotters, and a pastry casing made predominantly from fat. Okay, even I will admit it doesn't sound great when you put it that way.

The pork pie has an image problem. If you ask most people to describe the average pork-pie eater, they will no doubt conjure up a picture of a bearded man with a belly. In one hand, he will have a pint of real ale and, in the other, a copy of *Minstrel in the Gallery* by Jethro Tull. It would be highly unlikely that anyone of the opposite genital grouping has wanted to copulate with him since he last saw his feet.

This is, of course, hugely unfair. I eat a lot of pork pies and I don't have a beard.

Most pork pies sold in the United Kingdom, like so many traditional British foods, are basically inedible, made to as low a specification as the manufacturers can get away with and still call it by that name. They are solid lumps of stodge filled with graying meat and slimy jelly. Even I would not eat them, and I have been known to take tasty tidbits out of the garbage can if I am hungry and the can is within reach.

A real pork pie is a thing of extreme beauty, a filling of well-spiced, lean meat, encased in a protective jelly and surrounded by a casing of crisp pastry. A good pie has only six ingredients: pork, salt, pepper, flour, lard, and water—not an additive in sight.

The best pies come from the town of Melton Mowbray. And the best pies in Melton Mowbray come from one small company, Mrs King's Pork Pies, which actually originated, unlike some conglomerate-owned brands, with a Mrs King, and is now owned by the irrepressible Hartland family.

I first encountered Mrs King's pies when I bought one on my very first visit to London's famous Borough Market. I had a bite as I was walking around the stalls and almost went back and hugged the owner, it was that good. Over the years, few weeks have passed without me, or my brother, buying one of these beauties and enjoying it at home with a glass of shudder-making bitter, a slice of sharp cheddar, and a large spoonful of sharp piccalilli, a mustard-pickle sauce. The initial crunch of the pastry giving way to the soft jelly, then the spicy meat that requires effort to bite is one of the greatest tastes in the world.

Co-owner Ian Hartland agreed to let me come up to see for myself how my favorite snack is made. Walking in on the Hartland clan making pies is like walking onto the set of a Marx Brothers movie. They bicker as all brothers do, with Ian playing mediator and his son, Adam, seemingly doing all the work. They turn out one thousand of their miraculous little beauties per week, all of which are snapped up by right-thinking people across the country.

Ian gave me a bit of a history lesson about the company and about pork pies themselves, which apparently were the snack *de choix* of the hunting set in the nineteenth century: the tough pastry casing protected the meat as the hunters jumped over hedges in pursuit of some poor creature or other. At that time, the law required that horses be changed exactly one day's ride from London on the routes up north. That point was Melton Mowbray, which is why it became the most famous source of pork pies. Over the years, however, little was done to protect their name or reputation, and anyone who produced any old junk anywhere was allowed to call his product a Melton Mowbray Pork Pie, which is why so many people's opinion of them is so low. Now, however, there is something called the MMPA, the Melton Mowbray Pork Pie Association, which sets a standard for a pie to bear the famous name including a minimum of 45 percent meat. Mrs King's takes it a notch higher, to 50 percent.

Lean and fatty meat is mixed to ensure enough moisture, then seasoned with a little salt and pepper. The pastry casing is made equally simply with lard and flour, then case and filling are combined using a pastry press and a meat press. Traditionally, of course, they were hand raised, which involved using a block of wood called a *dolly,* and lifting the pastry around it until it was high enough to cover the filling. The Hartlands used to do it this way when they first started but, as the business grew, they had to resort to the modern method of a pastry press. Their press is over two hundred years old and operated manually by whichever brother whose shift it is to press and pack the pies. Along with a whippersnapper of a flour mixer that is a mere one hundred years old, the press is their only concession to the industrial process.

Once packed, the pies are cooked at about four hundred degrees before being topped up with a jelly made from boiling pig's trotters. Then, they are allowed to set before being released to a waiting world.

Since I was not just visiting to watch, Ian soon had me unloading shelves full of heavy pies from the hot oven as they bubbled fiercely with their natural juices. He then showed me how he filled them with jelly with the aid of nothing more than a pouring jug and a knitting needle.

That's all there is to it, but, by God, they are good and, thank heavens, becoming increasingly popular not just in the United Kingdom, but also across Europe, where artisan products are treated with a great deal of respect. Spain, in particular, has developed quite a craving for

God's good pork pie, which, given their love of all things pork, is hardly surprising.

The Hartlands are under no illusions about their audience. Unless Madonna suddenly decided that a Mrs King's Medium Pork Pie is going to be on her contract for every concert, their audience is still going to be predominantly, if not exclusively, male, and, of that demographic of the nation's men, it is still going to be enjoyed most by men of a larger girth with an unhealthy interest in progressive rock of the early to mid-seventies. "Thank God, there are still enough of them around for us to sell as many of the things as we can make," Ian said.

When it was time to leave, I deposited my overalls with a little re-gret, and left the family to resume their good-natured arguments. Ian insisted on giving me a pie to take with me for the walk back to the sta-tion, which may well have been prompted by me pointing at one and asking pleadingly, "Can I have a pie?"

I thought about bringing it home to London and sharing it with the Great Salami. Such thoughts lasted until about ten minutes after I had begun my hike, when I passed a small pub in the nearby village. The sun was shining in a cloudless sky and I couldn't resist stopping for a pint. As I sat outside, looking at my notes from my visit, the pie called to me and I took it from the bag. "One small nibble," I promised myself. "Then I can put it back and give the rest to Robin." Ten minutes later, the pint pot was drained and the pie was no more than a dribble of jelly down my chin, with enough crumbs on the floor to attract a small group of birds.

What the Great Salami doesn't know won't hurt him.

A week after visiting Mrs King's, I arrived in Ireland in search of cheese.

Research told me that the United Kingdom and its Irish neighbors now have, combined, nearly as many, if not more, artisanal cheese mak-ers as France. It is a remarkable fact, given the British cheese-making industry was more or less destroyed during World War II, in part by rationing and in part because of laws prohibiting the making of any-thing but hard, long-lasting cheeses that could be stored to help the war effort.

The reason British cheese-making is now in a much healthier posi-tion is due almost entirely to one man, Randolph Hodgson, owner of Neal's Yard Dairy and the acknowledged godfather of the British and Irish cheese industry. The two Neal's Yard stores in London are now part of the landscape for any food-obsessed person either living here or visiting, and it is hard to imagine a time when they were not around.

My first visit to the original shop changed my life. As I walked in, my nostrils filled with an array of smells the likes of which I had never encountered. Before I had the chance to utter the words *Laughing Cow,* the staff, in blue hats and starched white coats, had given me tastes of about ten cheeses, and I found myself handing over ten pounds, a considerable sum for me then, for slices of hard cheese, soft cheese, goat's cheese, and sheep's cheese the tastes of which I can remember to this day. Neal's Yard Dairy has had thousands of pounds of my hard-earned cash over the years and I don't begrudge them a single penny piece of it.

When I decided that I wanted to meet some cheese makers, it made absolute sense to head down to the Neal's Yard branch in Borough Market to see who were likely candidates: Montgomery's Cheddar, Mrs. Kirkham's Lancashire, or Gorwydd Caerphilly? One of the approachable staff suggested, "What about Ireland? There's some great stuff there and you get to drink Guinness."

As he spoke, he handed over a thin sliver cut from an orange disc of a cheese called Milleen's, which I had tried quite a few times before, then moved to a larger round of blue cheese before handing me a sliver of that, too, and saying, "You could go to Cashel Blue, too."

One taste and I was going to Ireland. I bought some cheese, obviously, about thirty pounds' worth, if I recall, and headed home where I sat down to eat it with some oatcakes and a glass of organic cider, booked a flight and made a few phone calls. Milleen's and Cashel Blue were both very receptive and I soon had the dates written in large black letters in my diary.

Milleen's is just outside Castletownbere, West Cork, which involved a three-hour drive from the airport in Cork. Every slow-moving vehicle and tractor seemed to have been rolled out just for my benefit, but it did give me chance to admire the scenery, which is breathtaking.

Eventually, I found myself in Castletownbere and at my bed-and-breakfast. As I was not due to meet my first cheese maker until the next morning, I dropped off my car and decided to go for lunch and a bit of a hike. I was taking every opportunity on my travels to go for long walks to counteract the obvious effect of eating rather a lot of food. Ireland offers some of the best walking anywhere, so I was perfectly happy spending a few hours wandering through fields, along cliff tops, and into mysterious stone circles.

By midafternoon, I was ready to head back to town for a pint of stout. Now, while the rest of Ireland may come under the spell of the much better known Guinness, Cork is Murphy's territory and, in many ways, I prefer its richer, darker, more roasted flavor to that of its well-marketed rival. Whatever the pros and cons of the two drinks, they do have one thing in common—they each take an age to pour properly.

In the current climate of immediate gratification, it is a welcome change to have food or drink that is not, nor was ever meant to be, served quickly and, in Cork, they certainly followed the age-old traditions to the letter. As I entered McCarthy's Bar, Castletownbere, at about three in the afternoon, it was almost empty, and the old dear who was running the bar and its attached grocery shop was busy sweeping the floor. I ordered my pint of the good stuff and watched as she began to pour, the chilled liquid cascading against the side of the glass to produce that legendary head.

When the glass was about a third full, she sat it down on the counter, picked up her broom and continued on with her sweeping. Three minutes later, she returned to the glass and filled it to the halfway point before setting it down again and returning to her work. A final minutes later she topped off the glass, and set it on the counter with strict instructions to "Let it rest a while."

Good things cannot be rushed.

When I finally got a quick nod from her, I lifted the glass to my lips and took a long slow sip. It was worth the wait, with a slight bitterness at the end, which made me shudder agreeably. I had two pints, which meant that I did not leave McCarthy's Bar until an hour and a half later, and with a slight stagger caused by the strong, dark, black beer and the lack of anything to eat for over twenty-four hours.

Lunch by now would be an early supper, as I went in search of something to eat. Although the views in the town were astonishing and the stout sublime, the food on offer was disgusting. Another example, I thought, of a country with some of the best raw materials sending it all abroad, leaving their own population to eat bilge so bad that it could inspire war crime tribunals.

After walking disconsolately up and down the high street looking for somewhere that was actually open in the first place, I found myself entering a brightly lit café and taking a seat at a corner table. The place was packed and, as I entered, all conversation stopped and all faces turned towards me. None of these particular Irish eyes seemed to be smiling and my mind turned to scenes from *Straw Dogs* and *The Wicker Man*.

I hid myself behind a menu and a local paper I had bought from the shop next door, whose front page celebrated the return of a local dog whose disappearance had obviously formed the substance of the front-page headlines from the week before.

The owner came over to take my order. I had barely looked at the menu, but when I did, I saw it mainly consisted of something and chips so I pointed at the word *chicken,* and left it at that.

"It comes with the vegetable of the day," the owner said. "Do you want that?"

I nodded, assuming that, at the very least it would be some greenery, and returned to the story of the missing pooch's joyous return.

Five minutes later, a plate was plonked in front of me. Next to a piece of breaded chicken baked until nice and rock hard was a pile of oven chips, a large mound of gray, gloopy mashed potatoes, and a strange shape, fried. "I don't think I ordered mashed potatoes," I said politely.

"Mashed potatoes is your vegetable of the day," he countered and wandered off to deliver another plate of food. His logic was, of course, faultless. Even in my hardest-hearted moments, I can't argue potatoes to be anything other than vegetables.

On its own, the appearance of four types of carbs, counting the breading of the chicken and four slices of cheap white bread covered in margarine, my plate of food would have been enough to make me quail in terror. However, the strange fried shape at the side of the plate was daring me to look at it. At first, I thought it might be another slightly misshapen piece of chicken. When I prodded it, the way it yielded to my fork told me it was some thing that had never clucked. I prodded it again and then, heart in my mouth, cut it open.

Mother of God. It was a whole, breaded, deep-fried banana. I recoiled in terror like the victim in a Victorian melodrama, and very probably let out a little scream. Looking back on it now, I can't believe that I actually brought myself to try it. But I did, and it was vile and unpleasant.

I was hungry enough to eat the chicken, a few of the chips, and even a mouthful of potato, but I could not bring myself to go near the banana again. When the owner came back to collect my still pretty full plate, he looked down and said, "Will you not be wanting your banana, then?" before carrying it away with a disapproving sigh.

No, I will not be wanting a deep-fried banana in breadcrumbs. Not now, not ever, never. I don't care if my life depends upon it. I knew that in my travels I was going to encounter some weird stuff, but I suspected that few things would ever come close to being quite as nasty as that banana.

Recognized as the very first of Ireland's new breed of farmhouse cheeses, Milleen's farmhouse is situated in the small hamlet of Eyries, about four miles from the town. When I arrived, Quinlan Steele was hard at work making the cheese I buy at least once a fortnight. Norman, Quinlan's avuncular father, dragged a couple kitchen chairs out into the sun-dappled farmyard and gave me a brief history lesson while we waited for his son.

There are sixty-five farmhouse cheese makers in Ireland. Milleen's was the first, when Norman and his wife, Veronica, started making their now-famous cheese to use up the excess milk of their one cow, Brisket. The next thirty years saw large chunks of both good and bad fortune. On the one hand, their cheese was given to Ireland's only Michelin-starred chef at the time, Declan Ryan, who promptly put it on his menu. On the other hand, their entire herd of cattle was wiped out by foot-and-mouth disease, from which Norman still has not fully recovered, preferring to buy in his milk from neighboring farms because he just doesn't have the heart anymore.

Eccentric, garrulous, and everything I expected a cheese maker to be, Norman had a seemingly inexhaustible supply of anecdotes. As we waited for Quinlan to finish in the work shed, he told me about the time he caused a postal strike when sending out mail-order deliveries of runny cheese, and about the time a health and safety official came to visit and invited him to shave off his long, straggly gray beard, a request that was greeted with the shortest of shrift.

After about three decades, Norman and Veronica were, quite understandably, exhausted, and felt the business was going backward rather than forward. Enter Quinlan Steele, with a name more suited for a superspy than a cheese maker, and his lanky, slightly awkward good looks and bookish mentality.

At twenty-six and an IT graduate, he had come back home from Dublin and moved beyond his father's intuitive, self-taught methods of cheese-making to a technology-based approach that he supports by poring over the Internet looking for the latest papers on microbiology, which he feels helps the consistency of Milleen's without robbing it of its identity.

This slight quirkiness of its makers is reflected in the cheese and makes Milleen's one of my favorite cheeses.

Quinlan gave me a quick tour of the cheese-making shed, which was much smaller than I'd imagined. It turns out only ten tons a year of the small, washed-rind discs, and the Steeles have no great desire to increase that.

After the tour, Quinlan selected a particularly good example and wrapped it up for me to take back to the bed-and-breakfast. Frightened of what other food horrors the town might offer up if I braved another supper, I stopped off at a supermarket and bought some fruit, oatcakes, and a bottle of beer and had a rather splendid little picnic in my room before falling asleep with the pleasing scent of the little cheese filling the air.

The next morning, the owner of the bed-and-breakfast gave me rather suspicious looks as I ate my bacon and eggs. Later, as I was packing my car, I saw her peering into what had been my room and having a deep sniff.

To this day, she probably still tells people about a short, bald man who came over from England and performed some unholy ritual in one of her rooms that left a smell she has not been able to remove despite a couple of bottles of Febreze and a visit from the local priest.

I pointed my car north towards Cashel, a small, historic town close to Cork. Three hours later, after about a half-dozen calls to the farm to get directions, I pulled into the driveway of The J&L Grub Farm and was greeted by Sarah Furno. Like Quinlan Steele, Furno has taken on the running of the family business from her parents. Mind you, that is where the similarity with Milleen's ended. Although both these places claim to produce farmhouse cheeses, they could not be more different.

Where Milleen's produces ten tons, J&L, I was told, produces nearly 270 tons per year. Where Milleen's is the work of one dedicated cheesemaker, Cashel Blue is the work of a team of close to twenty and where, despite Quinlan's devouring of biochemistry papers, Milleen's is still a cheese made as much by intuition as by technology, Cashel Blue is a cheese made for consistency that is ensured by rigorous, carefully annotated tasting notes.

I donned the inevitable overalls and Wellington boots and dipped my feet in regular baths of disinfectant as I was given a tour of the impressive facilities.

Cheese-making is pretty similar wherever you go and whatever style of cheese you eat. Coagulating milk with rennet, which splits it to whey, which is then drained. The curds are collected, pressed, shaped, and aged. It sounds straightforward enough, but it is the possibility for variety at each stage that makes cheese such an endlessly interesting food, from the animal chosen to provide the milk—cows, goats, or sheep—to the pasture and feed on which the animals graze, to the type of rennet used to the flora of the environment in which the cheeses are stored.

Sarah is most concerned about monitoring this potential for variation and, after the tour, I joined her and husband, Sergio, for what they consider the most important part of the whole process: tasting. For well over an hour, Sarah plucked long cylinders of cheese from different batches made from different milks and we tasted them for acidity, fat content, and for the spread of the blue that is injected after the curds are collected and pressed. As with wine, the real skill of the taster is not about the ability to taste itself, but to articulate that taste. It is about developing the vocabulary. It does not take long and, by the end of my time with the Furnos, I was tossing around words like "length" and "graininess" with gay abandon.

I said my goodbyes and headed back to Cork for my flight to London and home the next morning. I headed down to Borough Market and Neal's Yard to recount my journey to the man who recommended I visit Ireland.

"Sounds good," he said as I told him about my trip. And then, of course, he sold me fifty pounds' worth of cheese.

Chapter 3
SYDNEY: UNDERWHELMED DOWN UNDER

If you are going to spend a year or more traveling around the world eating, it is inevitable that you are going to spend some time in Australia. Australians are exceptional self-publicists and have persuaded many that Australia is the best country in the world, even if the Aussies promulgating this myth are usually living elsewhere at the time and show little inclination to return. It is the same with their food. Cooking shows across the globe are populated by bronzed, healthy-looking Aussies extolling the virtues of Australia's new cuisine, which has taken its lead from the immigration explosion in the country of the nineteen sixties, seventies, and eighties, particularly from Southeast Asia.

Plus, of course, Aussies just love to travel. As an Aussie friend once told me, "It's our world, mate. The rest of you just live in it."

The Great Salami was less charitable, arguing, "If you came from Australia, you would want to travel, too."

Adventures in far-flung places such as Thailand, Malaysia, and Vietnam had a profound impression on a new generation of Australian chefs, weaning them from their previous national diet, a British legacy of pies and Sunday roasts.

Sydney and Melbourne, in particular, have worked hard to persuade people that they are among the best cities in which to eat in the world, so I felt that I would scarcely have been considered to have eaten my globe if I did not head off to visit one or both of them. A friend from the Internet food boards had invited me to come and stay with him and his family in Melbourne, and trawling the Net had provided a likely source of cheap accommodation in Sydney. Adding a few chill-out days in Perth, I was all set.

Nothing quite prepares you for the horrors of flying to Australia, the other end of the world. My cheap ticket meant that, apart from a twenty-minute stop in Singapore, I spent the best part of twenty-five hours sitting in a flying tube, breathing recycled air with all the health-giving properties of sucking through a sumo wrestler's codpiece.

How can I put this nicely? People of Sydney, I hate to ruin things for you, but Sydney is not, never has been, and never will be the greatest city on earth. No matter how many times you tell people and add the word "mate" at the end. No matter how many of those fiercely unimpressive opera houses you choose to build, and, definitely, no matter how many times you choose to let fireworks off that sodding bridge and expect the whole world to give you a round of applause.

Now that I have said all that, I can also say I actually like Sydney rather a lot. It is hard not to. It's certainly beautiful and the weather makes visiting there better than a weekend in Whitley Bay in January. Actually, just about anything I can think of, including recent root-canal work, is better than visiting Whitley Bay at any time. But the constant and slightly desperate bleating of every person from Sydney I ever met that their city deserves to be up there with the best of them, including London and New York, is just a little bit silly.

Once you get over that obstacle, Sydney is an agreeable place. I was going to be there for a few days, for which I had already made plans to eat, on my own and with some like-minded souls with whom I had been in contact.

Given my limited budget, my expectations of accommodation were markedly different from when I used to travel on business. I actually found myself using the word "hostel" for the first time in over thirty years, which, as it did then, brought out a cold sweat. If my savings were to last, I had no choice, so I set myself some guidelines. I was happy to share a bathroom. Whether anyone else in the accommodation who saw me in the morning was quite so happy, you will have to ask them. However, I was not prepared to share a room.

Quite apart from not wanting an audience for some of my more unsavory nightly activities, I considered this an act of altruism to protect people from my snoring, which can apparently be measured on the Richter Scale. Girlfriends have told me that my midnight emissions could knock down the walls of Jericho. It might explain my current single status, along with the description—and I quote an ex-partner—that I am "a selfish, self-absorbed, self-righteous pig."

A single room it had to be, and at a price that would allow me to spend the rest of my budget for the trip on food, which is how I ended up at a hostel in Surry Hills, knocking on the door at ten at night lugging a ninety-pound rucksack on my back and looking like the oldest backpacker in town. In fact, as the owner showed me around, I realized that I was the oldest person in the place by at least twenty years. Seemingly hostile pairs of teenaged eyes surveyed the middle-aged newcomer with undisguised contempt.

As soon as I was shown to my room, I locked myself away like Charlton Heston in *The Omega Man* and looked around. You don't get a great deal for twenty-two dollars per night in Sydney, but my room, while basic, was clean and tidy and would certainly suit me. In the corner was a bunk bed and the lower half looked pretty inviting. I threw my bag on the top bed, lay down fully clothed, and promptly fell asleep. The only thing that awakened me from my jet-lagged slumber the next morning was the sound of a young, German couple having wild monkey sex in the room next door. In fact, they seemed to do this most mornings, and their Teutonic grunts, groans, and spanky noises became a very dependable alarm clock. I am many things, but I am not a killjoy, so I left them to their squeals of pleasure and dragged myself to the showers to clean away the filth of the previous day's journey.

Although I had made a few plans to meet people when I was in Sydney, for the most part, I was going to be on my own. A lot of people find solo dining an unpleasant experience, and it is certainly true that many restaurants can make it intimidating as they lead you through a crowded restaurant to a seat where you will be so conspicuous that you should have a large neon sign above your head reading "Sir William of No Mates." Others in the restaurant will stare at you, many will compose their facial features to express pity, others contempt. All will be hugely glad that they are not in your situation.

I have no problem at all eating on my own, sitting with a book or a magazine to keep me company, but usually perfectly happy to sip on a chilled martini or glass of wine, as I watch other diners come and go, and try to catch snatches of their conversation. I love eavesdropping. It is a family tradition. My Welsh grandmother would have been a world champion at the sport if there were an award for such things. She could pick up gossip at a hundred yards and, in any social situation, her ears would be twitching. Her particular favorite location was the beach and, if juicy tidbits were not forthcoming, she might move the whole family en masse to a more favorable location.

Being on your own also gives you the opportunity to mooch. *Mooching*, to put it at its most basic, is the ability to pass hours of time wandering around with no particular purpose or destination looking at whatever happens to cross your path. It sounds simple, but it is, however, an art form. It takes a great deal of work to get to the point where you can mooch apparently without effort for hours on end.

I am not immodest in suggesting that I am a particularly fine exponent of this. I am the Moochmeister. I could mooch for my country. If there were a league for mooching, I would be its MVP. Suffice it to say, I give good mooch.

On my first day of mooching around Sydney, I had breakfast at a local institution, Bill's, the eponymous restaurant of Australian uberchef Bill Granger. What I would call "the acceptable face of modern Australian cooking," Granger is blond, blue-eyed, with a fixed grin, a symbol of everything Australia wants its cooking to stand for in the pantheon of cuisines: simple ingredients of high quality not screwed around with too much. And, on the whole, he succeeds. Certainly he did with a breakfast of scrambled eggs run through with a creamy, house-made ricotta, and served on a slice of crunchy sourdough toast. Just the job to fuel me for my day as I went in search of one of Sydney's treasures and indeed one of Australia's great contributions to the world: the meat pie.

I love pie in all its forms, but meat pies in particular are a constant source of wonder. Everywhere in Australia, pies are available. As the genre has developed, they have tried to finesse the whole thing a bit with new and unusual fillings. But, the truth is that the Australian meat pie, in its unadulterated form, is a beautiful thing on its own.

In Sydney, there can be only one choice: Harry's Café de Wheels, a pie-dispensing caravan set close to the naval dockyards of Woolloomooloo (yep, I had to check the number of *o*'s, too). It has been there since the 1930s and still, to this day, attracts an incredibly diverse crowd of revelers, politicians, and celebrities who turn up at all hours to sample the legendary pies.

As I ordered a standard meat pie with a large dollop of mushy peas, I looked at the pictures that were pinned on the wall. Unless someone in the forties had developed a primitive version of Photoshop, it is pretty safe to say that both Frank Sinatra and Robert Mitchum had enjoyed the same meal as I had. Not bad company, although there was no one old enough behind the counter to tell me what Ol' Blue Eyes made of this Australian specialty. This pie was a perfect example of the art, packed with chunks of meat in a rich gravy topped with a covering of good, flaky pastry. On top of the pie a large mound of mushy peas, cooked down until thick, had a taste that took me back to my own childhood days when my parents would bring home pie, chips, and peas for a Saturday lunchtime meal spent in front of the television. So often, these pies can be all filler no killer, but Harry's pie really was a lovely thing, and fortified me for the long walk back to my hostel, to brave the stares of the young folk in the communal area and to catch up with some much-needed sleep, which may well have involved a dream about the legalities of marrying a meat pie.

At about six that evening, my deep, pie-filled dreams were disturbed again by the wild sounds of youthful sexual bliss from the room next door. I needed to leave anyway, for what I anticipated would be one of the highlights of my time in Sydney, the fourteen-course tasting menu at the eponymous restaurant of the now legendary Tetsuya Wakuda.

Among gastrotourists, people who travel the world solely for the purpose of visiting every fine dining establishment they can, Tetsuya's is regarded as one of the very best in the world and, in 2008, again was voted into the top five of the world's best restaurants by the six-hundred-strong panel of the trade publication *Restaurant Magazine*. This being one of the eating world's hot tickets, Tetsuya's doesn't make things easy for you. Faxed confirmations, phone confirmations, recon-firmations, and vials of blood were deposited at a secret location (okay, that last bit is a fib, but you get the picture). Then, for three hundred Australian dollars you get to experience a meal that justifies its position in the pantheon of fine dining.

My meal was far from flawless—with that many courses it was bound to have dishes that misfired—but one dish would have been worth the money: Tetsuya's signature dish of Ocean Trout Confit in local olive oil, served with daikon and baby fennel. The fish is poached in barely bubbling olive oil to the point that it is still medium done. This is one of those dishes, not just for me, but obviously for the whole restaurant. Table after table went from noisy chitter-chatter to stone si-lence as each diner in turn lifted his first taste of this dish to his mouth. It is a dish that would be included if the good lord decided to create a tasting menu in heaven. Other dishes came and went, but this was the highlight and the rest of the meal is a blur, a pleasing blur, but a blur nonetheless.

It would be fair to say that, the next morning, I was feeling a little bit under the weather. Fourteen courses with matching wines will do that to a man. Through my fog, I realized that, the day before, I had booked myself on a coach trip up to the Hunter Valley, one of Australia's primary wine-growing areas. I loathe organized coach trips at the best of times, and my banging hangover made the prospect horrific. But an organized trip seemed to be the option since Australia's police apparently take a dim view of bald men in rental cars hurtling through the countryside swilling enthusiastically from open bottles of Shiraz. Except that I was no great fan of Australian wines.

Well, that is not fair. Let's just say that I am no great fan of the Australian wines that find their way into the U.K. market, which is cheap, mass-produced plonk, whose lower price has been promoted so heavily by the U.K. supermarkets that most people would come out in hives if they were asked to spend more than five pounds on a bottle. Every Aussie has a built-in concept they call "fair goes," which basically means that you have to give people and things a chance. It would have been churlish of me not to have given Australian wines a chance, now that I was in striking distance of where some of the better ones were supposed to be made, even if my previous experiences with them involved spitting, choking, and swearing.

When I reached the departure point for the coach, my heart sank down to my walking boots. I was the only single person on the whole trip. The rest of the group was made up of young couples, holding hands and whispering to each other, elderly couples doing much the same, and a group of seven Filipinos who had never had a drop of wine between them, but were on the journey because one of their number had watched *Sideways* on the plane over from Manila.

In an enclosed environment when everybody else is paired off or in a group, it is hard not to feel self-conscious, as the others in the group stare at you like someone they have seen on a poster outside a police station. The Filipinos seemed particularly perturbed by my solitude, and kept on pointing at me during the journey. Points that were followed by whispers and then, rather disconcertingly, suppressed giggles. Steve, the driver, took pity on me and invited me to join him in the front of the van, which at least meant I had someone to talk to.

I was expecting lush, green, sun-dappled, rolling vineyards in idyllic surroundings, where I would be at liberty to wander around the fields before having a sample of some of the area's finest wines served to me by rose-cheeked young women desperate for my considered opinion of the latest vintage. What I got was a little different.

First of all, the Hunter Valley is not that nice a place. People from Sydney refer to it as the C*nter Valley and to its main town, Cessnock, as Cesspit, because of the amount of violent crime there. Secondly, the weather was appalling; it poured almost from the minute we set off to the minute we arrived back in Sydney.

The tour itself was harmless enough, in reality, a buying opportunity. Our visits to two small, boutique wineries bookended a few hours in a wine resort, where five or so wineries have come together to create a destination with restaurants, shops, and hotels to encourage people to stay longer and spend more. A passable lunch was thrown in and I got to sample enough wines to give even my jaundiced liver a bit of a buzz. But therein lies the problem.

The wines were just not any good, awful, in fact. By four in the afternoon, I had tasted enough overoaked Chardonnay and figgy Semillon to last any number of lifetimes. If another person had offered me a fruity red, I would have drowned him in a barrel of the reprehensible 15 percent ABV slop. I slept soundly on the way back to the city as did most of the rest of the group and, when we got close to the nearest drop-off point to my hostel, Steve gently nudged me awake and let me off the bus. What can I tell you? I still think Australian wines are lousy.

Australia's Asian community has had enormous impact on the country's food and I found, in Sydney, offerings of incredible quality from all corners of Southeast Asia at prices that made me shed a tear of pleasure. Many of these places are to be found in food courts, a Sydney treasure. Unlike the dreadful slop houses found in malls in the United Kingdom and the United States, food courts there take their lead from places in Singapore and Beijing, where regional dishes are served from small stalls for a few bucks a dish.

I met food blogger Helen Yee for lunch in Sydney's impressive Chinatown, where she introduced me to *banh mi*, the crunchy, delicious Vietnamese sandwich. As we ate, she pointed me in the direction of many other places I should try, restaurants specializing in food from Xian province at the beginning of the Silk Road, and Cantonese places serving traditional roast meats. I returned more than once to my own favorite, BBQ King, for a portion of their crispy pork where the crackling skin was supported by a creamy layer of fat.

Outside of the enviable array of Asian food, Sydney's dining scene was vibrant but small. The top restaurants in Sydney do not disappoint. But, in the midrange, while there is consistency and talent, there is too little originality to suggest a city close to finding its own culinary identity.

Young Aussie cooks, eager to show off their chops in the new wave of cooking, have created a "Hey, lemongrass is on special offer" cuisine. Ingredients from disparate places are flung together to form dishes of jarring flavors and inappropriate tastes. I couldn't help but question why, just because they had traveled around Vietnam on a motorcycle, I should have to suffer.

A meal I shared with Simon Thomsen, the coruscating food critic for the *Sydney Morning Herald*, at a relatively new place called Bentley's, exemplified this trend. The cooking was more than competent, drawing on the Ferran Adriá school of foams and fancies, but little about it suggested that I was in Sydney as opposed to a midlevel restaurant in any other decent-size city on earth.

Where I expected Sydney to be good, it excelled. There are, as they like to keep reminding you, few more lovely cities on earth and few places with as many ways to enjoy yourself. Magnificent national parks surround it and few people in this world know how to enjoy their city as well as the Sydneysiders enjoy theirs. Jogging, kayaking, windsurfing, diving, cycling—no wonder they are so bloody fit. They know how to live a good life and can probably teach the world a lesson or two on that subject.

Now all they need is someone to teach them how to make wine, create their own cuisine, and to stop trying so hard to convince the rest of the world that Sydney matters.

Chapter 4
MELBOURNE: EATING WITH THE DEVIL

Children like me.

Don't laugh. It's true. Kids love me. I may look like the child catcher from *Chitty-Chitty Bang Bang*, but, for some reason, children seem to take to me. At dinner parties, I am inevitably the one sitting in the corner with my host's kids playing games rather than indulging in serious adult conversation. On the few occasions when I am invited to christenings or weddings, I invariably plunk myself down at the children's table to talk to them rather than listen to some stranger tell me all about his career as an accountant while spitting bits of cold poached salmon in my direction.

Kids just love their adorable Uncle Simon.

Eric Balic, however, hated my guts.

One of the first invitations I received when I put out the word about my trip was from two friends in Melbourne, Adam Balic and Rebecca Hewlett. While Rebecca is a normal, well-adjusted type with a proper job, Adam is a brainiac scientist with a passion for food history, which had drawn him to the same Web sites I had frequented. We had met only a handful of times in the United Kingdom when they lived there, but had swapped countless e-mails and indulged in long arguments on important matters such as "the origins of Pinotage" and "Why does a durian fruit smell?"

By the time I started my trip, Adam and Rebecca had moved back to their hometown of Melbourne, with Adam acting as house husband until he found a job that involved test tubes and the opportunity to cackle fiendishly. He extended an invitation to me to come and spend a week seeing what Melbourne has to offer with him as my guide.

Melbourne has a reputation as one of the great eating cities, primarily because of the bewildering number of nations whose citizens have washed up on its shores. People from all regions of China, Indians, Turks, Jews from Eastern Europe, thousands of people from southern Italy, and more Greeks than in any nation other than Greece itself, all brought with them their cuisines and techniques. Because of this, no trip with the lofty ambition of going everywhere, eating everything could possibly be complete without a visit to this city on the coast of Victoria.

When I arrived in Melbourne after a long flight, Adam was waiting at the door of his home. In his arms was eighteen-month-old Eric. From the look on his round, freckled face, partly hidden by a shock of pure ginger hair, it was obvious that no one had explained to the poor mite that he would be sharing the loving attention of his parents with a visitor for the next week.

After a hearty handshake with his father, I turned my undeniable charms towards Eric and went to give him a peck, which would, of course, win him over to my side. It always does. As I leaned forward, whispering all the required "cootchie-coo" noises, the little sod delivered a swift, accurate right cross to the bridge of my nose, a punch that carried unexpected force and made me utter expletives that no eighteen-month-old child should ever have to hear.

That set the tone for the week. I tried all my best moves. I smiled, I made normally irresistible faces, and even tried bribing him with cookies when his parents were not around, all to no avail. He hated me and insisted on trying to beat me up on sight. Fortunately, for much of my time there, he was in preschool or confined behind the bars of a playpen, which I could not help thinking, a little uncharitably, would give him valuable experience for later life.

Methodical Adam had my week all planned out, like a scientific experiment that would see me cover every ethnic cuisine in Melbourne, and a significant number of cafés and restaurants in seven days. I suspect he had a chart somewhere.

It began the next morning as I emerged from the shower and deftly dodged Eric's attempt to do me bodily harm with a toy tractor.

"Hurry up and get dressed, we're going to the market."

I needed no prompting. I love markets, the proper ones, mind you, not the new-fangled ones filled with baby strollers and stall holders who think they are doing you the favor by being there. In real markets, rough-looking men with callused hands shout things like "lurvely-tomsapoundabowl" and shovel fruit into brown paper bags with a well-practiced twist, saying "That'll be pound fifty in English money, guv." They're the only people apart from London cabbies who can say "guv" without deserving a good slap.

We set off on the short tram ride from their home in Flemington to the Queen Victoria Market. After the relative disappointments of Sydney and its contests with London and New York, Melbourne was an immediately appealing city. Its laid-back inhabitants seem content to live in a great Australian city, and it really is a great Australian city.

The Queen Victoria Market in Melbourne is the real deal, and immediately tells you this city is extraordinary when it comes to food. Alongside the stalls selling all the usual fruits and vegetables, Asian stalls are piled high with mounds of fresh, glistening herbs. Next to these, the varied communities of the Mediterranean are represented in splendid arrays of tomatoes in many hues, purple heads of plump garlic, and mild onions to form the base of dishes from countries where wine and good conversation flow in equal measure. German butchers with more ways of making sausages than you ever thought possible sit next to Chinese fishmongers with live carp flapping around in their buckets waiting to be brightly spiced wok fodder. The market was everything I wanted.

In my rush to get out to see the market, I had declined the offer of breakfast and was now close to a dead faint. Adam obviously had it covered. In the section with the German butchers was a Melbourne institution, a stall serving hot bratwurst so plump the meat was almost bursting from their skins, served in crunchy rolls topped with the sweetest sautéed onions. One bite told me that being in Melbourne was a very good thing indeed, a feeling compounded as Adam and I used Melbourne's fantastic tram system for our week-long gastronomic tour.

Right now, however, we needed a bit of sweetening up, so we met up with Rebecca before heading over to Lygon Street, one of the centers of Melbourne's considerable community from southern Italy. Rebecca appeared pushing Eric who, though feigning sleep was obviously planning his next attempt on my life. As we approached Brunetti's, another Melbourne institution, he sat bolt upright and started howling, which meant that if he did not get cake and get it soon, there was going to be trouble. For once, I was in total agreement with the little monster, and we squeezed our way into an already crowded shop while I went in search of pastries. I came back laden down with some of the specialties of the house including flaky "Lobster Tails" the local name for the Neapolitan sfogliatelle pastry, piped full of sweet cream, and cannoli so authentic you could hear the theme to *The Godfather* as you ate them. I even picked up some mini ones for Eric, which gave me a few minutes respite from his threats of violence. Everyone was a winner.

When I first noticed Adam on a food Web site, he was posting graphic accounts of his attempts to re-create classic dishes of the past gleaned from the hundreds of cookbooks he bought over the Internet, and from the pages of Epicurious, including scary puddings offered up by Mrs. Beeton to sate the Edwardian appetite. His descriptions brought me out in a sweat just reading them, and Adam took detailed, stylish photographs that he posted to universal acclaim from all the other obsessive food types.

Like me, Adam had soon tired of the Internet forums and set up his own site to showcase his search for the great meals of the past, which he called The Art & Mystery Of Food. To Adam, cooking is akin to alchemy. Go and look it up, I think you will agree, he is a genuinely scary individual.

When I dragged myself out of bed the next morning, Adam was long gone, and had taken Eric kicking and screaming to preschool. We had agreed to meet at Flinders Station, a Melbourne Landmark where courting couples for decades have met under the clocks before heading off to do what romantic couples do.

Adam had organized our day down to the minute. First, a walk through the Botanical Gardens followed by some lunch, and not just any lunch. This proved to be one of the top ten tastes of the whole of *Eat My Globe.*

After a short tram ride to Chapel Street, the Greek enclave of Melbourne, Adam wanted me to taste the souvlaki at Lamb on Chapel. For all intents and purposes, souvlaki is the Greek equivalent of the Turkish doner kebab—not that I would ever say that to a Greek person for fear of being separated from my manhood quicker than you can warble Nana Mouskouri. There are few meat-and-bread combos I have not tried in my forty-four years, from the lowliest ballpark hot dog to the clubbiest sandwich in all of clubdom. But this little beauty was something else.

Imagine, if you will, thirty whole shoulders of lamb, boned and threaded onto a large skewer above smoldering, white-hot coals. As the skewer rotates, the thinnest layer of the meat cooks until it is crispy, before the cook slices it off with a blade that would make a samurai blush. He wraps the slivers of crispy meat and fat in a fresh, warm pita bread with a few extraneous bits of crunchy salad added, then douses the lot with a pungent garlic sauce. The first bite is good as the pita is ripped apart to release the combined flavors of meat, garlic, and lemon juice, but it just gets better. That the cook was a large, hairy, pot-bellied man in a sleeveless undershirt, and I still wanted to kiss him, tells you just how good this was, or it tells you that I have some serious issues to resolve.

It was going to be hard for Adam to try to top that. But, God he tried, and we hurtled all over the city to sample the best that was on offer, from simple street snacks to a fifteen-course degustation menu at Vue de Monde, one of Melbournes most highly regarded restaurants.

It was not all good. The Turkish food we tried was tired and listless compared to that back in London, and I will never begin to understand the almost pathological appeal of the dim sim to Australians. A grim, ersatz version of Chinese dim sum dumplings, the dim sim is the snack *de choix* of every hungover Melbournian. Based on the few I tasted, I would rather have the hangover. However, for the most part I experienced a quality, variety, and price that make it perfectly understandable why the citizens of Melbourne seem to eat out more than anyone anywhere.

A week in Melbourne passed very quickly and, before I knew it, I was stuffing my clothes back into my large rucksack, which I had now christened "Big Red," because it is, er, big and red. My taxi arrived bang on schedule and I prepared to say my goodbyes. Another hearty handshake from Adam, whose glazed eyes showed that he had already forgotten my existence, and was thinking about what to cook for supper. Eric ran towards me his arms open wide and a big grin on his face. Had Uncle Simon finally won him over? Was this the moment we finally bonded and I kept up my 100 percent record of child adoration?

As he reached me, he dipped his head and butted me as close as he could to the goolies.

I guess not.

Little bastard.

PART II

JAPAN, HONG KONG, CHINA, MONGOLIA, RUSSIA, AND FINLAND

Chapter 5
JAPAN: EATING LIKE A SUMO FROM TOKYO TO KYOTO

Until 1978, my only knowledge of Japan came from episodes of *M.A.S.H.*, in which Hawkeye and Trapper John would wangle a forty-eight-hour furlough to that magical place of sinful abandon. Then, one Christmas, I used some cash from my grandparents to buy an album called *PS 78*, by the now long defunct Dutch punk band, Gruppo Sportivo, which contained an insanely catchy but irritating song called "Tokyo." I sang that song constantly for a month until the Great Salami quite rightly beat it out of me with a wet towel.

Soon, albums like *Cheap Trick Live at Budokan* and the impossibly ugly Scorpions' *Live and Dangerous* in Tokyo joined my nascent record collection, previously filled with scary hand-me-downs of unwanted progressive rock albums donated by the Great Salami, and the notion of Japan began to seem quite hip. Thirty years later, although those records had long been consigned to the bargain bin of my life, I had developed a passion for Japanese food. Based more on enthusiasm than expert knowledge, it was a passion I indulged at every opportunity in London's growing number of Japanese restaurants and, even more often, on my regular visits to the United States where most neighborhoods seem to offer decent sushi and sashimi.

Japan, I decided, would make the ideal starting point for an itinerary that would also take in Hong Kong, China, Mongolia, and Russia. I also decided that, rather than travel independently, I would like to do this trip with a group. Not a large group, as I had no desire to walk behind someone waving an umbrella in a reenactment of *If It's Tuesday, This Must Be Belgium*, but I knew that some local knowledge and language would be useful. A company called Intrepid seemed to fit the bill. Decent itineraries, groups no bigger that twelve people, and just expensive enough that people on gap years would avoid it like soap on a Sunday.

I left for Tokyo a few days before my official trip began, so I could explore. After a painless flight via Munich, I was soon at my hotel and checked into my windowless, airless, and unwelcoming room, dumped Big Red, and headed out to find some supper in the neighborhood of Ueno, where my hotel was located.

I have been told that yakitori literally translates as "grilled bird," but I expect some expert out there will correct me. In effect, yakitori is a range of chicken items on skewers that are grilled to order and either sprinkled with salt or dipped in sauce and served with a cold draft beer or the fierce local spirit, *shochu*.

Yakitori bars can be smart or, as in Ueno, makeshift units with seats made from beer crates and tables from wood slung between two more crates. They seem primarily to be the haunt of salary men on their way home from a hard day at the office and, as I chose one at random, I had to squeeze my ample frame in between two men deep in conversation on their mobile phones. After I gestured for a beer, a rather frighteningly large bottle of Sapporo appeared, but, just as I reached out for it, a man on my right reached over and took hold of my bottle. Where I was brought up, in Yorkshire, touching someone else's beer is worse that goosing his wife. It will inevitably lead to a fight and there may well be broken glass and teeth involved.

"Pouring own drink bad luck," said the man with his hand around my beer. So, I allowed him to pour my beer and we began a very faltering conversation.

The skewers I had ordered appeared, as did those of my new friend, Koji. The inevitable swapping followed along with more orders as we sampled crispy chicken skin, chicken hearts and livers, beef tendon, roasted garlic, leeks, and many more forgotten in a haze of never-ending bottles of beer. Koji insisted on paying the bill, then walked me back to my hotel, both of us swaying happily. After dropping me off at the door he headed into the night, never to be seen by me again.

Once you get over the initial fear, Tokyo's subway system, its main method of public transportation, turns out to be an absolute delight. Even when it is heaving with people, as it always is, and even though the map looks like an eighty-year-old woman's knitting basket after the cat has got at it, the cars are air-conditioned which, for someone coming from London, is enough to make you refuse ever to get off. I was tempted to take off most of my clothing, pack a picnic, and make a day of it. It is also impossibly punctual, as indeed are all the trains in Japan. I took advantage of the fantastic value metro card and whizzed from district to district trying to cram in as much as possible.

Just about every department store in Tokyo devotes its basement floors to food. On one floor is a food hall and, below that, a range of restaurants that would make any food lover swoon. Tokyo Food Hall in Shibuya was a perfect example, about the size of a couple football fields with a staggering range of products on offer, including stands selling smarter versions of yakitori to those selling steamed and grilled unagi over rice to Western cakes and chocolates. I spent a good hour walking around slightly heartbroken that I did not have the opportunity to buy more than a few bits and pieces to eat on the hoof.

Another brief subway journey, and I was in the altogether more up-market area of Ginza where many of Tokyo's well-to-do shop. However, I headed to the wrong side of the tracks to the yakitori alley where yet another array of rather challenging shop fronts and stalls offered workers on a break or commuters on their way home the chance of a plate of something grilled.

I wanted to try *unagi*, freshwater eel, grilled, then steamed to reduce the fat content, then grilled again before being basted in a slightly sweet sauce and served over rice or on skewers. It is a specialty of Tokyo, and some places there have been serving it for well over a century. I popped into a local fast-food joint, sat at the counter, did a bit of pointing, and got my plate of unagi over rice three minutes later.

It may not have been the finest example of the art, but the combination of crispy skin, sweet dressing, and creamy flesh was just what I needed to combat jet lag as I headed up to Kappabashi, about two blocks to the west of the Senso-ji shrine in Asakusa, the area of Tokyo in which stores supplying the restaurant business ply their trade, not with food but with kitchen equipment, menu holders, place mats, and just about anything any self-respecting place would need—including, I was delighted to see, a man-sized model of the Statue of Liberty.

Best of all, however, Kappabashi was home to two stores specializing in the plastic models of food that Japanese restaurants display for potential customers. Originally, the models were made of wax but are now plastic and can be found everywhere from high-end sushi restaurants to fast-food stands all over the country. They are fantastic things, offering everything from plastic dumplings to complete bento boxes with miso soup, rice, and noodles. Incredibly realistic, too, and, if I had not been on the road for another three months, I would have definitely purchased a very realistic plate of egg and chips as a keepsake.

I then had to rush back to my hotel to move Big Red from my small single room to a twin, which I would be sharing with one of the other single travelers in my party. The group turned out to be an agreeable mix of Australians, New Zealanders, and Brits, with one unfortunate American, Adam, drawing the short straw and getting to call me roommate for the next two weeks.

After the initial tour briefing, with our guide, Yuka, the assorted throng headed out together for a local supper. I had other plans. I was going to eat like a sumo wrestler.

The Ryogoku area of Tokyo is best known as the Sumo district. It's anchored by a large stadium, which is surrounded by stores selling everything that a stable of sporting fatties could need. Just as retired soccer players used to open pubs, so retiring sumo wrestlers often open restaurants specializing in *chanko nabe*, the sumo stew responsible for building up their impressive girth.

A subway ride later, I was opposite the Tokyo Edo museum, peering cluelessly through the windows of restaurants in search of chanko. They don't give you much help. The restaurants are dark and the sliding doors prevent you peering in, so all but the most inquisitive might pass them by. One place looked promising, however, and recognizing the Japanese lettering for chanko that Yuka had written on a scrap of paper, I slid back the door and stepped hesitantly inside. A rather severe-looking man came over shouting something entirely incomprehensible to me. It sounded rather fearsome, but I was determined.

"Chanko?" I said hopefully.

"Chanko?" He replied as if it was the first time he had ever encountered the word.

"Chanko." I nodded.

"Chanko?" He countered again with not the slightest sign that he knew what I was talking about.

This could have gone on for some time, particularly as it never crossed my mind to show him the piece of paper Yuka had given me. One other table in the small room was occupied by a family and the father came over to see what the commotion was. He looked at me quizzically, so I repeated the only word I knew, "Chanko."

He turned to the owner and said, "Chanko."

"Ah, chanko," replied the owner as if the scales had fallen from his eyes.

"Chanko, chanko, chanko," he said, a few times more, smiling as if the word were getting good to him. Then he gestured for me to take off my shoes and pointed to a table in the corner. He brought over a menu all in Japanese and pointed to three vertical lines of lettering with the word "Chanko" He obviously just loved saying that word now. You could hardly stop him.

Not being able to read the menu, I just pointed at random and sat back, hoping for the best. An elderly lady appeared with a large cooking pot filled with broth and a burner, on the side of which were some oversized cooking chopsticks and a ladle. She left, then reappeared with a plate the size of a satellite dish filled with seafood, fish and a mound of white cabbage and began to place them into the pot of broth, cabbage on top, before leaving it to cook slowly. Returning five minutes later, she began to serve me, filling my bowl with a little of the soup and a small amount of each of the ingredients.

It is little surprise that sumo are so huge, eating like this every day. I barely made a dent in the pot and the elderly woman looked most disapproving when, after about half an hour, I gave up, chanko sweat pouring from my brow. It is really meant to be shared by at least two people, which is reflected both in the size of the meal and its price. As I left, the owner, whose pictures of his sumo heyday lined the walls, gave me a cheery wave, a thumbs-up, and a hearty goodbye, saying, "Chanko."

On our last day in Tokyo, our group was left to its own devices before departing for the famous town of Nikko. I headed to the ultramodern region of Shinjuku, famous most recently as the location for *Lost in Translation*, which has everything one would expect to see in Tokyo, from many-storied neon lights towering overhead to hordes of people at street level heading in every direction. Legendarily hard to navigate, Shinjuku Station has nearly two million people a day passing through its halls, which is intimidating, to say the least.

I was searching for a small street called Memory Lane, but called by the locals "Piss Alley," a more accurate description of one of the few narrow lanes in Tokyo to have survived the bombings of WWII. I had read that it was due to be knocked down shortly to become part of a megadevelopment, so I was determined to see what the fuss was all about before Memory Lane was nothing more than a memory. The fuss, as it happens, was about a handful of bars run by cross, fat men with beards who grilled odd bits of animal over coals. The few I tried were no better than I had experienced in Ueno, although one place did come up trumps and was, alarmingly, run by a smiling young woman who, after placing one of those large bottles of beer in front of me, proceeded to cook me a bit of everything she had available including an indecent amount of grilled garlic cloves to which I had become addicted.

Coming from the United Kingdom where train travel is, quite frankly, a dreadful experience, I found traveling by rail in Japan to be an unending delight. Trains run on time, seemingly to the second, so that one is able to plan journeys down to the finest detail and cover large amounts of the country in a very short time with no fear of being stuck in the middle of nowhere being offered an irregular replacement bus service as in Britain.

The journey to Nikko was relatively short, but, as we would be arriving at our destination rather late, we were advised to pick up some supper at the station to eat on the train. Every station, even the small ones servicing local trains, offer a range of shops selling bento boxes that would make even high-end London Japanese restaurants blush with shame, so high is the quality. Any time it was suggested we should eat on the hoof, we were easily able to return with trays containing rice, pickles, eggs, katsu, sushi, and sashimi of very decent quality to keep hunger at bay. The Japanese train station bento box is definitely one of the world's great foodie treasures.

Nikko is only a couple of hours outside Tokyo, and we were soon settled in our traditional Japanese inn or ryokan, with its tatami floors, and donned traditional slippers and robes. A large private hot spring bath overlooked a tumbling river. We all fancied a drink, which led to a discovery of another great pleasure of Japan, the ubiquity of its vending machines. There are over six million of them in Tokyo, alone selling everything from books, a bewildering variety of soft drinks and beer, and water to some rather more unusual things—including, I kid you not, used women's underwear and, in one case, whips and chains for that quiet night in. In London, these machines are invariably out of order within minutes of being situated, and are instantly covered with graffiti. In Japan, vandalism seems almost nonexistent.

The main reason for our being in Nikko, apart from the fact that it is achingly beautiful with misty mountains and rolling rivers, is the vast complex of temples surrounding the Tosho-gu Shrine, dedicated to the first Shogun of a united Japan, who later became venerated as a god. After a quick tour as a group the next morning, we split up, which allowed me to go exploring on my own, then to head off in search of lunch. Some excellent tempura, cold soba noodles, and unagi gave me enough energy to climb back up the steep hill of the main drag to the Imperial Villa, the residence of the imperial family outside Tokyo.

After the obligatory removing of shoes, I was able to spend another hour or so wandering around the palatial interior of this villa of one hundred or so rooms. Although the heavens had opened outside, it turned out to be the last defiant gesture of the rainy season whose end, it appears, can be predicted with incredible accuracy to the day as well as to the time of day in different parts of the country. Even the weather runs according to schedule in Japan.

Supper at a local restaurant was harmless enough, a few more skewers and some yaki soba (fried noodles), but it highlighted the problems of traveling with a group. Not everyone has my penchant for bits of the animal that might otherwise end up in pet food. Consequently, when we had meals together, our guide had to work to the lowest common denominator and find restaurants that would provide sustenance for those whose tastes were less adventurous than mine.

We were not meeting up until one the next afternoon, which gave me the chance to try a solo lunch of *yuba*, a local speciality of Nikko, made from the skin created when soy milk is boiled, then removed and dried so it can be stored during the rainy season. When needed, it can be soaked for use in soups and stews and is often served, as it was for me, in spirals in a small amount of broth with some ramen noodles and meat-filled gyoza dumplings. It was a filling and cheap lunch, and just about set me up for the task of lugging Big Red through three changes of trains and a bus ride to the next inn.

One of Japan's primary holiday resorts because of its pleasant climate and extraordinary scenery, Hakone attracts the rich and famous. The region is littered with stunning housing complexes and smart restaurants ranging from haute French to, bizarrely, a handful of German wurst shops. Although the weather is cool and there are enough attractions to keep a family occupied for an extended vacation, I found little to beguile me about the town itself, and felt slightly heavy-hearted when we set off to hit the tourist trail first thing in the morning. I cheered up, however, when Yuka promised that food might be involved, including the best dumplings in Japan and, more intriguingly, black eggs.

The region of Hakone is not far from Japan's most famous of mountains, Fuji, and was created by volcanoes. As we walked, we could see the toxic fumes rising off the sulphurous pools in the rocks above us. Signs along the path warned against breathing in the fumes.

Locals believe that eggs cooked in the sulfurous pools bring good luck and longevity, providing an extra seven years of life per egg. Baskets of white eggs are trundled to the top of the mountain on a creaky pulley system before being dipped in the hot water and served to a long line of customers. I tried a couple. Not much to them, really, just ordinary-tasting eggs with shells turned black by being cooked in the sulfur, but you now have to put up with me for another fourteen years.

The night before, Yuka had told me about the gyoza center of Goza. "The best gyoza in Japan," she promised, so we headed there.

Small dumplings akin to the ones made familiar in Chinese restaurants, gyoza came to Japan from China, after the Japanese invasion of China in the late 1930s. The dumplings are steamed, then fried on one side with a little added water so that a pancake is created that surrounds them and allows the order to be served in one piece. I don't know if they are the best in Japan, but they were delicious and I ate more than my fair share just to make sure. With Yuka's help, I got to talk to the owner, who showed me the kitchen where the dough and fillings were made. I was told later it was the first time he had ever let a visitor into the kitchen.

Takayama is a small city renowned for its well-preserved seventeenth-century houses and its morning markets. As in Nikko and Hakone, we stayed in a traditional inn, perhaps the nicest of the whole trip and the most traditional, requiring slippers to be worn at all times, and for us to wear our robes for a good part of our stay. The town itself was pretty, but unremarkable and would have been quickly forgotten, but for three reasons. The first is that included in our trip's cost were two formal meals prepared at our inn by one of the best-regarded chefs in the area.

Sitting cross-legged at small tables, we were each served small courses, representing the very best ingredients of the region from mountain vegetables and herbs harvested by hand and braised gently in miso to local river fish fried on a hot plate and doused in sweet soy sauce to more of the exquisite yuba I had first tried in Nikko.

The second reason was thin slices of the local beef known as Hida.

Although Kobe beef has become well known around the world, appearing on menus everywhere, few people outside Japan are aware of its cousin, Hida. From the same Wagyu breed of cow as Kobe, Hida beef is regarded by locals as superior because of its impressive marbling of fat. I can't claim enough expertise to make a true comparison but, when the beef is cooked slowly over a tea candle, with a small amount of broth and a few local vegetables, so that it melts away on contact with the tongue, it is a taste that stays with you for a long time.

I had the good fortune to meet a wealthy local Hida beef butcher in a bar on the evening of our arrival, and was invited to take some pictures of his shop the next day. It was no ordinary butcher's shop. This was serious stuff, with the head cutter in action slicing the local delicacy as if it were the finest sashimi, and joints of beef on display costing more than enough to feed a family for a month.

I shall also remember Takayama because of a small *izakaya*, or bar, located in an alleyway near our guesthouse. On our first night, after the Kaiseki meal, I was still hungry, so I persuaded most of the group to come with me on a bar crawl.

After a couple of nondescript places with nondescript food, we wandered into our last bar of the evening where I spied a bowl of glistening pork belly that had been marinated and braised in sake, soy, sugar, and star anise before being grilled until crispy.

If God ever came back in pork form, this would be it.

The devastating effects of August 6, 1945, and the aftereffects of the A-bomb inform every person's conception of what Hiroshima was and is. And, of course, they inform every aspect of this amazing city, too, from its understated monuments to the dead and to peace and to the shape and nature of the city, much of it has been rebuilt along its old lines.

Hiroshima was exactly my kind of town, just the sort of place you think of when imagining modern-day Japan. Lively, bustling, and frenetic, it still manages to have an air of civility about it, as well as some of the best food of the trip. Among its many claims to fame, Hiroshima is the spiritual home of *okonomiyaki*, to all intents and purposes a pancake that, while being cooked with great skill on a hot plate, is layered with a huge range of fillings, including noodles, meat, vegetables, and seafood. It is not fine food, but for hungry travelers, it was everything we needed.

So well known is Hiroshima for this delicacy that it even has an okonomiyaki district that houses the greatest density of restaurants serving them in Japan. We all decamped to a place that Yuka declared her favorite, and watched in awe as the meal was prepared. A thin layer of batter spread out like a crepe was layered with ramen or udon noodles, then shredded white cabbage, strips of pork, shrimp, and vegetables, before being topped with an omelet and flipped one last time. Served with a hot sauce and a cold beer, it is little wonder that it is the snack of choice for the wage slaves of Hiroshima.

The Japanese attitude to the A-bomb is interesting. In many ways, they are quite matter of fact about it and openly account for the war and its tragic ending to "mistaken domestic policy." Whatever one's views about the dropping of the bomb, the human reality is hard to avoid and provokes incredibly strong emotions.

The A-bomb Dome is the only building in Hiroshima that survived the blast and is now preserved as a monument to the dead. I will not deny holding back a few tears as I walked around the memorial to the one hundred forty thousand who died on the day itself, and another one hundred thousand who died in the following two years from their wounds and radiation poisoning. A gentle reminder to future generations.

After walking past a small monument on a side street, which marked the spot above which the bomb exploded, I needed to forget about the war and all its horrors for a while and see what the rest of the city had to offer.

In particular, I wanted to find a local specialty of grilled conger eel, known as *anago*, which I found in the small fish market located next to the Hiroshima railway stations. Unlike unagi, this eel is grilled whole before being doused in a sweet sauce, which gives it a stunning combination of crispy skin and fatty flesh that was enough to whet my appetite for lunch.

Fast food in Japan is a huge business and a number of chains have arisen to feed those who want to eat and leave in the space of fifteen minutes. In most, you choose from a menu outside before setting foot in the restaurant, buy a ticket for the corresponding meal from a vending machine inside the front door, and hand it to the server when you sit down at the counter. About a minute later, your meal is in front of you, along with some free water and green tea.

I chose a peculiar Japanese specialty, *kareh raisu*, which can trace its roots, I was told, back to British naval visitations in the nineteenth century. A sweet curry with soft chunks of meat and sometimes fruit in it, it is Japanese comfort food, their hangover remedy, and their chicken soup.

I am not going to lie to you. By the time we got to Kyoto, I was all shrined out. Which is a bit of a shame as Kyoto is officially the home of two thousand shrines. It is littered with them. Everywhere you look, you will find the telltale red signs that something or someone is being revered in shrines ranging from the truly magnificent to the tiny and discreet.

After another rapid train journey to Kyoto, Yuka sat us down in the lobby of the last ryokan of our journey to explain the shrine excitement that lay ahead in the next two days. When, after the meeting, I sidled up to her and asked if she minded if I gave it all a miss, she did not seem the least bit surprised. So, the next day, while the group headed out for a day of visiting famous and important sights, I had a bit of me time, which involved nonshrine-based explorations that led me to the Nishiki Market, an enclosed strip where Kyoto comes to shop for some of its finer delicacies. Many high-end restaurants outside Kyoto claim to serve food in the Kyoto style, meaning that they adhere to the extremely high standards of this city.

The market, while not huge, was a delight and much more a shrine to the things I hold more holy than anything with incense and a bell. For me, the smoke drifting from a small grill topped with little, delicate fish to be served doused with sauce is as important a sign of our relationship with the divine as any church. I spent an hour or so wandering up and down the strip, looking at fine lengths of *yuba;* tiny crabs ready for frying and eating in one bite; vegetables pickling in fermenting rice; and enough unrecognizable things that I did not regret missing a temple or two.

Yuka had recommended a kaiten sushi restaurant called Musashi for lunch, describing it as being the best of its type in the city. As the conveyor belt moved around at a stately pace, I helped myself to ten or eleven plates including one, I found out later, that was a sashimi made of horsemeat. To my right, an elderly man had ordered a dish not on the belt from one of the chefs and was wolfing it down with considerable enthusiasm, so I pointed and ordered one for myself.

A small blubbery sac on top of the normal vehicle of vinegared rice arrived. I ate it in one go and almost threw up on my neighbor. He howled with laughter, made the sign of a fish swimming, then what I am convinced was the universal sign for masturbation. Later, I showed a picture of my dish to Yuka. Her laugh was louder than his.

"You ate cod sperm, Simon."

On our last day, Yuka had arranged for me to meet a Kyoto housewife, Tomoko Osashi, a member of the Women's Association of Kyoto, whose aim is to form links with people around the world through cooking and culture. After the short walk to her home, and after I had donned a pair of beguiling pink slippers two sizes too small, Tomoko gave me a morning of cooking lessons that included much deft twirling of chopsticks on her part and much ham-fisted shambling on my own. By the end of it, I had learned the correct way to make miso soup with soft tofu and local greens.

"It is all down to the quality of the dashi," Tomoko instructed

I also learned how to make a dish of spinach with sesame seeds and how to properly roll maki sushi.

"Roll first, now press, now turn over, and roll, roll, roll."

A particular favorite, a chirashi sushi, is composed of the rice remaining after the maki sushi has been made. It is basically a rice salad mixed with egg, offcuts of fish, and herbs presented in a wooden dish. Nigiri sushi, fish on top of a pile of rice, is seldom made at home but is available in restaurants, Tomoko explained.

Best of all, I learned the secret to perfect tempura. According to Tomoko, few housewives in Japan make their own batter anymore. One reason is that it can be a bit of a pain in the backside. The other, more important, is that tempura powder gives a crispier end result. I must have looked skeptical and a bit crestfallen, because Tomoko suggested that we do a comparison. We took the same items—raw shrimp and vegetables—and fried them in each type of batter. We did a taste test, which entirely proved her point.

After a few hours, we sat down to enjoy the fruit of our labor. Between us, we had created a meal that, she announced, would not disgrace a Japanese housewife.

It was not the end of my time in Japan, but the end of my time with this particular group of travelers. The next day I caught a train to Tokyo, where I had one more important place to visit—the Tsukiji Fish Market. One of the most remarkable places I have ever been, it can be confusing and intimidating unless you know the places to go and the rules involved.

I had agreed to meet Aaron, my Australian guide, at five in the morning, so that we would be sure to see the auctions in action. Apart from a fluent command of Japanese, Aaron counted among his skills an amazing capacity to retain facts and, as we walked around, he gave a wonderful history of the market and how it works in modern times.

In existence for over 350 years, the fish market was originally established to sell the fish not eaten by the nobility, by the same eight families who are in charge today. They rank among the wealthiest in the country, owning as they do the fishing fleets, auction houses, and distribution network of the fish from the market to all parts of Japan. As Aaron explained, the fish bought in the market can be in Osaka or Kyoto by lunchtime; on any given day, one in every seven people in the country will eat fish that was sold in the market that morning. It is an unfathomable feat of logistics, and also explains why both the buyers and sellers of fish have to be there from one in the morning.

Everyone knows about the incredible tuna that is sold in the market, but to see the auction in process was extraordinary. Frozen fish from the Japanese seas are brought in by small shuttle ships that go from trawler to trawler, allowing the larger boats to stay at sea constantly. The fish is brought in by one of the eight families and then examined by licensed buyers who buy from the same auctioneer. The buyers have contracts with numerous clients from high-end restaurants, department stores, and even convenience store chains to provide fish, so the pressure is really on them to buy the right product at the right price. With tuna going for nearly 5,000 yen per kilo, it is little wonder that they recently beat the one-million-dollar mark for a single fish.

After we had been to the auction area, Aaron led the way to the inner market, which is normally open only to wholesalers. Unlike most of Japanese society, this is not a place where the men hold sway. Here, women are in charge. As the men cut fish, the women sit in small wooden cubicles, do the deals, and keep track of all the cash.

The array of fish is beyond staggering. Abalone and eel sit next to tuna that would cost more than an arm and a leg back in London if, that is, one could actually get fish of that quality. Along with fish that I recognized must have been about one hundred types on which I had never set eyes before, and which Aaron said had no English name that he had ever been able to find.

Over thirty thousand people work in the market and it is, in effect, its own town within Tokyo, which means it also houses a vast network of support services, from restaurants to feed the workers to shops selling razor-sharp knives, and a general market to supply the public.

After our long stroll through all the areas of the market, we went for breakfast at Jiro's, named after its cheerful owner, Kujiro. Kujiro's family has been running a restaurant at the fish market for more than three hundred years, primarily serving the local porters and fish cutters. He spoke decent English, and explained that the morning's assortment of sushi fish had not yet arrived, which was a real disappointment, but offset by a bowl of rice topped with more of that unagi of which I had become so fond. It is not to everybody's taste, as the oiliness of the skin and the fatty nature of the flesh is unusual, but glazed with the slightly sweet sauce it proved to be the perfect breakfast.

After a quick walk through the back streets around the market, including a stop for a squid ink ice cream, it was time to head back to the hotel and check out.

In a little over two weeks in Japan, I saw a lot, but actually so little of what this country has to offer. I tasted amazing things, but only a fraction of the extraordinary variety to be found. I ate incredibly well, from the simplest skewers of bits in the yakitori bars of Ueno to the formal setting of our Kaiseki meal in Takayama. But, most of all, as *Eat My Globe* was meant to do, the food brought me in touch with people. People like Koji in Tokyo who treated me to my first meal in Japan, Tokomo in Kyoto who stood patiently by as I made a pig's ear of my attempts at maki sushi, and Yuka, our guide, who guided me to some of the best food of the trip.

Chapter **6**

HONG KONG: FEAST MEETS WEST

Hong Kong has a reputation for food to equal any on earth. From Chinese street food to the very highest examples of Western fine dining, Hong Kong's got the lot, representing its colonial past, its Chinese future, and its current economic strength, which make it a home to expats from many nations.

I thought it would make the perfect staging post to become accustomed to the Chinese way before I hit the mainland.

David and Francine Holden are a true Hong Kong mix. Francine, Hong Kong born and bred, David a relatively new interloper from New Zealand. They were friends of friends and had generously agreed to put me up for a few days as I ate my way around the former British colony. Their lovely home was set in one of Hong Kong's multitude of gated communities with security guards, live-in maids, and all the other accoutrements I associated with the expat lifestyle. However, I was soon put straight when Francine told me that over 80 percent of the population in these communities was now Chinese and that the expat population was on the decline as the Chinese mainland influence began to exert itself. Whatever the demographics of these communities, they are certainly welcome havens of peace and quiet compared to the rest of Hong Kong, as I was to find out in the next few days. But, for now, I just wallowed in the luxury of a family home and an incredibly hospitable welcome.

Next morning, I set out on Hong Kong's efficient public transport system to my first planned port of call. Mong Kok is everything you might imagine Hong Kong to be. Bustling streets of restaurants and shops selling just about everything, alongside stalls selling everything that the shops may have forgotten to stock. It's a wonderfully seedy area with hundreds of strip clubs and girlie bars nestled unapologetically alongside other shops. Large neon signs advertise hourly rates of the hotels and list the services provided.

I noticed lots of hairdressers with their unmistakable signature of swirling candy-striped poles extending over the pavements, hundreds of them. Did people in Hong Kong really have their hair cut that often? Later, when talking to David I found out that they were split into two very different categories, those that offer a cut and blow-dry and those that offer a cut and blow job. Apparently, you can tell which is which by the direction the pole is swirling.

The main artery through Mong Kok, in fact through the whole of Kowloon, is Nathan Road, which I used as a reference point as I wound my way through the backstreets, past the Po Street Bird Market, the Flower Market, the Ladies Market, and Temple Street Night Market, until I hit the southern tip of Tsim Sha Tsui. Although I had stopped for a breakfast snack of beef tendon soup at the start of my walk, I was in the mood for something a bit more elegant, and made my way to Sweet Dynasty, a restaurant popular for its dim sum and noodles and famous for its spectacular desserts. I ordered a silky, custardlike tofu and a pot of black tea, both of which slipped down a treat.

David and Francine had invited me to join them at Crown Wine Cellars, a former World War II bunker set high up towards the top of Hong Kong's towering Victoria Peak, that has been converted into a restaurant and a cellaring facility for the fine wine collections of Hong Kong's great and good. Tables were communal and as people ordered their own food, they brought out bottles from private collections to share with others at the table, who reciprocated.

It made for a fun evening and Francine, being in the wine business, opened some memorable bottles. By the end of the night, we must have each had twenty glasses in front of us, which had contained everything from gentle old-world pinots to jammy Australian fruit bombs. We didn't drain them all, but enough for me to know I would regret it in the morning.

I am not sure, however, that I shall be invited back. I am never backward in expressing my opinion, as you may well have gathered, and when I have had a drop, there is no stopping me.

One woman offered us a glass each of her favorite Pinot Grigio, a thoroughly nasty little grape in my opinion. I let her have both barrels, announcing to her and the world in general that "I begrudge the five minutes of my life it took me to drink that horrid little wine."

Little wonder that I used to get beaten up so regularly as a child.

To the bewilderment of my hosts, I decided to work off the next day's hangover by returning to Mong Kok and walking the whole length of Nathan Road, about eight miles, before crossing over to Central, the business district, for lunch. Among the stupid ideas I have had, this ranks pretty high, the weather was approaching ninety degrees, and the humidity meant that I was soon dripping like a leaky tap, but, like all mad dogs and Englishmen, I carried on regardless, ducking down side streets, stopping at the food stalls for sticks of fried dough or steamed buns filled with char sui and snapping away with my digital camera until I reached the ferry.

The Star Ferry has been crossing from Kowloon to Hong Kong Island since 1888, with only a short break during World War II. Until 1978, when a tunnel was built, it was the only way to cross between the two points, and a glorious symbol of British colonialism with whites only allowed to travel on the breezy top deck, and the local Chinese confined to the diesel-fume-smogged lower decks. Even today, when anyone can sit anywhere, you still have to pay thirty cents more to sit on the top deck. I am a man of the people, and thus took my place below stairs with the common herd as we crossed over the water to Hong Kong's business hub.

I headed for Lan Kwai Fong, the part of Central that houses most of the cafés and restaurants, and found that I had arrived just as most of the workers in the district were leaving their offices for lunch. It was mayhem, and every storefront and stand was six deep with people slurping bowls of noodles or shoveling rice into their mouths with chopsticks at a furious pace.

I forced my way to the counter of a place called Dragon Roast Meat and ordered a plate of crispy goose with rice. As I ate it, I noticed an article on the wall about Anthony Bourdain, sitting where I was sitting and eating more or less what I was eating. What little delusions I had of myself as a culinary Magellan flew out of the window in a puff of goose-flavored steam.

At my next supposed discovery, Mack's Noodles, I fought for a space at a communal table and ordered a plate of chewy noodles topped with crispy roast pork. This, at least, I was convinced, was virgin territory. A real find.

The man next to me finished his own plate of noodles, stood up, collecting his newspaper to reveal another picture of Mr. Bourdain, under the glass, sitting at the same table eating the same meal.

Both places, I found out later, were local institutions and had been featured in his television show, *A Cook's Tour*. I walked back to the subway with the sound of my application to the Explorers Club being ripped up ringing in my ears.

It was my last night in Hong Kong and the eve of Francine's birthday, so David had planned a special celebration at one of Hong Kong's most notable venues, the Derby Restaurant at the Hong Kong Jockey Club, where they were both members.

Recently refurbished at a cost of seven million Hong Kong dollars, the restaurant had also brought award-winning chef Donovan Cooke from Australia to take charge of the kitchen. Originally from the United Kingdom, he had worked with notable chefs such as Marco Pierre White and Gordon Ramsay. We had a memorable meal of more than ten courses of classical French cuisine combined with a New World flair for ingredients. Ravioli injected with egg yolks and poached in a pork knuckle broth, lobster tail cooked *sous vide,* and a linguine of squid tail were among the ten courses. Each came with a perfectly matching wine and, at the end of the meal, we sat back with large glasses of our chosen digestives and waited to thank the chef.

"Now, then, how was the meal?" A recognizable accent came around the corner. Donovan Cooke it turned out was originally from Hull, a town close to my hometown of Rotherham. We had a long discussion, as I told him the purpose of my visit.

"Eating around the world, eh? Like my mate, Anthony Bourdain?"

My heart sank.

"Aye, he were in here not so long ago. I think I get a mention in his book."

There was the sound of that application being ripped up again.

Next stop, China.

Chapter 7
CHINA: GREAT EXPECTORATIONS

China is a foreign country. They do things differently there.

I became only too aware of this as the crew on my flight from Hong Kong came through the cabin collecting any so-called Western media before we landed at Guilin Airport. It was confirmed when I was pulled aside by some frighteningly young customs guards who decided to give both Big Red and my computer a thorough going-over. They indicated that I was to sit down like a good little boy, then spent the next half hour looking at my photographs of Australia and Tokyo's fish market, before barking at me to move on and stop wasting their time.

I was to join a group a few days later for the journey north from Yangshuo to Beijing, but first would attend the well-regarded Yangshuo Cooking School.

The school had arranged for a driver to pick me up at the airport and, almost as soon as I stepped into the arrivals hall, my driver took Big Red from my shoulders and began to sprint across the car park with my ninety-pound rucksack as if it were a fluffy pillow. I finally caught up with him when he stopped by a battered red car, where he was using my case as a seat as he rolled himself a cigarette.

The road to Yangshuo was in an appalling state and my driver's strategy appeared to be to aim at every pothole he could find. Road designations seemed to be optional; he was carving out a route right down the middle giving way to no one and nothing, whether aged farmer on a cycle or two tons of metal truck. Near miss after near miss seemed to be avoided only by him leaning on a horn that gave out nothing but an apologetic "parp" by way of warning and, after two particularly close calls, I decided the best option was to follow the lesson of the ostrich:

"If I can't see it, it can't hurt me." I closed my eyes and buried my head into the comforting folds of Big Red, which was on my lap.

No sooner had I retreated into my little haven of security than I was dragged back from it by the sounds of singing. I use the term very loosely here. What came out of the driver's mouth was like the unutterable scream from a character in Dante's *Divine Comedy* and, as the driving got more dangerous, the caterwauling got louder. I am not sure if it was my own delirium by this point, but the wailing began to take on familiar sounds and, I am pretty sure that by the time we arrived in Yangshuo, I had endured much of the canon of Messrs. Gilbert and Sullivan, together with a strained rendition of "The Candy Man" from *Willy Wonka and the Chocolate Factory*.

My driver had one more surprise for me. Before we arrived at our final destination, he needed to take a leak. So, did he pull over to a safe spot and find a bush? No. He stopped in the middle of the road. When I say stopped, I mean he slammed on the brakes. Only the welcome presence of Big Red stopped me from plunging through the windshield. He then got out of the car, which was now parked in the middle of the road with trucks whizzing by either side, and began to pee against the front wheel. As he stood there, hands on hips and trousers open to the world, he gave me a wide grin and a big thumbs-up.

Oh, goodie, we'd bonded.

A few minutes later we were in Yangshuo. He couldn't have hung on for another five minutes? Obviously not. He dumped my bag by the reception desk and headed out of the hotel without a second glance at me as he lit another cheroot and mumbled another tuneless refrain. Unsurprisingly, I went straight to bed and had a fitful sleep filled with dreams of customs men riffling through my clothes and drivers giving me gummy grins.

Yangshuo is easy-access China; I could immediately see why the travel guides refer to it as a backpackers' colony. Its population of forty thousand is swelled by thousands of tourists from all over the world and, increasingly, from China itself, who come here to take advantage of the astonishing scenery of the Li River and the recent development of Yangshuo as a center for rafting, caving, and hiking. Yangshuo's main drag, Xi Jie, was renamed Western Street by the locals; it was filled with cafés selling an odd fusion of local dishes and Western food along with everything a backpacker could possibly need. There is a lot of hustling going on, and everyone has something to sell or a service to offer. But, unlike many places I was to experience later in the trip, it was done in an amiable way with very little hassle. I began to rather like Yangshuo.

I wandered around the market, my first experience of one in China, and not something I shall forget in a hurry. The sights, sounds, and smells were an assault on every sense and levels of cleanliness were, shall we say, variable. Live carp splashed in buckets of water to clean the river mud from their systems before they were chopped up to order, their heads tossed on the floor to gasp their few last breaths. Butcher blocks held every bit of animal imaginable, and the putrid smell of the meat brought a wave of nausea over me.

And, of course, there were dogs. There were live dogs cowering in cages and dead dogs hanging from hooks where the raw flesh was covered in a crispy skin from where blowtorches had been used to remove the fur. It is a challenge to see markets like this, with their opportunities for disease and morally worrying sights, but this is a way of life for much of the world's population.

I had seen the dogs in the market, and I thought I should at least try them in the flesh, so I decamped to a nearby restaurant where I was presented with a small bowl of braised dog with a less challenging side of steamed chicken dumplings. Dog was like a gamey version of pork and, when I was told later that the dogs are beaten before being killed because people believe that adrenaline in the meat makes it taste better, I decided that that was going to be my one and only dog experience.

Pam Dimond, an expat Australian who owns The Yangshuo Cooking School, told me this about dog. Fortunately, the food at the school was going to be a lot less challenging. Pat had arranged for me to be picked up by Amy, one of her managers, and taken the few miles from the polluted, bustling city to the serene surroundings of the cooking school where the classroom opened up onto the stunning vista of the region's Karst Mountains.

Over the next couple days, Amy showed me and my fellow classmates how to cook more than a dozen dishes, most of them specific to the region but others that I was to find later throughout the country. Carp cooked in beer was a local favorite, as is kung pao chicken, a dish from the Sichuan region, popular here because of the abundance of peanuts. The best dishes of all were also the easiest to prepare: vegetables stuffed with spiced minced pork, then steamed, were simple and delicious; and egg-rope dumplings, which involved making mini-omelets in a wok, then stuffing them with minced chicken before folding them over until they resembled Chinese dumplings.

After spending the morning cooking, we all sat outside in the court-yard to enjoy our food in view of the glorious surroundings. Our after-noons were free to go rafting down the river, kayaking, or caving. On my last afternoon, Pat organized a bicycling tour for me with a local farmer, Christina, around the rice paddy and peanut fields.

Bikes and I are not the closest of friends: the seat of this borrowed bicycle seems to have been specifically sharpened to cause maximum torture to my ample buttocks. The scenery may have been spectacular but, after two hours, my eyes were watering and my arse screaming in agony. So, when Christina, noticing my pain and knowing about my food interests, asked me if I wanted to help her prepare a meal for her family, I was off the bike before you could say "Maillot jaune."

It was a simple meal, but every last scrap of food on the table had come from Christina's small farm. She pickled her own garlic and used this to flavor oil before adding strips of home-cured bacon and green beans. She dug up taro, sliced it into fries, soaked it, and deep-fried it in peanut oil. She steamed fresh vegetables. It was everything I had hoped for on the trip; we were joined for our meal by her husband, her baby daughter, and her elderly grandmother.

I did not enjoy the next two hours as we completed our cycle ride and, when Christina deposited me back at the hotel, she let out an un-sympathetic chuckle, as I turned over the bike to her and wandered into the distance walking like John Wayne.

I guess a food writer's got to do what a food writer's got to do so— that evening I headed out in search of another unlikely ingredient, one that I knew would challenge my stomach more even than dog.

I headed to the night market where stalls selling food to locals and tourists alike were already busy. I looked for one I had chosen earlier, and began to point to a variety of ingredients for the vendor to stir for me in his already smoking wok. He didn't bat an eye when I pointed to the selections of vegetables or even the cured bacon. He raised an eye-brow when I pointed to a curly pig tail, but duly chopped it up. It was when I pointed to the real reason for my journey that he stopped and asked, "You know what is?"

I did. It was a cane rat, dried, and laid out, head and teeth in a rictus grin. I nodded and he shrugged, picked up the rat, and chopped it up, head and all.

He watched me carefully as he served the finished dish. All I can say is that it didn't taste like chicken; it tasted exactly like I imagined a dried cane rat would taste.

Let us never speak of it again.

Chapter 8
GORGING FROM THE THREE GORGES TO BEIJING

If you are of a nervous disposition, skip this section, because what you are about to read will not only make you sick, it will haunt you for the rest of your days as it haunts me.

My small tour group set off from Yangshuo on our month-long journey, which began with an eighteen-hour train ride north from Liuzhou to Yichang, and proceeded from there with a three-day boat trip up the Yangtze River. If anyone ever tells you that traveling by train is romantic, I want you to kill him for me and I want you to do it slowly. When traveling by train is combined with the traveling Chinese, it is one of the worst experiences imaginable.

The first indication of the horrors came as we were about to board the train. I suspected that the toilets on board might be a little challenging, so I headed to the public bathrooms of the station. (This, unsurprisingly, is the point at which the squeamish among you should look away, particularly if you are on public transport and do not want to throw up all over your fellow passengers.) I expected squat toilets. I even expected a bit of a smell. What I did not expect was half a dozen holes in the ground straddled by Chinese men grimacing and groaning in open view. One of the men also thought this the perfect opportunity to have supper at the same time and was eating a bowl of noodles.

I asked one of my new companions to go back to check to see if I had really seen what I saw. He returned a few minutes later looking decidedly green and confirmed it all.

On the train, things were little better. When we boarded, the state of our car in our chosen class, hard sleeper, even made our guide, Jackie, blanch and say, "This is the worst I have ever seen." The only challenge to the stifling heat was a sputtering ceiling fan, which did little but move around the dirt. We opened the window as we got moving only to be covered by a thin film of black goo from the engine and the heavy pollution outside.

I was in misery but, using my best Anthony Robbins's techniques, climbed up to my middle berth and tried to get to my inner happy place, which is a cocktail bar in a good hotel where I can get a free bowl of nuts. I managed to doze off, helped by the clickety-clackety of the wheels on the track, but was awakened by the sound of the stranger on the bottom berth voiding his rheum directly on to my sandals.

I had already realized that the sound of Chinese men spitting was going to be the soundtrack to my time there, but had not yet discovered how little they cared where and on what they spat. In the next weeks, I saw them spit in bars, in expensive restaurants, on the streets, and in buses. It was spitting dragged from the very soles of their shoes and I stopped wearing open-toed sandals.

As I joined the line of people waiting to use the grubby little bathing area, I wondered why every man, woman, and child was carrying a particularly pungent lighted cigarette. When I got to within twenty feet of the toilets, I realized that the smell was so bad, it would take your skin off at fifty paces. I quickly retreated to my car.

We had brought snacks with us on the train, and staff wandered around selling tea and soft drinks, but what I had seen, smelled, and heard had shriveled my appetite like a salted slug. By the time we got off the train at Yichang, our moods were as filthy as our clothes, and we said little as we climbed on the bus taking us to the boat.

Described as a basic Chinese-style tourist boat on our trip itinerary, ours was a medium quality boat, Jackie explained, allocated to us by the Chinese government. If this was medium, God help those on anything of lower quality. My first impression was that I would be spending the next three days on a floating sewer. The room I shared with my companion, Chris, had sticky carpets, dirty sheets, and slime caking the walls of the wet room. The so-called sundeck had already been commandeered by the Chinese men as a place to wash and hang up their baggy underwear; most of them were already sitting shirtless in the sun, practicing their spitting.

Jackie suggested we clean up and meet in the small restaurant for supper. The water from the lime-scaled showerhead trickled out in an uninviting brown and I came out feeling dirtier than when I went in. At least I was able to change clothes before I headed off to eat.

Remarkably, the food sent out from the tiny kitchen was perfectly decent. We were now in Sichuan province and it showed in the food, every dish of which carried the peppercorns and chilis for which the region is famed. The peppercorns, actually the dried berries of a local ash tree, have an anesthetic quality, which starts by numbing the tip of the tongue and works its way back through the mouth. The chilies, dried on the roadside in the heat of the sun, bring a soft heat and an unmistakable red tinge to many dishes.

The menu was limited, but the simple dishes of cabbage cooked in beef broth, Chinese sausage with zucchini, tomatoes tossed with eggs, and plenty of those chilies at least restored us to some semblance of good humor.

The boat trip also gave us an opportunity to see the Chinese in their relatively new role as tourists in groups. They wear matching caps so their guide can identify them and bark at them through a megaphone, even if they are only inches away. They stand when they are told to stand, take pictures when they are told to take pictures, and sit the hell down when they are told to sit down. God help any one of them who dares show some individual thought or initiative. I could not help thinking of the Borg, from *Star Trek: The Next Generation*. Resistance is futile.

In the evening, the men, never the women, would gather on the sundeck to watch their underwear flutter in the polluted breeze, drink vicious-looking brandy, and smoke powerful cigarettes. To keep cool, they would roll up their shirts, tucking them under their ample man boobs to expose their bellies, which they would then sit rubbing as they continued to spit with some professionalism.

I didn't go out on the sundeck much.

The boat made one brief stop at a small town, Fengjie, to which many people had been relocated when their homes were flooded by the construction of the Three Gorges Dam on the Yangtze River. Its market was filled with all the redolent ingredients of Sichuan food, Chinese broccoli, potatoes, endless varieties of tofu, dried meats and sausages, fresh chicken and eggs, and, on the floor everywhere, peppercorns and chilies laid out to dry. We had a terrific meal at a local restaurant that made full use of these, including pork with water chestnuts; tofu and shredded taro in a slick of red oil; and sausage and eggplants with more peppercorns and chilies than some of the group could manage.

I was delighted to be faced with new and deeply savory food. I ended up clearing a lot of the plates, which at least sent me back to the boat in my happy place for our last night on board.

I was very happy to arrive in Chengdu. In fact, I would have been happy to be anywhere but the floating diesel dustbin after three torturous days floating along the polluted Yangtze. When it was time to jump ship, I practically ran up the one hundred stairs, Big Red and all, and jumped into the waiting bus.

We were going to break our journey to Chengdu with an overnight stay at Chongqing, officially the fastest-growing city in the world, with a population of well over thirty million, most of whom have arrived in the last ten years. Not that we saw much of it. We were only there for the one night, and it is easily the most polluted place I have ever visited. While our guide was dealing with the laborious check-in procedure, I walked outside to snap a picture of the towering skyline, finding it hard to believe that ten years ago there had been only one building over ten stories high. The fug of smog hit me in the face within seconds and led to a prolonged coughing fit. My eyes were still watering the next morning. I ran back inside.

Although we had been sailing through Sichuan province for some time, it was our dinner that day in Chongqing that woke me to the possibilities of one of China's great cuisines. In London, I had always associated it with meat dishes, many with offal, swamped in a slick of overpowering red chili oil. Here, though, as we sat in a restaurant of Jackie's choosing, the flavors were more distinctive and elegant. The chili and peppercorns were there, of course—there is seldom a dish in which they do not appear—but a dish of crunchy green beans dressed with garlic and chilies was so good we had to order two more plates and, while Sichuan-style spring rolls and a dish of fiery pork went down well, the most universally favored dish was cucumber poached in a highly flavored stock.

The next day we were up and ready for the relatively short six-hour journey by train to Chengdu, the capital of Sichuan, which Jackie promised had the best food in the province.

It was a statement worth testing and, as soon as we had checked into our hotel in the Tibetan quarter of the city, we followed Jackie to the nearest snack street. These areas have been created all over China by local authorities concerned about the hygiene and standards of the old-fashioned hawker's markets, but even more concerned that markets could get in the way of potentially more profitable building development. Snack streets are fun and, not knowing if I would ever be there again, I tried to hit as many vendors as possible. Small cakes of rice came stuffed with barbecued pork; piping hot broth filled with noodles and chicken were laced with chilies; spicy minced beef was stuffed into bamboo canes, which cracked open to let the aromas escape. Sticky rice balls were filled with melting sweet tofu, and deep-fried pancakes with kiwi fruit resembled the best turnovers you can possibly imagine.

I would have been happy to work my way along the stalls all day, but some of my companions wanted to have tea in one of Chengdu's famous tea gardens. Chengdu has more tea gardens that any other city, oases of tranquility in an otherwise crazy town. Guests sit in bamboo chairs among greenery that filters out at least some of the pollution.

The Chinese are passionate about their tea, whether it comes from the thermos flasks that they carry with them for every meal, or the hugely expensive teas from the grand regions of the country. I wish I could have enjoyed it more, but the whole experience felt like a tourist trap. We were immediately surrounded by hawkers offering massages or to clean our ears; the tea was overpriced and frankly tasted like lukewarm water filtered through cat litter. I could not wait to get out of there.

Supper was a triumph, however, with that most classic of Sichuan dishes, the hot pot. When we arrived at our restaurant it was already packed with diners enjoying one of the ultimate communal meals. At the center of each table was a small burner and, on it, a large dish with two bowls. The inner bowl held stock and the outer bowl, an oil flavored with fresh and dried peppercorns and, of course, dried and fresh chilies.

We ordered thirty side plates of raw vegetables, quail eggs, and meat both cooked and raw, which we dipped in either broth or oil to poach. The tastes varied depending on whether you chose broth or oil, so those who were more squeamish about the potentially spicy heat could steer clear. Many also refrained from sampling traditional hot pot favorites, such as lung, hearts, and tripe, which I tucked into.

Hot pot is basically an offal fondue, and I can't think of a single thing wrong with that.

Before we continued on our journey, Jackie wanted us to experience a unique lunch at one of the most famous monasteries in the city, Manjushuri, which had a nationwide reputation for its food and also its own little secret. At the set menu feast, we sat around a large table with a lazy Susan in the center, as monks appeared and placed dish after dish after dish in front of us: plates of thinly sliced pink sausage; kung pao chicken, a classic of the region; sweet-and-sour pork, crispy and delicious; fish fritters in a lemon sauce topped off with chives and chili; crab soup thickened with sweet corn; green beans with quail eggs. The meal went on and on until we had well over thirty dishes before us. At the end, we could barely stand up to walk away from the table.

The monastery's secret was that not a single animal was harmed in the making of our meal. Every dish at Manjushuri was purely vegetarian. If veggie food tasted this good back home, not a single creature with eyes and a face would ever need to die for my benefit again.

There are forty million bachelors in China. This interesting fact was shared with us by our local guide as we sat on the bus taking us from Xi'an railway station to our hotel in the center of the city. "It is because of economic and demographic factors," he announced as if reading from an approved text.

As I recalled the twenty-hour train journey I had just endured from Chengdu, the spitting and hacking of the men, young and old, I couldn't help thinking that there may well be other reasons that Chinese men are bachelors.

There are two main reasons why tourists come to Xi'an. One is to use it as a base to visit one of the great archaeological discoveries of all time, the Terracotta Warriors. The second is that Xi'an has some of the most varied food in all of China.

The capital of Shaanxi province, Xi'an, takes its name from the Chinese words for "Western peace," a throwback to when the city was the beginning of the Spice Road between China and Europe. Still one of the most important commercial centers in the country, it displays its history everywhere: in the large, imposing Drum and Bell towers, in its sensitively restored city walls, and, most of all, in the faces of its people who are mainly from the Han majority and Muslim Hui minorities, both of whom bring their cultures and their food to the city. Xi'an has the largest Muslim population in China, which also significantly influences the food. I headed to the Muslim quarter as soon as we had deposited our bags at our hotel.

Muslim restaurants do not serve pork, which, after Yangshuo and Chengdu, where every possible part of the pig is served, came as a bit of a shock. In this quarter of Xi'an, mutton formed the basis of just about every meal. The most famous dish of all is the nourishing yang rou pao mo, a soup consisting of braised mutton in a broth thickened with the local wheat bread, which is brought to the table with side dishes of chili, pickled garlic, and cilantro to add according to your taste. It was warm and savory and, after twenty hours of toilet-avoiding starvation on the train, I was ravenous. Two bowls went in quick succession before the next course arrived, a dish of cold wheat noodles mixed with a sauce in which I could detect strong notes of garlic and vinegar. Akin to the cold soba noodles of Japan, it was an acquired taste that I never quite acquired.

After a stroll around the city walls, I met with the rest of my traveling companions to head to another famous Xi'an institution, a restaurant called De Fa Chang, which was acclaimed for its dumplings, and especially for its dumpling banquet. The locals have a saying, "If you do not have a dumpling banquet in Xi'an, you have not been to Xi'an at all."

It was certainly an experience. We were presented with more than thirty-five bamboo baskets of dumplings, containing examples from all over China: fish, chicken, beef, pork, seafood, and vegetables were all represented in boiled, roasted, steamed, pan-fried, or deep-fried form. Each presentation was different, the dumplings dyed in bright colors and served in a variety of shapes. The staff just kept coming until, by the end, even I had to push away from the table, turning down the offer of one last walnut-and-roasted duck steamed dumpling for fear of losing it all.

I had received an e-mail from a friend when I told him I was in Xi'an that read, "Funny, you go all the way there and the Terracotta Warriors are all over here in London."

I didn't have the heart to tell him that, while there may well have been an impressive display of a few examples on tour in the West, the Museum of Qin's Terracotta Warriors would not miss a few because there were thousands, in fact nearly seven thousand excavated so far in three pits, and thousands more still believed to be underground. An army created by Emperor Qin Shi Huang to protect him in the afterlife, they stand in their allotted ranks as they did on the day they were first erected, row upon row of them along with their armor and chariots, each warrior based on an actual person of the same status. The sights of the four main galleries of excavations formed one of those all-too-rare occurrences when expectations were matched by reality.

The first warriors were discovered in 1974 by four farmers, who have become superstars in the local community, playing the part to the hilt as they sit in the museum area every day, pimped up to the eyeballs, ready to sign copies of souvenir brochures and posters, for a fee, of course.

Two days was an all-too-short stay in Xi'an, but as we clambered on board the train for our last journey together, I was filled with genuine excitement about finally reaching one of the world's great cities, which was only slightly tempered eighteen hours later, when we arrived and faced an assault of the Chinese in full flow, as thousands of people fought to exit the station through the one door that was open. The notion of waiting seems entirely alien to the people of Beijing and, as I had countless times before on the trip, I found myself being pushed to one side by the aggressive locals.

The authorities had put in a queuing system at the station to bring some semblance of order to the chaos, but the locals just ignore it. As we stood patiently waiting for cabs, people screamed and jumped in front, shoving us angrily to one side. None of our group would be particularly proud to admit that we became quite aggressive in return, giving as good as we got until we could force our way into a couple of cabs to our hostel.

Having calmed down and showered, I went for a walk in the local area situated around Beijing's other main train station. The weather was in the high nineties, and the humidity meant that I was drenched within minutes of stepping outside. Looking for some respite from the sun, I ducked down a small alleyway and found myself in one of Beijing's famous *hutongs*, small warrens of alleyways built around a local water supply, the name apparently coming from the Mongolian for well. After years of threat from development, many are now protected, and the communities within them preserved. They are alive with energy, the streets filled with shops and food carts, steam rising into the air from the dumplings and noodles stored within. I was starving so, for a few pennies, I bought large round steamed dumpling stuffed with minced chicken.

The dish most associated with Beijing is, of course, roast duck. Everywhere you look in the capital, you see them hanging in the windows of restaurants, waiting to be served to tourists and locals alike. It's a dish I had eaten many times in the United Kingdom with my family. It had been the cause of many an argument as the waiter served the skin and the flesh only to take the bones, my favorite bit, away so they could use them to make soup for the staff.

Duck restaurants in Beijing come in many different styles, from the small family places to those in the grand hotels. Each has its own recipe and its own way of serving. Some serve the skin and flesh separately, others layer one on top of the other. Some make a meal out of the whole duck, offering hot dishes of soup and blood before the main event. All present the ducks to the table first, glistening and golden, before carving and plating alongside baskets of steaming pancakes, dishes of hoisin sauce, and shredded crisp vegetables for texture as well as flavor. Our first choice was one of the family-style places; we demolished two ducks and plenty of side dishes. The crispy skin, the melting fat, and the moist flesh worked in harmony with the slightly sweet sauce as I rolled more than my fair share of pancakes.

"You need for energy," Jackie said, rolling herself another dumpling, "for walking the wall."

I had not actually been that bothered about walking on the Great Wall of China, put off by images I had seen of sections restored to former glory filled with throngs of tourists following obediently behind their flag-waving guides. I had planned to give it a miss and head to Beijing's snack street instead.

"No, we not do like that," Jackie argued, explaining that there were still sections of the the wall in total disrepair after years of being plundered for their stones by local farmers and, if we were prepared to suffer a four-hour ride in a cramped minibus to the faraway sections of Jinshangling and Simatai, she would promise us a very different experience.

She was right, what followed was an unforgettable five-hour hike along the wall, where we often had to climb up crumbling parapets on our hands and knees, along ledges and down steep slopes along parts that had not been repaired, I would imagine, since they were built. There was barely a soul in sight and, for well over an hour, I found myself walking alone. My thoughts turned to my mother and my eyes began to water. I knew it had been one of her dreams to see the Great

Wall and, as I stared out in the silence, I offered up a small prayer that she could share this part of my journey.

The following day was my last with this group and we had one more sightseeing trip planned, to Tiananmen Square, then to the Forbidden City. The names of both places resonate through history for very different reasons, and both places depressed me for entirely different reasons. I recall seeing, as a young child, blurry images of missiles being paraded in front of the Chinese leadership in Tiananmen Square seemingly for the benefit of those in the West. In later years, of course, a burgeoning democracy movement found its spiritual home in the same square and, as it was put down with ruthless efficiency by the authorities, the images were screened around the world, and indelibly printed on the minds of all who saw the massacre.

Unsurprisingly, the Chinese government brooks no discussion of such matters, and our official guide denied all knowledge of such events. No mention is allowed in the media and the Internet is scoured for any unauthorized release of related images. China may be opening up but, at times like this, you sense that it is still very much a closed country. As a visitor, you are allowed to see what they want you to see and allowed to hear what they want you to hear.

The square is impressive. Built on the gardens of the original city of Beijing, which was destroyed by Mao, it has a capacity to hold over one million people and is still the center for many celebrations and concerts. Topping and tailing the square are reminders of China's hard-line past and its most significant leader, with a mausoleum containing the mummified body of Mao Zedong at one end and the instantly recognizable portrait at the other end.

Mao is more than just a dead political leader to the majority of Chinese, but his influence is definitely on the wane. The older generation revere him, almost to the point of divinity; to the younger generation with their exposure to Western culture, he and his school of thought are increasingly anachronistic, a piece of history, which greatly influenced where they are now but is of little relevance in their daily life.

My thoughts inevitably turned to the anonymous man with the shopping bag who became a symbol of the failed push for democracy as he stood in silent challenge in front of row after row of tanks. No one is quite sure what happened to him, but it is fairly certain that the Chinese leaders did not give him one of the luxury apartments they kept aside for their cronies.

Our guide led us from the square into the Forbidden City. It was impossibly crowded with tour groups, primarily Chinese, who followed dutifully after their flag-waving guides who were barking at them through plastic megaphones as they moved in irresistible waves through the grounds. Half an hour of wandering around saw me right royally pissed off at being shoved from pillar to post. I decided to head off to find something forbidden of my own, in the form of the more unusual snacks offered on the streets of Beijing.

Beijing's snack street is not for the squeamish. It specializes in things on skewers, like seahorses, silkworms, slugs, lizards, and scorpions impaled and all wriggling around as they are selected, dipped in oil to meet their deaths on a sizzling hot griddle. I tried some, so you don't have to. The silkworms were chewy and the seahorses chewier still. I could not bring myself to eat a lizard but watched in horror as it shriveled in its death throes as it was cooked for eager customers.

Across the road, I saw a sign saying "Gourmet Street," pointing down under one of Beijing's huge, modern shopping malls. Following the arrows, I found myself in an enormous food court, stretching hundreds of yards into the distance, filled with stalls selling food from every part of China. Spicy Sichuan hot pots, Cantonese roast goose, Silk Road noodles and mutton soups, fiery Hunanese fish, stir fries, dumplings, and braised pork knuckles. The quality was exceptional. The stall holders filled the air with amiable banter persuading you to come to their stalls as opposed to those of their neighbors.

"Eat this. Good. His stuff smell bad, very bad, make you sick."

It was enormous fun and large plates of food with the inevitable *bing pijiu*, cold beer, costs little over a pound each.

One day later, I was ready to say my goodbyes to my companions, but still had one more treat in store, thanks to Jackie, who offered to show me what she considered the best street snack in Beijing. She led me to a small stand where a man was busy cooking on a hot plate.

"Juanping," she told me.

It was a thick crepe brushed with hoisin sauce, lined with a crispy dough stick then sprinkled with chili, dried chicken, and spring onions before an egg was broken into it and the whole thing was folded over for easy eating. We stood outside the market eating our snacks. Jackie smiled. "Something to remember China by."

I thought of eating dog and rat in Yangshuo, of the train journeys and the boat trip up the Yangtze. I thought of the spitting and the man who ate noodles while using the bathroom. I thought of the melee at the train station and the horrors of the pollution. Then I thought about the cooking school, the simple meal I had helped Christina prepare for her family, the Sichuan hot pot, the snack street of Chengdu, the pao mo and the dumpling banquet in Xi'an, and, of course the roast Beijing duck here in my last port of call.

"Don't you worry, Jackie," I said. "I have plenty to remember China by."

Chapter 9
INTO AND OUTTA MONGOLIA

On the thirty-six-hour train journey from Beijing to Ulan Bator, I made the acquaintance of the companions who would be joining me as I traveled on the Trans-Siberian Railway to Moscow. We got to know each other over many bottles of cold beer provided by hawkers at the regular train stops and by becoming embroiled in a series of bitter, hard-fought card games. It was a small group of singles and couples, the youngest only twenty-four, the oldest a couple from Australia well into their seventies, not a bad feat considering that this had all the hallmarks of an arduous journey.

By the time we reached Ulan Bator we were all slightly disheveled. After a day's journey through the Gobi Desert, which filled the whole train with dust for at least five hours, we were all glad of the chance to have a long hot shower before heading out to see what Mongolia's capital had to offer.

The recent history of Mongolia is one of subjugation and tyranny. Since the time of Ghengis Khan and the decline of the Mongol empire, this small country has been under the control of other nations, first the Chinese, then, more recently, the Soviet Union. For nearly seventy years, Ulan Bator was a Soviet outpost with all that entails, the economy strictly Soviet socialism, religious observance outlawed, and all places of worship, including centuries-old monasteries, destroyed or turned into municipal buildings.

In the early nineties, when the Soviet Union shattered into nation states, Mongolia was cut loose to fend for itself. With no apparent source of revenue and no export market to the former USSR, it quickly descended into poverty, and would have also descended into chaos but for one factor: the incredible resilience of the Mongolian people. Brave, passionate, proud of their country, intensely close to their families, and unendingly hospitable, few people I encountered on my travels were quite like them.

Although the majority of the three million people of Mongolia live a traditional nomadic lifestyle, Ulan Bator's population just topped the one million mark. With no state funds to support infrastructure, the city's pavements are crumbling and road surfaces almost nonexistent. Medical services are negligible, and there is horrendous poverty everywhere you look. It is one of the ugliest cities imaginable; guidebooks describe it as a carbuncle on the face of the earth, with its architectural legacy of its Soviet days and high levels of pollution.

In a remarkable contradiction to this tale of gloom, there is a spirit of energy and renewal about Ulan Bator every bit as strong as the Chinggis vodka they seem so keen on drinking. Mongolia has a very stable education system and high levels of literacy. Many Mongolians speak excellent English, which they have to if they are to work abroad. The country also has some of the most advanced communications networks in Asia and, because of foreign investment in the mining of Mongolia's rich deposits of minerals, it now has large expat communities from all over the world, which inevitably means a large numbers of restaurants, cafés, and bars to serve them.

By far the largest group are the Germans and, whither go Germans, so goes beer, which also means that Ulan Bator is filled with pubs and bars selling the local beer, Chinggis, whose bar at the Chinggis Brewery is a fully decked-out German Bierkeller, with all the Mongolian waitresses dressed in dirndls, the traditional dress seen in Munich's beer halls.

Food in Ulan Bator is robust and has a lot in common with that of its former Soviet overlords, including lots of smoked fish accompanied by heavy stuffed pancakes, called kushuur. It is also the only place, outside France, where I have been offered horse.

For our first meal there, I ordered a horse rib. What came reminded me of the opening credits of *The Flintstones* when Fred orders a Bronto burger so big it tips his car over. I tucked into it with gusto. It was very highly flavored, gamey, and stringy, but perfectly acceptable, and after a few days on a train eating Pringles, I gnawed it down to the bone.

We only stayed one night in Ulan Bator before setting out into the

Mongolian wilderness for a couple of days at a ger camp, named for the traditional tents of the Mongolian nomads. Our guide, Nemo, was a perfect example of what was both laudable and unforgivable about Mongolia. He spoke perfect English, was witty, educated, and loved his country. By training, he was a urologist, but had not been paid for over two years by the government, so was supporting his family as a paid tour guide for Western visitors.

Nemo's passion for Mongolia was tangible and, as we drove to the camp, he took time to show us things that we would otherwise have missed. Small pyres of stones, topped with flags around which you walk three times to invoke a blessing and wish for a safe return, men at the roadside with their arms extended carrying hooded eagles used for hunting, and, best of all, an encampment of Mongolian nomads with whom he was acquainted.

He pulled our van into their camp and led us to one of their tents, with a promise that we were going to sample some traditional nomadic food.

When I told people I was going to Mongolia, to a person, they all asked, "Are you going to drink the fermented yak's milk?"

This is one of those fallacies that have become accepted over the years, but has no basis in truth. The Mongolians certainly keep yaks, thousands of them in great herds over the Mongolian wilderness, but only for their wool. They produce very little milk. *Airag*, the fermented drink so associated with the region, comes, in fact, from mare's milk.

Nemo showed us how it was produced. Mare's milk is poured in a bag made from a cow's stomach, which can hold nearly twenty-one gallons of the stuff. About 10 percent is kept back each time as a master culture and refilled each day with fresh milk.

The bag is stirred vigorously with a paddle every time anyone passes, in order to incorporate the new milk with the old. If children misbehave, they are punished by having to paddle the milk for an hour and any visitor entering the tent is also expected to give the bag a good stir as a thank-you for hospitality. The milk reaches a strength of around 5 percent and remarkably, Nemo told us, Mongolians can drink over a gallon a day. It is little wonder that they have one of the highest levels of cirrhosis of the liver in the world.

Nemo passed round a bowl so we each got to try some. I would love to say that I liked it, but I can't. It really was a noxiously dreadful drink, tasting as you would imagine a musty bowl of white horse piss would taste.

Other products we were offered, all made from horse milk, were equally challenging, including a tough, sour curd biscuit, a so-called vodka distilled from horse-milk yogurt, and a couple of hard cheeses. One item, however seemed to meet universal approval: *orum*, a cream with a thick skin, rather like clotted cream and made in a very similar way, by heating milk in a pot over simmering water.

We headed off for the camp and, as we pulled up to the small lines of tents, we all murmured sounds of approval. It was a small space, with about twenty circular ger tents, often used by Mongolians from Ulan Bator when they want to get away from the chaos of the city. Idyllic it certainly is and, after dumping my kit, I wandered off into the hills behind the camp. After the chaos of Beijing and the grime of Ulan Bator, the clean air and tranquility came as a welcome relief; when I returned to the camp, I could see it had had the same effect on the others in the party.

The next twenty-four hours passed very gently. People went riding. Not me, mind you. I eat horses, I don't ride them. People tried their hand at archery and went for long hikes. It was good to be out and about in the clean air and to have the opportunity to see the Mongolians doing things that have been part of their culture for centuries. Particularly riding.

It is said that "Mongolians are born in the saddle and die in the saddle," and it is true, they are incredibly at ease on horseback. The next morning, I awoke at about six and slipped out of my tent to enjoy the chill morning air.

As I wandered, I heard thundering hoofbeats. Climbing a hill, I looked out and saw two men on horseback herding their cattle. Hurtling along at full gallop, they were standing up in the stirrups, hands on their hips, as if the horse were simply an extension of their bodies. A magical sight.

When it came time to leave the camp, we all felt a little deflated. It was such a beautiful place to be, and the quiet and calm so welcome that we were all loath to go, but we headed back for one more night in Ulan Bator before the beginning of the next stage of the journey—the Trans-Mongolian/Trans-Siberian Express which, after all, is what the trip was all about.

Chapter 10
THE TRANS-SIBERIAN RAILWAY: RIDING THE RAILS FROM ULAN BATOR TO ST. PETERSBURG

It's a bloody big place, Outer Mongolia. So big that the next stage of the journey would see us travel for over forty hours and across two borders before we even hit our first stopping point in Russia, Irkutsk.

En route to the train station, we had stopped at Ulan Bator's state-owned department store to buy snacks for the journey, having been warned that there would be precious little food on board. Even though there was a dining car, we would be dependent on what we brought and what we could buy from the housewives who lined the platforms at each stop, selling pastries filled with cabbage.

We boarded the train at six in the evening, stowed the bigger luggage under the seats, and soon settled into the long journey with games of cards or Scrabble, reading from the floating library of books on offer, or simply sitting with a bottle of beer or glass of vodka and watching the world go by outside.

After my first train journey in China, I was beginning to enjoy these extended train rides, incredible though that may seem. I had figured out a routine to keep reasonably clean and the enforced periods of inactivity with nothing to do but listen to the rhythmic rattle of the train over the tracks was strangely pleasing.

Not so pleasing was the interminable wait at both the Mongolian and Russian borders. Five hours at the former challenged both patience and bladder, as our carriage attendants decided it was a good idea to lock the toilets.

The delay at the Russian border was more tolerable. After we cleared customs and our passports were taken away for our visas to be checked, we were at least able to get down from the train and walk into the nearest settlement to top up our supplies. The first thought, obviously, was to try the Russian beer, Baltika, available in grades from three to ten, with the lowest being the light, refreshing beer the Russian men like to drink during the day, and the highest being a dark, rich, black beer akin to stout.

It also gave us time to buy some of the weird and wonderful snacks, including tubs of dehydrated mashed potato and croutons, an odd mixture that became strangely more palatable as the trip progressed, as we reconstituted them with hot water from the samovar available in each carriage.

After we were cleared to go, we settled back in to our routine for the next twenty-four hours, until we reached Irkutsk, the capital of eastern Siberia, where we immediately boarded a bus to take us a short way to the Listvyanka, on the edges of Lake Baikal. There, we were split into smaller groups and billeted to spend the night as the guests of local Russian widows who rented out rooms in their apartments to raise extra income.

I paired off with Karen, another single traveler, and Andrew, our guide, joined us in the home of Ludmilla who, for some reason I never quite figured out, spoke to us only in German. Whatever the language difficulties, she was incredibly welcoming and soon had us sitting in her kitchen with cups of strong black Russian tea, plates of fresh vegetables, and bowls of *pelmeni*, small dumplings in broth, in front of us.

Despite the slightly forbidding appearance of the apartment blocks, remnants of Soviet times, the homes themselves were comfortable and warm. Much restored, we left our luggage and walked down to the edges of Lake Baikal to meet with the others.

The largest freshwater lake in the world, Lake Baikal contains over 20 percent of the earth's total unfrozen freshwater reserve, so pure that it is pumped from the lake straight to the homes of local people. It also provides a ready supply of fish to the local restaurants; just about every meal contains fish in some form, be it smoked, in patés, or freshly grilled.

At the local market, plump, stern women sold fish that they smoked themselves at every stall. The fish hanging from hooks above them swayed gently, giving off a wonderful smoky scent in the breeze. I just had to try some. They were still warm and bubbled with the oils released during smoking. The flesh fell from the bones and was deliciously sweet as it dissolved on the tongue. It spoiled me for other smoked fish.

Tradition dictates that visitors to Lake Baikal must indulge in one of Russia's favorite pastimes, the *banya* or sauna, which in this case meant sitting in a hut at the edge of the lake, slowly being boiled alive by steam coming from a wood-fired burner, drinking vodka, then throwing yourself in the ice-cold lake. There are no written statistics of fatalities, but I suspect the lake bed is littered with the bodies of middle-aged men clinging to vodka bottles. The combination of heat, cold, vodka, heat, cold, vodka made sure that, when we all congregated the next morning, we made little noise except a few gentle moans as we boarded the bus back to Irkutsk.

A growing city of nearly one million people, Irkutsk clings fiercely to its place in Russian history as the home of exiled revolutionaries from the Decembrist movement of the nineteenth century. It is also proud to declare itself a city built by women, in honor of the wives of the exiles who also chose to give up their lives of comfort in Moscow and follow their husbands to what was then a bleak outpost. The term "Decembrist wife" is still used in Russia to describe a woman who shows loyalty to her family in the face of extreme adversity.

Next to modern buildings lie side streets lined with the wooden buildings of its first incarnation, which made for a pleasant interlude before our next, longest part of the journey. These neighborhoods also provided us with our first close interaction with the Russians themselves.

For centuries, the people of Russia have had little or no individual freedom, first during feudal serfdom, then under harsh Soviet rule, they had been told what to do, say, think, and believe. They compensate for this lack of influence by now clinging to any scrap of personal power life might give them, and by making life miserable for anyone else who might need them to perform the services that they have been appointed to provide. They have an ability to appear exasperated at anything and everything no matter how good or bad that thing may be. Purchasing anything in any store involves eye rolling and shrugging of shoulders by the clerks who give you the distinct impression that your purchase is a terrible inconvenience to them, an insult from which they might never recover.

Checking into our very Soviet hotel had been challenging enough, but much better was to come.

A favorite drink of Irkutsk is *kvass*, beer made from fermented bread.

On just about every street corner, elderly women sit by large barrels dispensing glasses for a few rubles a time. Getting them to hand it over, however, is immensely hard work.

ME: "Kvass, please."

OLD CRONE: "Kvass?" Looks mystified as if she has never heard of it before despite the fact she is sitting next to a barrel with the word *kvass* written on it in letters two feet high. She makes sure to turn to anyone passing to show how unfair life is expecting her to deal with people like me.

ME: "Kvass," pointing to the two-foot-high lettering.

OLD CRONE: "Ah, kvass." Looks at me as if I had spoken gibberish and why was I wasting her time. Wearily pushes small button to dispense beer into the plastic glass as if it pains every bone in her elderly body.

ME: "Thank you," handing over exact change.

OLD CRONE: Stares at exact change as if I had given her a one-million-dollar note, rolls her eyes, looks around again to make sure everyone knows just how miserable her life is, then gives me one more look of withering contempt.

Unfortunately, the beer was not worth all that effort. It was cloyingly sweet, and I poured most of it away. Out of sight of the old crone, of course.

The next day, we were due to get back on the train for the longest stretch of the journey, some eighty hours across country from Siberia, in the Asian part of Russia, to Vladimir, a mere couple of hours' drive from Moscow. If Siberia were a country in its own right, it would be the biggest country in the world, which explains the length of the journey, but I was actually looking forward to it. I didn't even mind when we were confronted by the terrifying female attendants who would watch over us for the duration of the trip, and who barked instructions at us as if we were prisoners on the way to Stalin's gulags.

I slightly uncharitably christened them "Kong" and "Mighty Joe Young" and, at the advice of Andrew, our guide, went to try and buy them off with a bar of Russian chocolate. It didn't elicit even a hint of a smile as the bars were snatched from my hands.

There is a reason that Russian men have a life expectancy of only fifty-nine years, and almost always die before their wives.

They want to.

Apparently, some people are institutionalized after having traveled on the Trans-Siberian Express, having become so used to the routine, that, when it comes time for them to leave, it is a shock to their system.

Until I made the journey myself, I thought this had to be absolute nonsense, but it turned out to be true. After nearly four days of riding the rails from Irkutsk to Vladimir (near Moscow) with precious little to break the routine other than a leg stretch on a station platform or a walk down to the dining car, I had quickly become used to the rhythm of train on tracks, the water bottle showers in the morning, and the diet of dumplings, crisps, and pasties washed down with beer and vodka.

I had become used to reading, playing cards or board games, listening to music, and, as the guidebooks advised, just staring out the window for long periods of time. For someone who had almost fainted with misery on his first train journey through China, I really enjoyed the Trans-Siberian ride, and getting off the train in Vladimir was indeed a shock to the system in more ways than one. Not only did we all experience serious wobbly-leg syndrome, but we detrained into the cold winds of Europe in the same clothes we had been wearing in the humid warmth of Asia, and stood shivering on the station platform until our bus came to collect us.

We spent our first night in the pretty town of Suzdal, an eleventh-century capital of Russia, famous for having the highest density of churches in the country and for being where the tsars sent their wives to live in convents when they got fed up with them. After a good night's sleep and a huge breakfast, everyone, me included, was in good spirits as we boarded our bus for Moscow.

I had been to Russia's capital in 1998 for the Moscow Book Fair, accompanied by a literary agent who not only translated for me but guided me through the complicated etiquette of doing business with the Russians. This consisted mainly of drinking umbrella stands full of vodka or whisky before every meeting. By midday on the first day of the show, I was horribly drunk and had to leave the conference hall to go be violently sick at the feet of a large statue of Lenin.

I had not been back since, but knew that it had changed considerably. A friend who had been there more recently told me that the change was not for the better, that it was a dirty, ugly, corrupt, and dangerous city. It is all of that, of course, but also has elements of both a frontier town and a city that is rediscovering itself after years, even centuries, of deprivation and struggle.

Our hotel block was extraordinary. Converted from accommodation built for athletes during the 1980 Olympic Games, it was now one of the world's largest hotel complexes, with more than eight thousand beds. It was a short metro ride from Red Square, which gave us a chance to marvel at one of Moscow's great treasures: the stations of Moscow's underground railway. They are like nothing else on earth, certainly a far cry from the grubby subways of New York and London, and a damn sight more efficient. Towering bronze statues of Soviet heroes line the platforms, a testament to the power of Stalin during whose time they were built.

When we emerged into the autumn sunlight of Red Square, however, our plan to visit Lenin's tomb fell by the wayside as the mausoleum was closed for repairs, so we split up and headed in separate directions.

I was glad of the opportunity to be on my own, and planned to go for a budget-busting lunch. I worked up an appetite with a long walk along the Moskva River past the impressive monument to Peter the Great and through the grounds of the Red October Chocolate Factory, where production left a permanent sickly sweet haze hanging in the air, then headed up to Ostozhenka Street where I had chosen a restaurant called Tiflis for lunch.

Considered the finest Georgian restaurant in Moscow, it was also the lunch venue *de choix* for the country's oligarchs. It had suffered recently from the sanctions levied by President Putin after a spectacular fall-out with the Georgians, because of which they were not able to offer any Georgian wine or beer. However, it was a lovely place to have lunch, even if the prices brought tears to my eyes. Georgian breads stuffed with *suluguni* cheese, soft rolls of curd in yogurt, a salad of pomegranate seeds with chopped walnuts, and an expertly grilled lamb shashlik. After the privations of the train, it was everything I needed, and my heart only stopped for a couple beats when they presented me with the one-hundred-pound bill, which, to be fair, did include a small cup of tea.

We had considerable time to ourselves in Moscow, and I gladly took the opportunity to mooch and, after buying a bowl of borscht from a roadside stand, found a small park filled with neglected statues of Soviet heroes. I sipped my bowl of soup with its fragrant beetroot steam wafting into my nostrils, watched silently by my dining companions,

Lenin, Brezhnev, and Andropov, before heading back to meet my companions for an overnight journey, which, after our recent travels, was an unchallenging eight hours, allowing us two full days in Peter the Great's capital, which is an astonishing work of construction, rightly compared to Venice for both its beauty and its network of canals.

Now, in autumn, St. Petersburg was in all its considerable glory. Its courtyards, churches, and gardens looked impossibly beautiful in the watery sunlight.

Ten years before, after the Moscow Book Fair, I had readily agreed to spend a week in St. Petersburg over the New Year's holiday with the literary agent with whom I had become more than friends. I had enjoyed the city on that visit, but Russia in winter was, unsurprisingly, ferociously cold and we spent quite a lot of time in our comfortable hotel room. That in itself was no bad thing, but I did not see anywhere near as much of the city as I wanted to, and what I did encounter was through the thin slot left by a woolly hat and a thick scarf. Now, I had plans to catch up on lost opportunities.

The Russians, however, had different ideas. I had purchased a train ticket to take me from St. Petersburg to Helsinki for the next leg of the journey, and had arranged with the tour company to have my tickets delivered to the hotel.

Once we checked in, I asked politely if they had arrived.

"No," the woman at reception barked at me. "If they were here, I would have told you," giving me that all-too-common look of contempt.

I decided to give it until the next day and headed off with the others to spend time in the Hermitage, but found myself unable to concentrate on the wonders in one of the world's greatest museums. I called my ticket agent, who assured me the tickets had been delivered, so I headed back to the hotel to ask again.

The same woman was behind the counter.

"Are you calling me liar?" she snarled looking across at her colleague. "He is calling me liar."

I checked once more that evening, before supper, this time with another woman, who also denied all knowledge of my tickets. I felt a slight air of panic, and Andrew suggested that I consider alternative travel options on the overnight busses, which ran between the two cities every day.

Next morning, the staff remained obdurate, and I headed out to buy a bus ticket only to realize when I got to the station that I had forgotten my passport.

I headed back to the hotel, angry and frustrated, and stomped to the lift.

"You," a familiar voice snapped. It was the receptionist. "Do you not want your package?" She waved an envelope at me.

"*What?*"

"Do you not want package? It has been here since yesterday," she added with an innocent look.

I took the envelope and opened it, hardly surprised to see my tickets come tumbling out onto the counter.

"Bu, bu, but I asked you about these yesterday," I stammered.

"No," she shook her head. "You never asked me. It must have been some other person," she glanced across at the same nodding colleague for support.

I almost cried. At least now I had the tickets, so I could go out and enjoy my last evening.

For the last few weeks, I had been a backpacker. I may have been a lousy one who moaned a lot and was generally a bit useless, but I had been a backpacker. My companions along the way, being experienced travelers, had all helped me, but now it was my turn to drag them into my world, a world of smart bars, well-mixed cocktails, and plush leather seats. I gathered together a willing handful and led them the short walk to St. Petersburg's famous Grand Hotel Europe.

I commandeered a circle of seats in the corner of their lavish bar and called over the manager.

"Six Beefeater Martinis, up with a twist. Very, very cold. Very, very dry. Oh, and some crisps."

The drinks came soon and we raised them, by the stem, of course, not by the bowl, and made a toast.

I had been grateful to all of them, and the others on the previous trips for their support. Now, however, with my first shuddering sip of martini, I was back in my world and all was right with it.

Chapter 11
FINLAND, PERTTI, AND THE PRINSESSA

Sitting in my train carriage as it chugged away from St. Petersburg towards Helsinki, I experienced an agreeable shiver of pleasure as the Finnish customs official took a cursory look at my British passport, smiled, and said, "Enjoy your time in Finland."

After passing through the Chinese, Mongolian, and Russian borders accompanied by bladder-bursting waits on locked train carriages and unsmiling men with guns, to be back in the European Union felt pretty good.

It took an even sweeter turn when my taciturn companion in the train compartment offered his own Russian passport, only to be given the third degree and a thorough bag search that left him spending the rest of the six-hour journey grumbling and trying to fit his saggy underwear back in his luggage. I assumed a concerned expression, and even joined in with his Russian shrugs and eye-rolling at the general unfairness of life, but it felt good, really good.

I had added Finland to my itinerary because of my friend Martina Rydman. When she heard about *Eat My Globe*, I was buying her dinner, my frequent vehicle of communication, she suggested I should go to Finland. I had actually laughed so hard that I snorted a rather good Argentinean Malbec out both nostrils.

"Finland?" I shrieked. "That is the only country with a worse reputation for food than England!"

Martina began to wear me down with descriptions of how good the food was. Not an easy task because my only experience had been something called *korvapuusti*, a doughy breakfast bun more suited to hand-to-hand combat than eating. She won me over, however, when she said she could arrange for me to go hunting with a family friend who was well into his seventies.

Planning details of my visit was placed in the hands of Martina's family, and I arrived in Helsinki to be greeted by older sister, Paola, who helped me lug Big Red into her small car and pointed us north. I was not actually certain what was ahead of me, but with so much of the past two months having been organized to the last detail, it would be good to have some surprises. Paola explained that we were heading up to Juupajoki where the family shared a holiday home.

After a two-hour drive, we turned off the road and into the pages of a storybook. Their picturesque house sat on the edges of a lake whose surface shimmered a golden reflection of light from the low sun. The welcome from the Rydman family, too, was like something from a storybook, and their immediate, genuine hospitality contrasted starkly to many of my experiences in Russia and China.

Baggy, comfortable sweaters were provided to combat the chill in the autumn air, and my unsuitable footwear was quickly replaced by a large pair of Wellington boots, padded with thick Finnish socks. Snug as a bug in the proverbial rug, I was sitting at a table where they made sure I finished off at least two bowls of thick pea-and-ham soup mopped up with large chunks of bread, while they padded around and prepared my makeshift bed on an all-too-welcome-looking couch.

After such an early start, I could have dived under the covers right then. However, Paola had plans for me, and I was instructed to wrap up against the chill, as we were heading out to forage in the local woods.

Foraging is not a pastime for the Finns. It is a way of life and takes on a spiritual quality, influenced by the fact that their abundance of wild food kept the nation from starvation in the dark days after World War II. In fact, so sacred is the right to forage that it is enshrined in law that any person is allowed to go picking fruits and mushrooms on any land in the country within a given distance of the owner's house.

Our eyes and stomachs were set on mushrooms and berries. The woods surrounding their house have a thick carpeting of sharp, tangy lingonberries, which the Finns revere for the vitamins they provide. Alongside these, but much more scarce, appear clumps of meaty chanterelle mushrooms. I was warned to watch where I was treading in case I put my size tens on a patch of fungal goodness.

In a short time, we had filled up two buckets with prime specimens, and Martina's mother, Maija, headed back to the house to start preparing them for supper. In the meantime, I was prepared for the next stage of my adventure: hunting.

I originally had planned to arrive in Finland in time for elk-hunting season, when over fifty thousand of these mooselike creatures are culled, then butchered and prepared to provide meat for the rest of the year. I was heartbroken to find that, because of my schedule and the short season for hunting, I would miss it by mere days. Martina's brother-in-law, Henri, and friend Niko told me that we were going hunting anyway, this time for wild duck and grouse.

Hunting in Finland is a way of life. The Finns do not think that their meat and fish come in choice cuts wrapped in plastic. The birds we shot that day, if indeed we killed any, would end up in a pot, not as a trophy. Of course, when I say "we," I don't mean that I was going to be let near a gun. In a very wise decision for all concerned, I was briefed to stand perfectly still when we reached the hunting site and not to do anything that might make them think I was a bird. I strongly suspect, at this point, I was the subject of a dry Finnish joke. I can just see the headline, "Bald, one-hundred-eighty-pound man with large ears, wearing highly decorated sweater, shot when Finn mistakes him for small game bird."

We met up with our fellow hunting partner, Pertti, who owned the land on which we were about to hunt. Easily into his late seventies, and with a face marked with a crease for every one of them, he had been hunting since childhood and had probably killed more birds in that time than I had eaten.

We split into pairs and I headed off in pursuit of Henri, who was striding through the brush towards a small copse. Niko and Pertti went in the opposite direction, towards a spot overlooking an open field. Then we waited and waited and waited. Nothing. We had more chance of catching pneumonia than a bird. I didn't mind. The scenery was beautiful with blue skies patterned with wispy clouds passing over forests of green pines and trees shedding their autumn leaves. The air was clear and crisp.

Henri seemed disgruntled, however. He moved around a bit, letting out weary sighs that expressed his general dissatisfaction with the birds' failure to land in front of his gunsights. Then, he decided to make some peculiar noises. Meant, I expect, to sound like a lady duck with loose

morals, they really sounded like a desperate man making cartoon duck noises in the middle of a forest.

An hour or so later, still nothing, and even I was slightly disappointed. This hunting lark was hardly the joyous carnage I had been led to expect, with birds popping out of the sky at regular intervals. Eventually, Henri gave in. With another sigh, he broke his gun and called me over just as I was having a pleasant daydream about Sichuan barbecue.

"Did we catch anything?" I asked innocently, already knowing the answer, but unkindly looking forward to the sheepish reply.

"No, but Niko and Pertti did," he said, a mite too tersely.

How did he know? I hadn't heard any shots ring out. Perhaps there was an intuitive connection between brother hunters in Finland built up over centuries. Perhaps, after years of hunting, he could smell a mixture of cordite and death in the wind. Perhaps, this particular group of hunters had developed their own form of communication involving hoots and squawks that a novice like me would have mistaken for animal sounds.

"They texted me," he said holding up his Nokia.

The others had indeed caught a couple of beauties, plump and ready for hanging. Pertti, who was sitting on the front of his car with the ever-present cigarette dangling from his mouth, posed for a picture with his prize as his two young disciples looked on, birdless.

Pertti set off home to his wife so she could prepare the birds for a meal the next day to which we were all invited. We headed back to the Rydman house, Henri and Niko talking about just how close they had come to shooting some beauties of their own. 'Course you did, boys, 'course you did.

That night, it was fish on the menu. A dish called *loimu lohi*, which is one of the simplest dishes you can imagine but impossibly tasty. It's prepared by nailing a whole side of salmon to a plank of wood and leaving it to smoke gently for a few hours over the embers of a fading fire.

Dishes like this appeal to me. Get a great ingredient and don't screw around with it too much. When supper was ready, I cut a large slab of oily fish and ladled a spoonful of the mushrooms we had picked earlier, cooked in a little cream, onto my plate. It was a truly delicious meal in the welcoming surroundings of an equally welcoming group of new friends.

It is little wonder that, as soon as I dived under the covers of my put-me-up, I was asleep and dreaming of duck noises.

The next morning, it was time to meet Pertti's wife, whose real name was Kiti, but was known to one and all as the Prinsessa. It is hard to know how to describe a woman who, like so much I had experienced in Finland, stepped straight out of the pages of a fairy tale. A plump woman with a face brightened by a constant smile, Kiti's entire existence seemed to involve making sure that everyone she met was eating all the time.

As I arrived at their picturesque house, Kiti was already hard at work baking and, as I sat down, poured me a large glass of fresh rhubarb and ginger juice that she just happened to have made. She gave me a tour of her house, filled to bursting with a lifetime's collection of bric-a-brac, before sitting me down to talk about her greatest passion, food. I fell in love immediately. She was a kindred spirit and, as we talked, we cooked together. We prepared more of those meaty mushrooms, we stuffed wild ducks with apples and garlic, made salads, and we laughed. A lot.

I had not really spent that much time cooking with my own mother. The kitchen was her domain and I just enjoyed the end results. Now that she's gone, I have added it to a long list of regrets. But sitting there with the Prinsessa, I got just an inkling of what it might have been like.

By the time people began arriving for lunch, the Prinsessa had already laid out enough food to cause the dining table to sag under its weight. Alongside the ducks, which had been braised in cream, were rolled herrings, wafer-thin slices of cured elk, a whole poached salmon, and chanterelles served three ways: pickled, in cream, and tossed with apples and walnuts. As tradition required, Pertti read a quote about the joys of sharing the harvest of the land and then we all tucked in. Almost everything served had come from their land or the skies above it.

Among all this abundance was a small dish of new potatoes from the garden. I popped one in my mouth. It was the best potato I had ever tasted. Needing no accompanying salt or butter, it was sweeter than candy, and I returned to that bowl many times to sneak more. We ate until we had to be rolled away from the table. We then moved to their parlor to take tea with a slice of apple cake. While everyone helped themselves to a slice, I am not too proud to admit that I sneaked back to the dining table and stole the last potato.

If *Eat My Globe* were about anything, it was moments like this. Sitting with people who were, until recently, complete strangers, sharing their delicious food. At the end of what would prove to be one of the hardest legs of the trips—China, Mongolia, and Russia—to be cocooned in the welcoming arms of a loving family, even if it were not my own, was a very special thing. I shall never forget it.

That night, as I went to bed, however, my mind was on other things. I had already turned my attention to the next stage of the journey.

I was off to look for America.

Visas

IT IS THE RESPONSIBILITY OF THE PASSPORT BEARER
TO OBTAIN NECESSARY VISAS

Given leave to enter the United
Kingdom for an indefinite period.

IMMIGRATION OFFICER
* (035)
-7 JUL 1978
HEATHROW

IMMIGRATION OFFICER
(386)
EMBARKED
-5 OCT 1978
HEATHROW (2)

-5 JAN 1979

UNITED STATES, MEXICO, ARGENTINA, BRAZIL, U.S. WEST COAST, SCOTLAND, MUNICH, AND ICELAND

Chapter 12
AMERICA: FED, WHITE, AND BLUE

I love the United States. I always have, since my first visit in the early 1980s. It is a country of endless variety and, whatever your heart's desire, you can find it somewhere.

I love the uniquely urban landscapes America has given to the world. I adore driving through the country and seeing signs that say, "Gas, Food, Lodging." I giggle with delight when I see signs for "The World's Largest Thermometer" or "See the Bible Written on a Grain of Rice." Most of all, however, I love the people.

Americans get a bad rap, partly because of American tourists abroad who, for decades, believed that every country in the world had to modify itself so that U.S. visitors could see the sights, but still feel as though they were back home, and not have to come in contact with any nasty foreigners and their strange food. This has changed, although there are still elements of what I once heard beautifully described as "nervous Americans with bum bags." These days, however, the modern American traveler is savvy, more enthusiastic, and more adventurous than ever before.

In the United States, I have found Americans to be extraordinarily engaging, frighteningly open, and the most passionate and loyal friends any man can have. I count myself fortunate to have many.

I like eating in America, too.

I am not just talking about the dining scenes in major cities like New York, Los Angeles, or Chicago, where, to be frank, the restaurants can be as mediocre and overrated as anywhere else in the world. I am talking about the food that Americans seem almost apologetic about and are often loath to admit liking—dishes that, when made well, are simple but stunning: Barbecue, a legacy of German butchers; baking, a legacy enriched by Jewish immigration from Eastern Europe; and simple things like meatloaf and hamburgers, which can be utterly delicious.

This was the food I was in search of. Oh, of course, somewhere along the way, I was sure to poke my curious nose around the entrance of a few high-end restaurants, but that is not where the great stuff is, that is not where the great people are, and it is certainly not where the real America is.

Kansas City, Missouri

Kansas City is an odd place to begin an eating tour of America. In fact, it's an odd place to visit without a good reason. A pleasant city with a vibrant community spirit and bags of culture paid for over the last century by cattle, rail, and lumber magnates, Kansas City still feels as if it never quite recovered from turning down the opportunity to be the central hub for the transcontinental rail lines back in the nineteenth century, an opportunity that went to Chicago instead.

Mark Cordes, the most wholesome man I ever met, uses phrases like "gosh darn it" with no sense of irony at all and calls so many people "sir" or "ma'am" that I kept thinking we were on the set of *Little House on the Prairie*. We became friends while doing business together and, for years, he had been inviting me to join him at the American Royal, arguably the biggest BBQ competition in the world where, my research told me, nearly four hundred thousand pounds of meat were cooked and consumed in two days every year.

With the exception of my sister who never touches the stuff, meat is rather important to the Majumdar clan. In fact, along with the Great Salami, I have predicated entire holidays on it, heading to Texas and Louisiana to spend two weeks on the trail of great barbecue or to the harsh landscape of Spain's Extremadura in search of the best ham in the world. We talk about meat a great deal, and love pressing our noses against the windows of local butchers, watching in awe as they use their skills to produce glistening cuts of things that once made cute little animal noises. We have even been known to secretly rub the fat on joints of beef, pork, or lamb, while emitting plaintive little sighs.

So, of course, I was interested in going to an event where thousands of midwesterners cooked and ate vast amounts of meat while drinking beer. I am many things, but I am not crazy enough to turn down that kind of opportunity. I would have gone sooner but business commitments prevented me from making it. Now, there was nothing stopping me and I turned up at Mark's house two days before the event and made myself comfortable in his guestroom before he had the chance to say, "That's swell."

The barbecue competition is part of a bigger American Royal event that brings together people from all over the Midwest to celebrate the cattle industry. There are rodeos and farm shows and events lasting a few weeks. The barbecue competition is the centerpiece, with more than five hundred teams competing in two events. The Open is for anyone who can afford to rent a space, and the Invitational is for the serious professionals who already have a championship under their belts.

It is hard to explain the scale of the event even if I tell you that it covers a space at least the size of ten football fields. It is immense.

Barbecue is serious business in America. It is not even closely related to barbecue in the United Kingdom, which usually means lots of rain and swear words, pieces of supermarket chicken charred on the outside and life-threateningly red on the inside and, lots of tears as what should have been a nice family occasion all goes tits up in withering blasts of accusations and salmonella.

In America, barbecue involves huge hunks of meat being smoked over different woods for hours on end, in smokers the size of a small European car, so they are cooked to succulent perfection. It involves slabs of pork or beef ribs marinated in secret rubs and cooked until the meat begins to fall off the bone. It involves chicken cooked until the skin is crispy and the flesh moist and it involves links of plump, spicy sausages with the juices bubbling under the skin ready to release their flavor at the slightest tooth pressure.

Barbecue varies from region to region. In Texas, it is all about the cow. In Kentucky, you may even see mutton on the menu. In the Carolinas, it is pork. In Kansas, it's a combination of fatty beef brisket cooking next to pork butt and baby back ribs. Every American thinks his state's barbecue is the best. Those arguing usually have guns, so I tend not to express an opinion.

(Cough, "Texas," Cough.)

I had been invited to join Burn Rate, a motley assortment of Mark's friends who barbecue in order to do a bit of male bonding. In the Midwest, barbecue is very much a male event, where the womenfolk stay home and the men erect a marquee and prepare two large smokers for the three days ahead.

"We are barbecue widows," team member Paul Diamond's wife, Kathy, sighed. "The boys do this and we take care of the kids for a few days. But, next month, all the girls get to go to Cancún or up to Chicago for the weekend and the men look after the children."

It was hard work, lugging hay bales to mark our patch and erecting fences to create a perimeter, but, cooled by cans of beer pulled from garbage cans filled with ice, and fueled by some ribs that had been thrown on the smoker to test the heat, we were able to turn an assortment of cases, freezer boxes, and offcuts of wood into an attractive party space with a working kitchen.

After we had more or less set up our space, Paul tossed me a nice cold one and asked, "You wanna rub some butt?"

I am not normally that kind of boy but, in this case, yes, I did, I wanted to rub some butt very much indeed. We headed over to the kitchen area and I was handed gloves of the sort that make me want to run and hide when my proctologist puts them on, before Paul opened one of the freezer boxes and produced a large piece of pork.

"About five pounds," he announced proudly. "We have about fifty of them. I'm not sure it will be enough." He was deadly serious and passed me one to work on.

First we smeared each of them with French's mustard "to hold the rub on," Andy Roscoe, another team member, explained.

Then we heaped dry rub on to the mustard and began massaging it into the meat which, I will admit, was a slightly sensual experience.

"There's oregano in there," Andy explained, "a little rosemary, garlic, lemon pepper." The list went on longer than the credits from a *Star Wars* movie. Americans love to explain their ingredients at great length, but I didn't mind, I was just happy rubbing away, grinning like a buffoon.

"I can't ever recall seeing you look so happy," Mark said.

He was right. Buzzed with a couple or three beers and cheerily giving a foot rub to a dead pig, I was rapidly coming to the conclusion that this was one of the happier days of my life. It got better. A rack of ribs, the first, was taken from the smoker for us to try, and the whole team gathered around the table grabbing handfuls of succulent pork, moaning in pleasure as we took our first bite.

"The rules say that the meat should fall from the bone only where you are biting and not off the whole rib or it is overcooked," said a teammate. "These are good, but they are not good enough for the competition."

By now, it was beginning to get dark and, our setup done, we prepared more meat and began to chill out after hours of hard work in the hot sun. Jeff Teeven, another team member, produced the biggest bottle of Jack Daniel's I have ever seen and poured me a three-finger slug and then the same for himself, which he topped off with Coca-Cola.

"We've earned this," he sighed, taking a long draw from his plastic cup.

Because of strict food laws, the American Royal is not, as I had imagined, an opportunity to flit from one stand to another sampling barbecue. It is more like a series of private parties to which friends and relatives are invited along with sponsors, often the companies for whom the team members work.

We were all set up for the following night, and most of the team looked like they were ready to drop. Some, in fact had already begun to flag and were draped over hay bales. Others had retired to the back of the van, where they had placed sleeping bags and pillows. I can only take male bonding so far and Mark, thank God, felt the same, so we left them to it and drove back to the comforts of his house for a good night's sleep.

By the time we arrived the next morning, the team had already been hard at work preparing the meat both for the competition and the night's party. The two smokers were stacked to capacity with brisket and pork butt; chicken and ribs were marinating happily in freezer boxes on the floor. There was not a lot left to be done. Most of the team were having breakfast, which from the appearance of ribs and whiskey on the table seemed remarkably similar to supper. I was not quite up to this breakfast of champions at eight-thirty in the morning, so headed off with Mark to see the rest of the showground.

All the teams were getting ready for action and ranged from small mom-and-pop teams out to have a weekend's fun to serious contenders with large banners, enormous smokers, and even stages for live music to be played during their party. Best of all were the names. I thought our own Burn Rate was good, but it paled by comparison to Whiskey, Women, and Wibs; Motley Que; The Master Basters; and, finest of all, hats off to Morning Wood.

Mark had arranged for me to join a press tour of some champion teams in The Invitational, so I could see how the professionals did things, so I made for the arranged meeting point. There, I found Chris, one of the organizers, talking urgently into his cell phone. He waved me over.

"Are you Simon, Mark's friend?"

I nodded that I was. He seemed relieved.

"Okay, here's the deal. My father has been taken ill and I have to rush off. Here is the map showing where the teams on the tour are situated and there . . . , " he added, pointing at a small group of people, many wearing Stetsons, "is the group that needs showing around."

And, with that, he headed off, flipping open his cell phone to make another call.

Which is how a bald forty-something from London ended up guiding visiting press from all over the United States around the world's biggest barbecue competition. Some of the group began to ask me questions about barbecue in general and the American Royal in particular. It was too good to resist and, with my accent, I knew they were going to fall for whatever baloney I happened to be spouting.

If you have ever read in your local newspaper that barbecue was invented in England and brought over to America on the *Mayflower* or that the American Royal was first held in 1875, is normally opened by David Beckham and Posh Spice, or that the Queen of England likes a bit of fatty brisket, you know who to blame.

The members of the major pro teams were a little perplexed when the group arrived headed up by an Englishman, but were soon handing over samples and explaining their methods of making championship barbecue. I thought the taste of what we had done at Burn Rate was pretty good, but these guys were the business. Their pulled pork had a fabulous char created by adding brown sugar to the rub, their brisket fat just melted on the mouth like cotton candy, and their ribs had just enough bite to make the hunt for meat worthwhile. Little wonder that some of these people spend every weekend of the year competing, and can earn up to two million dollars in prizes and endorsements.

Evening was drawing in and the parties were just getting underway. Country music blared from speakers all over the campground, and I threaded my way back through the crowds to the Burn Rate marquee where the party was well underway. The wives of the various team members were gathered, staring in horror into the back of the truck where their husbands had been sleeping, a space that now looked like a cross between *Lord of the Flies* and something from Alexander Solzhenitsyn. Their children had already begun to dive headlong into the food we'd laid out: nearly four hundred pounds of meat, I was told, as well as salads, coleslaw, beans, bread, and desserts. It was easily enough to feed five hundred or more and I was glad to see a steady stream of people arriving to party.

"You're grinning again." Mark nudged me, and I realized I was just standing there with an overburdened plate in my hand and a huge smile on my face, still trying to take it all in. Not just the scale of the event, the amount of work it had involved, and the unbeatable taste of barbecue—my reaction was more about the people. Over the course of the evening, each one of the team had come up to me and personally invited me to come back again anytime I wanted. Some had offered accommodation if I ever got fed up with staying with Mark, and others had said just to come over anytime anyway, just for the hell of it.

This was what this whole trip had been about—the chance, through food, to meet people whom I could genuinely call "friend." And here, in America's Midwest, I had found a whole group of them.

I forked a large mound of pulled pork into my mouth, turned to Mark, and just nodded.

Next stop, Chicago.

Chapter 13
CHICAGO: DOG EAT DOG

I am slowly beginning to evolve a theory about American food. It is by no means fully gestated but basically is that the United States' greatest contribution to world cuisine is . . . the sandwich. This is, assuredly not meant as a criticism. If you ask me the same question about the United Kingdom, for example, I would cite the pie. And that is a very good thing, indeed.

Oh, and before all the amateur food historians head out to buy a ladder to climb on the highest horse they can find, I know the Americans didn't invent sandwiches, the British did. But, as with soccer, we sent the sandwich out into the world for everyone else to do better.

In America, the concept of slapping incredible ingredients between slices of bread has reached its highest point. Americans, in fact, have raised the sandwich to an art form. I am talking about portable food, originally designed to feed honest, hard-working folk on the go for small amounts of money, that has become iconic. I am talking about the po'boy and the muffaletta I was hoping to see in New Orleans. The cheese steak I had marked out in Philadelphia; the pastrami on rye, which some say New Yorkers cannot live without; the barbecued brisket sandwich I had eaten in Kansas and was looking forward to in Texas; and, of course, hamburgers and hot dogs, perhaps America's biggest contribution to the world's culinary landscape, exported to and copied in every corner of the globe.

This theory began to find fertile soil in my brain as I headed off for three days in one of my favorite cities anywhere on earth, Chicago. To my mind, Chicago is one of the truly great American cities. New York, like London, is a city of the world and operates on a different level. Chicago, on the other hand, could never have been imagined or built anywhere but America.

Its architecture, its location, and, of course, its food make it stand out from any other city in the United States. Every time I walk its streets or take a nighttime cab ride, I find myself staring open-mouthed at its skyline, with buildings that represent some of America's greatest achievements, from the towering Gothic splendor of the Wrigley Building to the International style high-rises of Mies van der Rohe. Chicagoans also offer a uniquely American combination of brusque charm, brashness, and a childlike enthusiasm for their own town.

I had been particularly pondering the evolution of the sandwich because, as I get older, I find myself increasingly underwhelmed by so many restaurants' meals. It may be that, after thousands of them, I am jaded, or it may be that, after years of eating food that has been messed around with by chefs keen to show their skills, my taste buds just crave the simplicity of good ingredients.

Admittedly, while in Chicago, I did not trouble the very highest end of restaurant dining by visiting Charlie Trotter or Alinea, but the restaurants I did visit came well recommended by locals and were packed to the rafters with diners who seemed happy enough. The meals, though, were ordinary and fitted neatly into the identikit mold of midrange American dining.

I found myself much happier eating stuff between bits of bread, particularly, in Chicago, the hot dog. My first was at a legendary joint, the Weiner's Circle, which is famous not just for its hot dogs, but also for the abrasive nature of the staff who are, shall we say, not the sort of people you would take home to tea. I had just had a blah lunch at a place called North Pond and, was feeling miserable and, even more shameful, still hungry. On the way back to my hotel I popped into the Weiner's Circle.

"What the fuck d'ya want, big ears?" shrieked a large African-American woman through the serving hatch.

"Er," I stammered, "I am not sure."

"What the fuck kind of accent is that?" she hollered. "Are you retarded?"

"No, I'm British."

"Same thing," she countered before turning to a hidden colleague in the kitchen. "We got the goddamn Queen of England out here."

Slightly shaken by this interesting approach to customer care, I ordered quickly.

"A red hot . . . er, with everything." I had no idea what a red hot might be, but I wanted to get the whole experience over with.

"That's five-forty, Big Ears," she extended a chubby paw towards me.

I handed over ten dollars and waited for my change. Instead, she put it in a large jar marked "IT'S FOR THE TIPS, BITCH" and glared at me.

"That okay with you, Big Ears?"

"Yes, ma'am," I whimpered and stood to one side to wait for my dog like a good little boy.

It was all schtick, of course, which would have mattered if the dog were no good. I need not have worried. It was a great dog and worth all the abuse and the 90 percent service charge extracted from me for the pleasure.

I am funny that way and just like being abused. Any takers form an orderly line.

If that dog was good, the next proved to be one of the most memorable tastes of the whole trip to date.

I was lucky, in Chicago, to have contact with Adam, the poor chap who had shared a room with me as I traveled around Japan, and who had seen me parading in little else but a variety of short silk robes. Adam lived close to my hotel and joined me for several meals. While he was working, he put me in the charge of his girlfriend, Saritha, who seemed happy to wander around with me as I looked for things to eat. I did what any gallant chaperone would do when accompanied by an attractive young woman: I made her walk with me through one of the rougher parts of town in search of another hot dog, in this case at Hot Doug's.

When I had done my research, Hot Doug's was the name that came up most regularly. A little bit more research showed that Doug was an old punk rocker and had named some of his offerings after the members of my favorite band of all time, the Buzzcocks.

It was obviously kismet.

When we arrived, Doug himself was seated behind the counter and, as the line shortened, I took in the posted menu. The Pete Shelley was a temptation until I realized it was a vegetarian option. I just couldn't do it. Saritha, however, was a vegetarian, which probably explains the additional whining when she realized we were going to a hot dog joint. She leapt at the chance of a Pete Shelley. I went for a standard frank with everything, some fries, and a diet Coke (well, I was having to watch my weight on this trip), and we took a seat in the cheerful little dining room.

Three minutes later, our food arrived. On one of their windows they had hung a sign which, to paraphrase, said that there are few things better in this world than an encased meat sandwich. They are right. This was fabulous even when splashed with that hideous green relish Chicagoans love. The fries were good, too, although I was disappointed that the variety cooked in duck fat, which I had read so much about, was only available on Fridays.

I only had a limited time in Chicago, having squeezed in a couple days between Kansas and an invitation to Ann Arbor. I did not really have time to explore the bewildering variety of food Chicago has to offer. I did not even have time to visit one of Chicago's legendary steak houses.

But I really wanted to tell you about those hot dogs, a simple sandwich that catalyzed my theory about what makes America such an amazing place to eat. For that alone, I am glad I went to Chicago.

Oh, I did have a burrito as big as my head before I left town.

Well, you are forced to, aren't you?

Chapter 14
ANN ARBOR: THE CULT OF ZINGERMAN'S

My friend, Gauri Thergaonkar, another of those people unfortunate enough to have made my acquaintance via a food Web site, is a long-time resident of Ann Arbor. As soon as she heard about *Eat My Globe*, she extended an invitation for me to head to Michigan and spend time with her.

A campus town for the University of Michigan, Ann Arbor is filled with bright, young idealists still waiting for life to come and beat the living crap out of them, and lots and lots of coffee shops for them to sit around in while waiting for that to happen. It might seem strange to cut short a visit to Chicago, one of the great eating cities in the country, to head up to Ann Arbor, where my own past experiences with restaurants could best be described as *nasty*.

I was going for one reason only. To visit Zingerman's.

Zingerman's styles itself as a Jewish deli and, in fact, the name is a composite put together by the founders to make it sound the part. However, to call Zingerman's a deli is like calling Fortnum & Mason a corner shop. It is an extraordinary collective of food-related businesses in orbit around the main store, all of which pride themselves on the superlative quality of their products and of their level of customer service. Alongside the deli, there is a creamery that makes cheese, a bakery, a vast mail-order business, and several restaurants.

Founded by Ari Weinzweig and Paul Saginaw in 1982, Zingerman's rapidly built an astonishing reputation nationwide, not only for the quality of its food, but also for its service, which borders on the pathologically attentive.

When I first met Gauri she was, like so many people in Michigan, working for one of the major car companies. But she found herself spending so much time and money in Zingerman's that she decided to make a total career change, and took a job as a line worker in the deli. Over the next few years, her enthusiasm and ability let her rise to become a manager and, because of her own big career shift, she understood completely when I told her about *Eat My Globe*. She sent me a supportive mail and, at the bottom wrote, "I'll organize for you to hang out at the deli."

That alarmed me ever so slightly as Zingerman's engenders a loyalty that borders on the cultlike. However, Gauri is used to getting her own way and, on a Saturday in mid-October, I found myself reporting for duty.

A few days before, I had arrived in town and toured the satellite businesses while the managers tried to inculcate me into the Zingerman's way. It's impressive stuff. I was shown around Zingerman's Bakehouse, where thousands of loaves of bread are prepared every day, as well as dozens of styles of cakes and pastries, including their famous coffee cake of which I was proudly informed they sell over thirty thousand at Thanksgiving alone.

I was invited to be part of the bimonthly tasting of all the products submitted to the deli by hopeful suppliers. It is here where you can see how Zingerman's has developed its enviable reputation, as a small team spends three hours tasting hundreds of products in dozens of different categories. Olive oils from Greece, tomato sauces from Spain, chocolate nibs from Ecuador, and cookies made by an old lady just down the street.

The others there were all experts, of course, and had all the right vocabulary. I just tried, without much success, not to make an oaf out of myself.

"F*ck sake, that tastes like crap," I said about an orange marmalade so nasty it could have been used for riot control.

"We try not to say things taste like crap," one of my fellow tasters said. "People have often put their heart and soul into producing these things."

"But, you're right," she added quietly. "It does taste like crap."

"I like this oil a lot," one of the managers said, dipping a small piece of bread into a bowl of lurid green olive oil. "It's fresh with a hint of citrus and the acidity is offset by a sort of creamy smoothness. What do you think, Simon?"

"I think it's as rough as a sandpapered arse," I said honestly. It was horrible, like eating fresh grass clippings. There was a spluttering sound to my right and I turned to see Vanessa Sly, who helped purchase oils for the deli, trying not to choke on a piece of bread.

We wrapped up pretty quickly after that. I am not sure if it was because the meeting had come to its natural conclusion or that they did not want to be exposed to any more of my imaginative descriptions, but I was ushered out and into a waiting car to take me back to Gauri's house.

Gauri had decided that the best way for me to understand the deli would be to volunteer for a day on the shop floor. I would get to hang out in each section of the store and, if the general reports at the next staff meeting were positive, they would tell me. If I were eligible, they would offer me a job.

My shift began at eight in the morning, but before that, Gauri had arranged for me to meet Ari Weinzweig in the Zingerman's coffee shop so I could get some background about the company. As always, he had arrived as soon as they opened and was sitting with half a dozen cups of their different coffees in front of him, doing a tasting.

"So, what do you want to know about Zingerman's?" he asked, slurping on a rich, dark brew.

"Well, how do you get your staff to drink the Kool-Aid?" I asked.

Ari looked up and gave me a thin smile. I was obviously not the first to make the comparison.

"Well, you'll just have to ask them when you are working today," he said, and added, "All we try and do is find people who are committed to achieving the same vision that Paul and I have for the company and its future. Some can fit in and others can't."

Ari explained that Zingerman's runs an open-book finance policy. Every employee can review the accounts. They also have other policies, official and unofficial, that they use to support their staff, from help with sometimes serious personal problems to promotions on merit and a definite recognition of individual abilities.

For a hugely cynical Brit like myself, it was all a bit hard to believe but, as I spent more time with Ari and the staff of the company, I could see it was genuine. The level of service is incredibly high, as is the level of staff loyalty; not just to the customers who were already flooding through the doors, but also to each other and to me, the odd, middle-aged man who had been dumped in their midst and whom they made feel immediately welcome.

I was really thrown in the deep end for my trial shift. Jess Piskor, who was looking after the cheese and meat counter where I was to spend the next couple of hours, explained, "It's the double whammy—it's homecoming and U of M has a game today." He may as well have been speaking Martian, but I gathered from the crowds even at this early hour, that it was a big deal.

The staff were swamped so Aaron, another staff member, handed me a plate of Montgomery's Cheddar and told me to head out into the store and let people try samples. "Give it your best British shit," he added. One of the few benefits of being British is the accent, which, particularly in America, can help you get away with anything. I played the card to the full, wandering around for the next eight hours giving it my best "British shit," trying on a range of accents from the "Cor luv a ducks" faux cockney of Jamie Oliver to the plummy tones of David Niven.

It worked. I moved from the cheese counter to the bread counter to the dry goods area, where Vanessa, who was in charge for the day, warned me, "Please don't say any of the oils are as rough as a sandpapered ass."

I sold, as some Americans might say, like a mo'fo. I persuaded people to buy fifty-dollar bottles of vinegar, loaves of bread stuffed with chocolate (admittedly that did not take so much work), and enough British cheese to keep the industry going for another year or so.

At four that afternoon, during a lull, Gauri came onto the sales floor.

"You look shattered," she said and it was true. I was knackered.

I caught a glimpse of myself in a mirror. I was covered from head to toe in flour (note to self, black is not a good color when working with bread), and my face was lined where beads of sweat had attractively cut tracks through the caked-on flour. Gauri was clutching a package. Inside was a black Zingerman's T-shirt, my reward for helping out.

"You deserve it," she said giving me a hug and she was right. It made me realize how much effort went into giving the level of service Ari demanded and how much I had enjoyed being part of it. I was a convert.

Now, where's that Kool-Aid?

Chapter 15
AUSTIN: DON'T MESS WITH TEXAS

I can understand why Texas gets a bad rap. It does precious little to ingratiate itself with the rest of the United States and, more than any other state, feels like its own country rather than part of a federal system. Signs along the highways that read "Don't mess with Texas" are not just talking about litter. Do not get in the way of anybody in a state where it is easier to buy a gun than an apple.

I had spent two weeks in 2002 driving around this vast state with the Great Salami in search of amazing barbecue. He, of course, had done his research and had a large map of the state with the word *meat* scribbled on it at places of bovine interest. We both came under Texas's spell and thought we might never leave when we drove into a gas station called Billy Bob's that sported a large sign announcing it only sold three things: gas, cracklin', and ammo.

Since then, the Great Salami has been known to suddenly giggle quietly and say, "Gas, cracklin', and ammo" to no one in particular.

If Ann Arbor had been about spending time with old friends, Austin would be about meeting new ones. I had pretty much the same barbecue intentions this time as I had had on my previous visit, but was resigned to the fact that I was going to have to make the journey alone, a double shame because there are few people who are better company when one is in search of meat than the Great Salami and, obviously, having only one stomach, there was only so much I was going to be able to eat.

Fortunately, the food Web sites came to the rescue again and, via mutual friends, I was put in touch with two locals, Jane and John King.

On my last visit, I had rather fallen in love with Austin. I liked its quirkiness and the laid-back vibe, which meant that everything happened at its own steady pace. I liked its independence and the demand on its inhabitants from the Austin Independent Business Alliance to "keep Austin weird." Five years later, there were more signs that the chains were taking over, but the old Austin spirit still seemed to be there, particularly in the utterly fabulous Austin motel with its sign, an extended middle finger, and its declaration that it was "So Close Yet So Far Out."

After an unmemorable lunch, a short walk to see the shabby titty bars and dreadful restaurants of infamous Sixth Street, my new chum, Jane, picked me up to spend an afternoon with her, her family, and various other members of the food Web site who had put together a Tex-Mex feast in my honor.

When we arrived at Jane's house, her husband, John, was busy unloading beer from his car onto the porch. I liked him already. Dressed in shorts, a gray T-shirt over his rounded stomach, and a straw Stetson worn without a hint of irony, he is impossible to dislike. This attraction was reinforced when he handed me the first of far too many shots of tequila with the words, "Welcome to Texas."

I knew almost nothing about Tex-Mex cooking, but expected that it was very different from Mexican, although I knew nothing about that, either. My experiences of it in London had verged on the disgusting, and I had assumed that it was just an excuse to use up residual amounts of bad cheese found in the back of the fridge. Well, it is certainly meat-and-cheese dependent, and there is no way you would ever call it a refined cuisine, but, on the evidence of what was put in front of me, it is entirely delicious.

Armadillo eggs were particularly good. Made of jalapeño peppers stuffed with cheese and wrapped in bacon, six of them disappeared down my maw before I realized that everyone else on the porch was staring at me with a mixture of horror, disgust, and nausea. Undeterred, I moved quickly on to chili con queso, a dip made with ground beef and yet more cheese. I did not give the Kings a chance to tell me not to stand on ceremony, as I stood right by the table with all the food on it and helped myself until they began to stare again.

Those dishes turned out to be just the starters. Soon a large bowl of beans and a huge dish of enchiladas stuffed with pulled pork appeared. Jane produced a pico de gallo in a vain attempt to keep things on the healthy side, but it was too late. The enchiladas were so good that it was all the guests could do to stop me stripping off and smearing the sauce over my chest.

After making a pig of myself, I flopped down on a pretty pink rocking chair and helped myself to yet another shot of tequila.

There is a saying that "Texas is just a state of mind." Well, I was in a hell of a state and no one seemed to mind.

The next day I spent with Jane as she worked in Central Market, one of the best food stores I had visited in a long time, and we spent the evening cooking Indian food together for more of her family and friends.

After supper, as I flopped back into the rocking chair on their porch, John came to sit on the couch next to me.

"When do you plan to go eat barbecue?" he asked.

"Tomorrow, my last day before heading to New Orleans," I replied.

"Do you mind if I come with you?"

Mind? I was thrilled. Not only did it mean I would have a dining companion, but I had just seen John eat. Few people can put stuff away like my dear older brother, but John looked more than up to the task of operating *in loco* Salami.

The next morning, as planned, John wandered into the café next to the motel as I sipped on my hot chocolate, Stetson very firmly on his head and looking ready for the fight.

"Big day ahead of us, my friend," he drawled. "I want us to hit four barbecue pits before we head home. Are you game?"

I had never been more game.

I love barbecue anywhere, but Texas barbecue is the *ne plus ultra*. Texas barbecue is special because it comes without sauce.

"If you need sauce," John intoned wisely as he drove, "then there is something wrong with your barbecue."

We were heading to a small town called Lockhart some thirty minutes drive from Austin, considered by many to be the barbecue capital of the world, with six major barbecue pits in one town, a legacy of its past, when German butchers would smoke meat to sell alongside fresh meat to local farmhands and cowboys.

We had plans to hit three pits there, then move on to another small town, Luling, to visit one more joint.

"We're going to have to pace ourselves," John warned as we pulled up outside Kreuz Market, our first stop, "or we wont be able to manage all four."

Kreuz was the most famous barbecue pit and, as we entered, a lunchtime crowd was lining up, while elderly ladies sliced huge slabs of brisket from large joints or beef ribs to be sold by the pound. The smell was incredibly good and John guided me through the ordering of meat with sides of pickles and sliced white bread. I liked it, but John the pro was harder to please.

"It doesn't quite have that smokiness going through to the center as it should," he nodded seriously. "Not bad, though, not bad."

We headed back to the car for the short drive to our next port of call, Black's, a much smaller place whose original clientele, I understand, were African-Americans. As John headed up to collect more brisket for our tasting, supplemented with some meaty sausage links, I went to claim a table. It was beginning to fill up: Barbecue really is a great equalizer. In the small dining room, obviously wealthy men in expensive suits sat next to Hispanic farmhands, students next to ordinary stiffs like us. Good 'cue knows no boundaries.

The sausages were spectacular with a sufficient bite and the right amount of spicing. John was still not happy with the brisket, however. "It's a little dry and there's not enough fat." A hard man to please. I would kill for any place that made close to this quality in London.

A short hop across the road was Smitty's, on the original site of Kreuz. Smitty changed to its current name because of a feud between surviving relatives of the original owner. The wooden walls are ingrained with the smell of a hundred years of smoke and so, too, it seemed, were the people serving. Generations of Texans had come to eat almost exactly what we were eating.

We ordered more brisket and some ribs and found a space in the long dining room. The ribs were spot on. Strips of fat had been rendered into crispy chewy strands that you worked your way through to the meat. The brisket was good, too.

"This is the best yet," John said, giving his seal of approval. However, I could sense that all was not yet right in his world, brisketwise. We wrapped up our remains in the butcher's paper in which it had been served and headed to our last port of call, City Market, in the nearby town of Luling.

By now, I was suffering. Beads of meat sweats trickling down my face and I was not sure if I would be able to face another slab. John, however, was made of sterner stuff and, to complete our day, ordered an extra big slab of brisket for us.

"Now, I'm going to show you how to construct a proper barbecue sandwich," he said, laying slices of brisket and pickles between two pieces of bread. I tried to keep up with him, but it was no good, I had to sit back and admire the master at work. He soon polished it off, licked his fingers, and said, "Let's head home."

John and I talked without a break on our short drive back to the motel. He parked the car and walked me to my room. As he reached the end of the parking lot, he turned, his body suddenly a rounded silhouette against the setting sun.

"Thanks for a great day and, by the way, thanks for the barbecue," he said with one last wave.

No, John, thank you.

That night, when Jane had finished work, she joined me for a last drink and a dish of ice cream from a store across from the motel. The saddest thing about meeting people on the road is that, at some point, you have to say goodbye. I was sadder about saying goodbye to Jane and John than just about anyone I had encountered so far, but, as Jane rightly put it, "You'll just have to come back and eat more barbecue."

Damn right.

Chapter 16
NEW ORLEANS: SIMON IS BIG AND SIMON IS EASY

New Orleans is a tough old bird of a city. Abandoned by its government and much of its population after the apocalyptic hurricane of 2005, many other cities would have crumbled. Not this one. Not the Big Easy. It may struggle in the face of federal indifference and public fear, but New Orleans is dragging itself out of the swamps and the floodwaters of Lake Pontchartrain and rebuilding itself all over again.

On my last visit, in 2002, the horrors of Katrina were all in the future and New Orleans in full flow. The Great Salami and I spent four days in the city, drawn to it by the food. By the end of our trip, we had eaten as well, if not better, than we had in any other city in the United States. Its unique atmosphere and languid pace had seeped into our blood.

On our last night, after a meal of crispy fried chicken at Jacques-Imo's restaurant in the Riverbend District, we sat on a small bench outside a bar with a bottle each of frosty Abita beer in our hands.

"Four days is not enough," the Great Salami said, draining the last drops from his bottle. "We have to come back." He was right. And I had come back. I knew that no visit to the United States could possibly bypass this resilient city at the mouth of the Mississippi.

I had been fortunate enough to meet Chris McMillian and his wife, Laura, at a bar show in London. A fourth-generation New Orleans bartender and one of the directors of the Museum of the American Cocktail, Chris was dedicated to preserving the heritage of mixed drinks in the United States. He was a mountain of a man but softly spoken and polite in the way that only people from the southern states of America can be.

"You'll just have to come to see me in New Orleans," he instructed. "I make a pretty good Sazerac."

Three months later, as I sat across from him in the Library Lounge of the Ritz-Carlton, he was busy mixing the promised cocktail.

"New Orleans in a glass," he said in an accent that could not have come from anywhere else.

Drinking a Sazerac is a very pleasurable history lesson. Arguably the oldest of all cocktails, its roots lie in the French origins of the city, when it was made with cognac. Now, it is made with rye whiskey, sugar, and local Peychaud bitters, before being strained into a chilled, absinthe-washed glass dressed with a lemon peel. The first sip is a great joy. The slight burn of the whiskey followed by the sweetness of the sugar and the citrus of the peel. Chris McMillian at the Library Lounge makes the best in the world.

I had plans to visit quite a few restaurants while I was in New Orleans but I wanted some local advice and asked Chris for more recommendations.

"Well, now, I'm not working until late tomorrow," he said, wiping the bar. "Why don't I give you the tour?" It was settled.

When Chris pulled up in front of my hotel the next morning, the hood of his big, old Lincoln arrived about five minutes before the rest of it. I could already hear the unmistakable sounds of New Orleans jazz filtering through the windows. Chris opened the door, leaned out, and drawled, "Mornin'. Y'all ready to eat?"

I climbed in, reclined into the luxurious leather seats, and let Chris take charge.

Chris loves New Orleans. He loves it in a way I had not seen from anyone in any city on the trip. He loves it in a way that a father who has almost lost his only child can love. He loves it because of and despite Katrina, and he will love it until he finally keels over and is laid to rest in one of its famous cemeteries.

Eventually, we drew up alongside the waters of Bayou St. John and into the parking lot of the Parkway Bakery, famous for serving one of New Orleans' greatest sandwiches, the po'boy.

As the name suggests, the po'boy or, poor boy, sandwich was created as a cheap, filling meal for those down on their luck. It consisted of a long roll, dressed with lettuce and tomato and then filled with deep-fried chunks of cheap local fish and seafood like catfish, shrimp, and oysters. Nowadays, of course, those ingredients are not exactly cheap, but the sandwich has remained a New Orleans classic.

I warned Chris of my aversion to oysters and let him amble up to the counter to order. He returned moments later with two huge cylinders wrapped in kitchen paper.

"I went for oysters, I got you a mixed catfish and shrimp with all the dressing. I hope that's okay."

I had already torn the wrapper off and had taken my first bite. There's no denying, this is one of the great sandwiches. We bit down on the soft roll, appreciating the crunch of the fish and seafood, which I had drizzled with lemon juice, and the bites of salad to give a semblance of health.

We ate our sandwiches in that silence that only middle-aged men can manage when they know something better is on offer than conversation.

Chris had also bought a bottle of Barq's root beer for us. He pushed my bottle towards me and motioned for me to take a sip. I ran to the nearest waste bin and spat it out. Singularly the most vile drink I had ever tried and, remember, I had drunk fermented horse milk. To many Brits, root beer tastes medicinal, like the stuff your mum used to rub on your chest as a kid when you had a cold. I pushed it away.

We finished our po' boys and headed back to the car.

"I think you need to see what happened," Chris said in a solemn tone, as we climbed back in and headed in the direction of the infamous Ninth Ward.

I had been surprised by how normal everything looked in New Orleans in my short time there. The St. Charles Streetcar was not running and some buildings in the Garden District were boarded up, but on the whole, it all looked in a good state of repair. As we hit the Ninth Ward, I saw the real story. Like pictures of Hiroshima after the A-bomb, row upon row of houses in block upon block of streets, all deserted and crumbling. At every fifth house or so there was an empty lot where the floodwaters had extracted the house like a rotten tooth. Roads had turned to mud tracks and all local businesses were shut.

"It's a dead area. Even if people wanted to live here, there is no infrastructure left to support them. No schools, no shops, no hospitals."

Chris parked the car and stared out the window. The sounds of WWOZ, New Orleans' radio station, provided an eerie soundtrack as we looked out at the devastation of the city he adored, not repaired even two years after the event.

When we finally drove on, a new tune blared through the speakers.

A hybrid of New Orleans jazz and Latino rhythms, the result of construction workers arriving in the city to help with rebuilding, joining with young local musicians to create a new sound.

"This is what makes me confident about the future," Chris smiled. "Whatever they throw at us, New Orleans finds a way to come through it. Now, let's go eat some more."

We drove back to the French Quarter and pulled up outside Central Grocery.

"Another sandwich?" Chris asked. "Italian, this time."

The muffaletta, unique to New Orleans, shows the Italian side of its heritage, or to be more precise, Sicilian side. A ten-inch loaf of Italian bread layered with meats, peppers, cheeses, and, most important, a dressing made with olives, pickles, and enough oil to soak into the bread. It's tasty, all right, but just too messy for my liking. Impossible to eat without getting oil into places where oil really shouldn't get. Chris seemed to have the knack, though, and polished his off in easy order, wrapping up my half sandwich to take home to his kids.

Chris had to head off to work. It had been a fantastic morning despite the depressing drive through the Ninth Ward. However, I only had a couple more days left in the city and, enjoyable as they were, New Orleans has a lot more to offer the food obsessive than those two sandwiches.

I crammed a lot into those two days with breakfast at Brennan's, which filled me up with turtle soup and eggs Benedict, then a bowl of Susan Spicer's mind-blowing garlic soup at Bayonna. Bags of ultralight beignets from Café du Monde came dusted in powdered sugar that I had to lick off my fingers as I walked, and which took the fire out of a bowl of crawfish étouffée I had bought to eat on the hoof. You could eat three meals a day for three days in New Orleans and not even begin to scratch the surface, but I had limited time and, on my last night, just about enough room for one more meal.

Upperline, in the University Area, had a menu filled with the sort of Creole food that made New Orleans famous, so I put myself in owner JoAnn Clevenger's hands, leaving her to order. A large plate of fried green tomatoes came topped with a shrimp remoulade spiced with grainy mustard. Half a roasted duck was accompanied by sauces of garlic and of ginger with peaches. Just when I thought I could eat no more, JoAnn carried out a large plate of profiteroles over which a bitter chocolate sauce had been ladled.

This was my sort of meal, well-made, unapologetic food, which has never striven to be fashionable and so has never gone out of fashion.

A cab took me back to the French Quarter and dropped me off at the beginning of the infamous Bourbon Street. I had avoided it until now, remembering the vile perfume of piss and vomit from my previous visit. My memory did not fail me and, despite the effects of Katrina, it was filled with drunk frat boys and girls.

I hurried towards my hotel. As I turned onto the street, I heard music, great music. I followed the sound and saw a parade of people, young and old, all races and colors, playing instruments, dancing, and having a ball. I joined the party and followed along for a while until exhausted. As I got ready for bed, I knew they would still be outside partying for all they were worth, not knowing what the future holds for them or the city.

I may not know the future either, but I do know one thing: New Orleans may be down, but it is most definitely not out.

Chapter 17
PHILADELPHIA: STAN AND LISA, PAT AND GENO

Just as I drained my second powerful martini of the evening at the bar of Smith & Wollensky in Philadelphia, a gruff but not unfriendly voice came from the person on the stool beside mine.

"You in town on business?"

"Sort of," I replied, barely looking up. It had been a long day and the juicy, rare T-bone I had just polished off, with its strip of fat and its salty, charred crust, was the only thing between me and bloody murder.

My flight from New Orleans to Philadelphia had been the stuff of nightmares. The flight was little over an hour, I could put up with that. Then seatmate number one turned up, little short of three hundred pounds and wearing shorts. As he took his seat, the flab from his thighs flowed from his trouser leg and began to create Lebensraum on my side of the divide.

Then seatmate number two turned up, a woman, scarcely a pound lighter than number one, whose Lycra-enveloped flab from her side of the border encroached on my other leg. A passing stewardess gave me the most pitying look imaginable as I sat being slowly consumed.

As we began to taxi, the vibration of the airplane made their fat undulate and, by takeoff, it was batting out a fierce rhythm on each leg. If I could have freed my arms to reach the sick bag, I would have thrown up.

By the time I had endured another round of thigh slapping as we landed and reached my hotel, my mood was already as dark as the October skies above Philadelphia. Few things can cheer me up when I am in this sort of mood and, since I did not have the latest Victoria's Secret catalogue to hand, thought I should probably just head out and get a steak and a couple of martinis.

"What does that mean? Sort of," the man persisted.

I turned from my empty plate to face a man in his fifties, graying hair and the sort of strong features that made me think I ought to be a little more polite. He introduced himself as Stan Cohen, a regular at the bar of the steakhouse, as his wife worked at the hotel above and he was waiting to take her home. I began to explain about my journey just as she appeared.

"Lisa," he turned to his wife. "This is Simon. He's traveling around the world to eat."

She turned to me. "So, are you going to have a Philly cheese steak?"

To be honest it was the only reason I had come to the city. I knew there was a lot to like about the place, I had been before. I knew that they had a great Italian market, and that the city was the home of soft pretzels and the Italian hoagie, another spectacular sandwich filled with cold meats, cheeses, sweet peppers, and onions. I also knew the city's pride in the Reading Terminal Market where some stalls were run by, and sold the produce and baked goods of, the Pennsylvania Dutch. However, I had not had a cheese steak on my previous visit and, on this trip, I only had one full day in the city that I had set aside for my first-ever Philly cheese steak.

Stan bought me another martini and, as I took a sip, he and Lisa gave me a history lesson. The first cheese steak sandwich was created by Pat Olivieri, who sold a sandwich he had made for his own lunch to a passing cab driver who was so impressed he brought his friends back to try them. His store, Pat's King of Steaks, opened in 1930, and had the game to themselves until Joe Vento opened Geno's directly across the street in 1966. Battle commenced and they have been rivals ever since.

In Philadelphia, you were either for Pat or for Geno, Stan explained. Stan was one of the few who had crossed sides, having moved to Geno's when he met Lisa.

"So, when are you gonna go try one?" he barked.

"I was going to go tomorrow lunchtime," I replied.

"Nah," Stan replied. "You have to go at nighttime when they're all lit up." He looked at his watch, looked at Lisa, and then back at me.

"C'mon. We'll take you now."

It was approaching one in the morning, on top of which I had just eaten twenty-six ounces of T-bone steak, and was buzzing from three martinis.

"Sounds good," I replied, despite the time and the fact that my colon might explode. My trip was not going to get any more real than having a couple locals drive me across Philadelphia in the small hours in search of a cheese steak.

"If you don't know how to order, they won't serve you," Stan shouted over his shoulder as he drove through the streets of South Philadelphia.

"You gotta order 'Whiz with' which means a sandwich with Cheez Whiz," Lisa explained.

"And you want to get it 'handicapped' so they cut it in half, " Stan added.

Even in the small hours, both Pat's and Geno's had long lines and, while Stan went to park the car, I was sent to get in line and collect our order. By the time they reappeared, I had our sandwiches wrapped and ready to eat. We took a table outside on the pavement and I went to add a little hot sauce to half my cheese steak.

It may have been the context, eating a meal not only in the town in which it was created, but also in the very restaurant, but that cheese steak—the soft Italian roll filled with sweet onions, wafer-thin strips of good beef, and topped with cheese—was as good as anything I had eaten on the trip.

Stan and Lisa were devouring theirs with a practiced air.

"They are never as good anywhere else," Stan mumbled between large mouthfuls. "It's the water we use to make the rolls."

As I sat in the glare of the large neon sign, with two people I had only met a little over an hour before, I was as happy as it would be possible to get. Unless, of course, someone produced that Victoria's Secret catalogue.

Chapter 18
THAT'S SO NEW YORK

However good New York is, it will never be quite as good as New Yorkers believe it to be. Nothing will ever be quite as good as New Yorkers believe everything in their city to be. If it is good, it is "the best," if it is high, it is "the highest," and if it is old, it is "the oldest." They deal in superlatives and have an enthusiastic capacity for hyperbole. This childlike enthusiasm—which finds its final expression in that wearisome phrase, "That's so New York"—is a demand for uniqueness that springs from the city's and the country's relative youth. Such a phrase would never issue from the lips of the residents of its elder European siblings, who have had thousands of years to, quite frankly, get over themselves.

This same enthusiasm makes New York what it is and makes New Yorkers what they are. They are easy to wind up, for a start, and just love it when I refer to the city as "London Lite," as I do at every possible opportunity. They are also more food-obsessed than most. Few cities are predicated on eating in the same way that New York is, and few people spend as much time eating and arguing about food as New Yorkers do. Every block of the city's five boroughs will provide multiple opportunities for you to stuff your face with great food from all corners of the globe.

The same youthful enthusiasm is evident when New Yorkers describe restaurants. I have regularly heard ethnic places described as the very best of their type in the world without a thought that there may well be some halfway decent examples in the countries they represent, or a thought that the person saying it may never have been farther than Queens. Mind you, in Queens you could probably eat the globe right there, as just about every race and nation is represented in the shops, diners, and restaurants.

This black-and-white, often blind, passion for things and people can be exhausting to deal with, but it also makes New Yorkers among the most loyal friends you can have, and I am lucky to count many as mine.

If I have many special friends in New York, I also have some very special relatives. Sanjoy, my father's cousin, and his wife, Evelyn, are contemporaries of my mother and father. They have become my second parents and I always stay with them when I am in the city.

Sanjoy is a typical Bengali man, whose life seems to involve sitting beatifically in the center of a maelstrom of his own creation. Bengali men are not lazy, but feel that it is the duty of the rest of the world to make their life comfortable and their duty to point out the failings of others, for their own benefit, of course.

When I arrived from Philadelphia, Sanjoy had just returned from work, changed into his loose Bengali clothing, and was already creating havoc as Evelyn prepared supper for guests who were arriving shortly.

"Sweetie, can I have a soda?" Sanjoy asked, sitting less than three feet from the fridge.

Evelyn rolled her eyes and walked across the kitchen to hand it to him. She is nobody's doormat, but in the years since they were married, she has recognized the fact that Sanjoy would starve if he were left to do anything for himself. He popped open the soda and read his newspaper circling random words with a pen, something he has always done, although why, I have never quite figured out.

Although originally from the Philippines, Evelyn is one of the great cooks of Bengali food, another thing she had in common with my mother. She had prepared a simple but delicious meal of dahl, chicken, and vegetables, and invited a group of friends over to share our food.

The meal went on until midnight. Both Sanjoy and Evelyn were happy, Evelyn because everyone declared the food delicious, and Sanjoy because he had offended everyone at the table and prompted a political argument, which had us at each other's throats while he just sat and watched with a smile on his face.

I had a big smile on my face, too. It felt like I was home.

In many ways, New York does feel like home. After London, it is the city I know best, having visited it approaching countless times for business and pleasure since my first trip in the early 1980s.

I know its streets, I know how to get around, and I keep up to date with its restaurants and bars. I based my first day on visiting three places that represented the incredible diversity of the city.

Katz's Delicatessen, on the Lower East Side, has been an institution in New York almost since it opened in the late nineteenth century and is most famous for one thing, a sandwich stuffed with pastrami, beef that has been spiced, brined, and smoked before being steamed, then cut into thin slices and piled high between slices of rye bread. The bread is nondescript, merely a delivery system for the incredible flavors and textures of the meat. With a little deli mustard to dip it into and a plate of pickles on the side, each bite is like a taste of New York; it would never taste the same anywhere else in the world.

It is a hefty lump of protein, however, and, as I had lunch reservations, I took the opportunity to walk from Katz's on Houston Street up to Midtown. The Lower East Side has changed out of all recognition since my first visits, the streets now filled with smart-looking shops and restaurants, a far cry from the mid-eighties when I ended up in the same area by mistake and was bundled into a cab for my own safety by a neighborhood policeman.

By one-thirty that afternoon, I had walked sufficient miles to make space for lunch and sat in awe at the sushi station of master chef Naomichi Yasuda, for one of the great eating experiences in New York. Yasuda's hands move at lightning pace preparing piece after piece of nigiri or maki sushi for the five or so people at his station.

I particularly requested uni (sea urchin), unagi (freshwater eel), and anago (saltwater eel), but was also presented with fatty tuna, scallop, and salmon roe marinated in a blend of different soy sauces, which led to a mouthful of popping, mildly salty fish eggs.

"Better than sex," Yasuda chortled.

"I don't know," I replied. "My memory's not that good."

I racked up a small bill of around sixty dollars before heading off into the afternoon sunlight for a good long walk to prepare for what I knew was going to be a major dinner.

The Kebab Café may only be a short hop by subway but is as far away from Yasuda as it is possible to get. On Steinway Street, in Astoria, Queens, it has become one of my favorite restaurants anywhere, since I was first taken there in 2002, not just because of the food but because of its Egyptian owner, Ali El Sayed. It's a tiny place with a kitchen the size of a small soap dish in which Ali produces some of the most delicious food in the world, with influences from across the Middle East.

One of my oldest and best New York friends, Cathy Loup, had warned Ali that I was coming. He knows my tastes and, as I arrived, he came around the counter, put his huge arm around me and said, "Here, Indian boy. Have some brains."

He handed me a piece of veal brain that he had just breaded and fried. It melted away on the tip of my tongue. This was only the beginning and, as I caught up with Cathy, he began to bring out dish after dish from his Lilliputian kitchen. Roasted eggplant and beets, calf's brains, tripe soup, stuffed hearts, tongue dumplings, roasted marrow bone, and, of course, some testicles.

New Yorkers may be prone to hyperbole, but everything you hear about these three restaurants is true, and only in New York could they exist so happily together.

I had experienced two boroughs of New York on my first day; my second day was going to take me to the far reaches of a third, the Bronx, where I wanted to get a taste of old-school New York and one of its oldest Italian communities. Another dear friend, Sandra Levine, agreed to show me around and I met her at Grand Central Terminal, now fully restored as one of the great landmarks of New York City.

We headed out on the short train trip to Arthur Avenue in the Bronx, which for many decades was one of the more predominantly Italian neighborhoods in New York. The perfect companion, Sandra knows as much as anyone about the history of the people and buildings of the city. The area is not what it was, she told me, since many of the original Italian families had moved out and were now being replaced with an influx from Albania. We mooched around for an hour or so, looking at the stores selling pastries, mozzarella, and Italian meats, before we found our way to Dominick's Restaurant, one of the old stalwarts on Arthur Avenue. It was already bustling inside and we squeezed into a place at a communal table.

Just as curry-house food in the United Kingdom bears little relation to food in India, so red-sauce American Italian bears little resemblance to what I was to eat later in Italy. It does not mean that it cannot be tasty, but this wasn't. Overcooked pasta in a heavy shrimp sauce was joined by a chicken Scarpiello, which should have been a crispy, garlicky treat, but was stewed and rather nasty. With a glass of wine I did well not to spit across the room the bill came to forty dollars—way overpriced.

"Because of your camera and your exotic accent," Sandra assured me. I knew they would both get me into trouble one day.

After I said goodbye to Sandra, I headed back into Manhattan to meet with two other friends, Beth Pizio and her husband, Peter Coughlin. They had been charged with trying to persuade me that pizza is not one of the most disgusting foods in the world. An onerous task, because I have expounded my theory that pizza is snot on toast on many occasions to any willing to listen and plenty who weren't.

They had chosen a well-known place in Spanish Harlem, Patsy's, famous for its coal-fired oven and excellent ingredients. The room looked the part, and it all smelled wonderful. That's the thing, pizza often does. We started with a couple of passable salads, and I left the ordering in the hands of Peter and Beth. Two pizzas, each the size of a small dining table, arrived, bubbling promisingly. One was topped with garlic, anchovies, and basil, the other with fresh ricotta and sun-dried tomatoes.

Two pairs of eyes were watching me expectantly as I helped myself to a slice from each pie. I wanted to like them, to have a Damascene experience and find yummy noises escaping from my mouth despite myself. But, I just smiled politely and ate little more than the slice I had taken. Perhaps I am just wired incorrectly, but I don't get pizza. I suspect I never will.

I certainly get steak, however, and there is nowhere on earth like a Manhattan steak house. Unapologetically masculine with wood-panelled walls, leather-booth seating, enormous wine lists, and even more enormous cuts of steak. Over the years, I have eaten enough steaks to form a composite herd of my own. I love them and would probably choose a steak house in which to have my final meal.

If you ask New Yorkers, however, they will tell you that the best steaks in New York are not in Manhattan, but across the Williamsburg Bridge in Brooklyn, at the legendary Peter Luger Steakhouse, which has been serving steaks from the same location for over a hundred and twenty years. It is not your typical steak house; the room is utilitarian, the waitstaff famously grumpy, and the wine list appalling, but it is worth it all for the steak.

The Peter Luger porterhouse is the stuff of a meat lover's dreams. Richly marbled with fat to keep it succulent and juicy, it is dry-aged for at least twenty-eight days. There are other things on the menu, but it has never crossed my mind to order them. Strips of sizzling bacon are perfectly fine, but just to pass the time until the steak arrives, cooked rare to perfection, sliced for you in sizable chunks, one end of the large plate resting on a bowl so the juices flow to a shining pool at the other.

I shared my meal with two friends from London who were in town. They both like their meat, but were still full from breakfast and left much of a porterhouse for three to me. I did not fail them and cleaned the plate, gnawing the last flesh off the bone before mopping up the juices with an onion roll. They looked a little queasy as they watched, but steak this good and its juices are simply too good to miss.

A meal at Peter Luger's could have been the perfect way to end my trip to New York, but my friend Cathy Loup had other ideas, offering to host an *Eat My Globe* party for me. I was up for it, in part because it would allow me to catch up with a lot of the friends I had not had a chance to see but more selfishly, because Cathy is a bloody good cook and, when she turns her attention to the large smoker in her garden, I have been known to do a little dance.

She had procured forty pounds of pork from Flying Pigs Farm in upstate New York and, after rubbing it with French's mustard and spices, had left it to smoke gently for fourteen hours. I arrived early and helped her carry it up from the smoker and pull it apart into moist shreds ready to be served. I made sure, of course, to sneak regular chunks of the charred crust, far too good to be wasted on others, for myself.

The others arrived with wine and side dishes or desserts and there were soon about twenty of us making pulled pork sandwiches with Wonder Bread and pickles and tucking into coleslaw, collard greens, and mac and cheese before attacking wonderful pies, cookies, brittles, and gelato.

In the end, I realized that Peter Luger would not have been the perfect end to my time in New York. Eating some of my favorite food in one of my favorite cities with some of my favorite people was.

No hyperbole there, it was just "so New York."

Chapter 19
MEXICO: MI CORAZÓN

Mexico was one of the first names on my list when I began to draw up the itinerary for *Eat My Globe*, not because I was a huge fan of the cuisine, but because I needed to learn more. My only tastes of it had been the vile approximations in the brown sludge emporia of London's Tex-Mex restaurants. Research made me think that a week attending one of the many cookery schools in the country would be as good a way as any to begin.

I posted about my intention on a food Web site and almost immediately received a reply from Cristina Potters, who lives in Mexico with her partner, Judy. "I am sure we can do better than that," she e-mailed and pointed me in the direction of her excellent Web site, Mexico Cooks.

I spent a good part of a day reading it and it became obvious that she had the passion for Mexican food that I was looking to discover. When she suggested I fly down to Guadalajara to meet with her and Judy for *El Día de los Muertos*, the Day of the Dead, a major holiday in that region, it did not take me long to shelve the idea of a cookery school and take her up on the offer.

When we met at Guadalajara Airport, I already felt as though I knew and liked her, a fact reinforced as she gave patient, detailed responses to some of my stupid questions about the country and its food as we drove to my hotel. I was starving, and Cristina and Judy promised me a great dinner.

The rumbling of my stomach reminded me that I had not eaten for nearly twenty-four hours. So, Cristina, keeping her promise, suggested that we make our way to a dinner of tacos.

Los Altos was everything I imagined a Mexican taco stand to be; it was already swarming with people when we arrived and joined the line. There I was instructed on the etiquette of taco construction. My first two contained goat meat cooked until slightly crispy on a double layer of corn tortilla, which I topped off with fresh salsas, lime juice, and chili from large communal pots. My first bite of the taco, in fact my first bite of Mexico, made it pretty obvious that I had made the right decision. The combination of crunchy savory flesh with the lime juice and chili was a taste that could not have come from any other country.

Cristina smiled and said, "I thought you might like these."

I was already up and in line again. I wanted to try two more stuffed with brains. They were just as good, if not better, and I was already to line up for more, but Cristina quite rightly cried "Enough" and suggested we go for some dessert.

Next door, men were busy stirring pots of Mexican ice cream in tubs of salt and ice. I ordered a small scoop of helado made with fresh pineapple, the perfect way to round off the meal, and indeed the day.

Jet lag had me awake hideously early the next morning and, because I was not meeting the others until later in the day, I went out to mooch around on my own for a while.

Guadalajara is a lovely small city, with a population of around one million, filled with charming squares and intriguing alleyways and interesting enough to fill a few hours until my body demanded breakfast.

I followed the crowds and found myself in a small, central market in the middle of which were counters crowded with people choosing from more tacos, tamales, and enchiladas. I saw a sign that read "Tacos de Tripa," and sat down on a high stool at the bar. Tripe has always been a favorite of mine, from the days I used my lunch break from school to buy a tripe and roast udder sandwich from Rotherham's last remaining tripe shop, to my more recent visits to Madrid where *callos madrileños*, tripe cooked in a tomato sauce, is a regular tapas order.

In this case, the tripe was boiled, then deep-fried until crispy before being served on a warm tortilla. Having learned the technique the night before, I scooped up plenty of fresh salsa from a bowl in front of me and squeezed lime juice to wake up all the flavors. Another winning combination and I had eight of them, which still cost well under a dollar, before heading back to the hotel to meet with Cristina and Judy.

Their plan for the day was to show me a local *tianguis,* or market, set up especially for the Day of the Dead. All over the central states of Mexico, El Día de los Muertos is taken very seriously. *Ofrenda,* or shrines, are created to remember people who have died; and these markets were where people came to buy ornaments and food.

The Mexicans have a unique take on death, both joyous and slightly macabre. The stalls were packed with skulls made of sugar, models of a skeleton, known as *La Catrina,* dressed in outlandish clothes, and models of coffins and headstones.

The smell of baking wafted towards my nostrils and Judy pointed towards a man grilling traditional holiday cakes, *gorditas de nata,* made with cream. Cristina held me back as I went to order.

"Wait until he puts a new batch on," she advised. "You have to eat them straight off the griddle." She was right, of course. When we did buy a batch, they were fresh, hot, and rich with a slightly soft center that oozed out as we ate them.

"They have a saying in Mexico *'Sin maíz, no hay país.'* Without corn there is no country," Cristina said. That evening, over a passable dinner at a local restaurant, Cristina and Judy began to map out our plans for the next day's lunch, *birria* from their favorite restaurant, El Chololo. *Birria* is a signature dish of the city and involves roasted meat, usually goat, served with a strong broth flavored with dried peppers. In the case of El Chololo, the meat is braised in the broth before removing it and roasting it to develop color and a crisp texture. The broth is served with bowls of hot salsa made of onions and coriander leaf, chilies, and lime juice to spark the flavors.

As we arrived at the restaurant the next lunchtime, a group of mariachi musicians were already unloading their instruments from a minivan. Resplendent in their fitted uniforms, studded with sequins, and topped off with wide-brimmed hats, they moved from table to table playing impossibly sad songs for tips.

The restaurant was huge and already beginning to fill up as we took our table. Cristina told me that it was such a popular place that they prepare more than seven hundred goats per week. The moment the food arrived, I could see why. There were more tortillas, of course, and I was shown how to take one, smear it with salsa and pile it high with savory roasted goat meat before rolling and taking a huge bite. I didn't need any second lesson. In between bites of the tortilla, I took sips from broth that was so spicy it brought tears to my eyes.

Cristina waved over the mariachi band and, after a brief conversation, she palmed the bandleader some notes. They gathered around the table and began to sing directly to me.

In Mexico, it is illegal to sing any song that does not make at least one reference to *mi corazón*, my heart, which, of course, this one did. When they got to the chorus, *"Volver, volver, volver"* Judy leaned over to say, "It means *return*."

As I mouthed another bite of *birria*, and thought about how much I had enjoyed my first few days in Mexico, I was pretty sure that was not going to be an issue.

I am rather partial to a prawn cocktail. The British one, in which pretty little pink prawns nestle on top of shredded crisp lettuce before being wrapped in a blanket of proper Marie Rose sauce (a mixture of ketchup and mayonnaise). It should be eaten, of course, with a squeeze of lemon and lots of slices of brown bread and butter. And, the American version with larger, less sweet prawns smothered in a red sauce made of ketchup and horseradish.

Before we left Guadalajara and headed to Morelia, Cristina and Judy wanted me to try the Mexican version, quite different, but so good I have been trying to re-create it ever since.

A stall in a market set up primarily to sell secondhand clothes did not strike me as a particularly promising. However, as I watched them being made, I could tell they were going to be good. A tall ice cream sundae glass was layered with ice, avocado, plump cooked prawns, and chilies before being topped off with lime and tomato juices. The whole lot was mixed together and served with a straw and a spoon.

I had soon eaten the almost impossibly fresh and zingy prawns and was slurping loudly to suck down last little droplets of juice. I could have stayed for another, but Cristina explained that it was a good five hours drive to Morelia and, as always, she had lunch plans.

Man cannot live by prawn cocktail alone and, although I enjoyed the almost picture-book Mexican view from the back of their car as we took the scenic route, I was pleased when, after three hours, we turned off the road and pulled into the small lot in front of a restaurant, which bore the sign "Carnitas Aeropuerto."

"You'll like this," Cristina turned and smiled at me, "it's pork." Already, she knew me well.

Similar to *birria* in many ways, *carnitas* uses pork butt, which is simmered until it can be pulled off the bone in shreds and then roasted to give a mix of soft, tender, and crispy, almost sweet meats which are, of course, served with tortilla.

Cristina had been there before and used my presence to scalp the lovely owners for some smart aprons with their name on them. I put one on and stood behind the counter with the large knife that they use to chop the meat in my hand. It felt good to me and I had to be dragged away kicking and screaming.

The following morning, we headed to Cristina and Judy's home in Morelia. It was a long drive and had taken its toll on us all. I let my hosts head home and checked into my hotel, which I was thrilled to see was described as the most romantic in Mexico. Unless I suddenly developed a fetish for Big Red, that was not going to be an issue for me.

The next day was the eve of Day of the Dead and the town was awash with the vibrant blue and orange marigolds used to decorate the *ofrenda*. People were already dressed in local costume and the shops had built their shrines upon which they had placed loaves of the specially baked bread, *pan de muertos*.

For supper that evening, Cristina had a particularly unusual suggestion. "We are going to church," she told me.

What she really meant was that we were going under a church, in this case the modern Church of the Immaculate Conception, whose construction had been part funded by a *kermesse*, a food court run by locals to raise money. It had become so successful that, even now that the church was finished, the locals kept it going as a hub of the community.

When we arrived, it was already packed with local families whose members ranged from newborn babies to elderly men and women with walkers. Around the edges of the basement, stalls served a huge variety of different foods and refreshments, and the smells of fresh cooking were already thick in the air. We had to shout to make ourselves heard through the happy din of chattering families.

We bought a book of vouchers and walked around to see what looked best and most popular, using the age-old theory that the stalls with the longest lines must be the best. We each took up a position in a long line and regrouped ten minutes later with plates laden with fresh tamales, enchiladas, quesadillas, and pozole, which we helped down with large plastic glasses of Fresco.

Mexican food is certainly not the prettiest but it is some of the most honest, and it is made and served with a generosity of spirit that makes it never less than tasty. Here, in the basement of a local church, as the locals milled about and pans clattered and fryers spattered, I had some of the best food in my whole time in Mexico.

Cristina was keen for me not just to taste the food but to see other aspects of the Mexican way of life, especially how families are so important to it and why families members come before anything else, "even if they are no longer alive." I must have looked a little puzzled because she added, "You'll understand tomorrow."

We were heading out to pay our Day of the Dead respects at the cemetery of Tzintzuntzan, about forty minutes' drive from Morelia. Half the state of Michoacan had the same idea; the roads were clogged with cars and pickup trucks loaded with entire families.

Inside the graveyard, all the headstones had been decorated, and some of the more recent graves were surrounded by large shrines with pictures of the deceased, along with a selection of their favorite records, books, foods, and sporting equipment.

"People will come and spend the whole night here," Cristina whispered to me as we wandered through the cemetery. Our respectful glances were greeted with genuine smiles of welcome.

At the top of a hill in the graveyard, a crowd had gathered around an elderly priest who was blessing the shrines. The crowd began to sing a quiet, impromptu hymn. It is a balm whenever I think about it, to this day.

When we returned to Morelia, Judy and Cristina invited me to have lunch with them. It was my last day and we had not yet had a chance to share a home-cooked meal. Their lovely home had a small, well-maintained garden where we sat chatting while Cristina made chilaquiles, a dish of eggs, day-old tortilla, onions, and chili.

I was heading to Mexico City the next day, which was exciting, but I was a little disappointed that I would not see it through the eyes of my guides for the last week, whose love and knowledge of the country had opened it up to me. They had introduced me to real Mexican food, and allowed me to share local customs and lives.

A song was playing on Judy and Cristina's radio. It was the same one that had been sung to me by the mariachi band.

"*Volver, volver, volver*," I sang along.

"Yes, you definitely have to come back and see us again," Cristina added.

• • •

Mexico City has a reputation for pollution, noise, corruption, and for being one of the most dangerous cities in the world. It's all true. It is dirty, and some areas make the Bronx look like the Upper East Side. It has a Chinese-quality smog, a fug of car fumes so thick in the morning that I could barely see past the end of my bulbous nose.

I rather liked it.

My opinion is based only on a two-day stretch there at the end of my time in Mexico and before I headed to Argentina. I did not do it justice. I did not have time to leave the city to see the astonishing sights of the Aztec pyramids, and I spent more time in doing laundry than inside its many museums, art galleries, or cathedrals.

I arrived from Morelia on a bus. I don't normally do buses. They remind me of my childhood trips from Rotherham to London in the 1970s when my parents would gleefully deposit me on a National Express Coach, with an egg-salad sandwich wrapped in foil, in the vague hope that my grandparents would be there to meet me at the other end. The coaches would often break down, leaving us stranded on the hard shoulder of the highway for hours on end.

Mexico's buses are another matter, however—smart, clean, efficient, and comfortable. They have to be because there is no train service in Mexico. Five hours after leaving Morelia, I was at my hotel in the heart of Mexico City.

Cristina had suggested I should visit the Mercado de la Merced.

"It's not like any market you will have seen before," she said, when I suggested that I was a little marketed out.

The guidebooks warned the market was in Avenida de Salvador, a sketchy area of the city, and suggested taking a taxi there rather than walking. I walked. It was a fascinating way to see the old city with its sprawling parks, churches, museums, and squares, as well as local neighborhoods doing what locals do on a Saturday morning, which is apparently haggle over cheap clothing and household items.

I stopped for a short while in the Zócalo, Mexico City's main square, one of the largest in the world, built in the same spot as the center of the ancient Aztec city. It was heaving with people. In one corner, people lined up in front of native Indians who were cleansing them with ritual smoke. In another corner, an early, open-air mass was being said, and in another, a rally for gay rights was being held by hundreds of men naked but for a picture of the Mexican president covering their crown jewels.

I could have easily taken a seat in one of the surrounding coffee shops and spent a good few hours watching the spectacle, but I wanted to get to the market before it began to wind down for the day.

The guidebooks were right. The Mercado de la Merced is hardly what realtors would call "up and coming" and as I approached, I noticed that the surrounding streets were full of streetwalkers, their pimps, and pushers offering stuff I didn't want and didn't want to understand. I did not feel in the slightest threatened, but I was more alarmed, as I got closer to the market, to see that every stall was now displaying posters for pornographic DVDs, many of which advertise the involvement of animals you could also buy at the market.

I was pleased when I finally hit the first stalls selling food, and could duck under the cover of the market hall. Cristina was right: It is an astounding sight, one of the biggest markets in the world. Everywhere you look, mounds of fruits and vegetables tower from floor to ceiling, butchers display hundreds, no, thousands of carcasses swinging from metal hooks, and the alleyways between the stalls have a constant flow of powerful men pushing carts containing everything from vats of milk to cows' heads with their eyes still open and their tongues lolling from the sides of their mouths.

I walked around for two hours, taking well over a hundred pictures, always asking, "*Puede* (may I)?" first. I was never refused. In one stall, where a man was busy feeding corn masa into a machine and churning out hundreds of tortillas every minute, I was invited in to have a go myself and found it harder than it looked to scoop the right amount from the dough and to keep the rhythm of feeding the machine. As I left, they kindly presented me with a packet of the tortillas I had helped make.

Mexico City, being the capital, has representatives of the cuisine of all thirty-two of the country's states. I couldn't try them all but Cristina had insisted that I try one particular place, Azul y Oro, so I headed out on the efficient metro system to National University's cultural center.

Ricardo Muñoz, the chef at Azul y Oro, is author of *The Gastronomic Dictionary of Mexico* and considered one of the finest chefs in the country. His simple, canteenlike restaurant has a short menu that shows the benefits of good ingredients and attention to detail. A small dish of candied jicama was placed in front of me while I chose what to eat.

A cream of cilantro soup with toasted almonds scattered on top was simple but perfectly executed, just enough to prepare me for the main course. I had wanted to sample a *mole*, one of the most famous of Mexican dishes from the Pueblo region. Cristina told me that Ricardo made some of the best, so when I saw *mole negro con pollo*, I chose that, ordering the version that came with meat on the bone.

Mole is made by the slow cooking of a huge number of ingredients: onions, chilies, peppers, and, most famously of all, dark, bitter chocolate, which thickens it and gives the sauce depth. The version served at Azul y Oro was revelatory. The chicken, while tasty enough, was just a vehicle for the *mole*. Black and glistening, it had layers of flavor I had never experienced before: heat, of course, but also smokiness, bitterness from the chocolate, and sweetness from the onions. It remains one of the most memorable tastes of the trip and I scooped up every last bit with a wheat tortilla before looking around to see that no one was watching, then picking up the dish up and licking it clean.

It was the perfect meal with which to end my time in Mexico. I had been in the country a little over two weeks and it had surpassed all my expectations. The people had been more welcoming than I could have hoped for and the food more varied and delicious than I ever possibly imagined.

Next stop, Argentina.

Chapter 20
BUENOS AIRES: LOVE ME TENDER

They say it's an ill wind that blows nobody any good and, arriving in Argentina, you understand what they mean. In the early part of this century, the Argentinean economy collapsed and their currency became worth a fraction of its former self. A horror for the locals, of course, but for the visitor to Buenos Aires it meant that this elegant, sophisticated city could be enjoyed at a sliver of its former cost.

I discovered this almost immediately when I arrived, deposited Big Red in my accommodation and walked to the trendy San Telmo district. When one thinks of Argentina, its steak springs instantly to mind. Argentinean steaks are different from those found in the United States or Europe, and the meat is fresh, not aged, which gives it an entirely different texture and taste. Both have their place, but here in Buenos Aires, I was keen to try it the local way.

At midday, El Desnivel, a local favorite, was already buzzing with a mixed crowd of tourists and businessmen. The menu was short and I chose a local *morcilla*, blood sausage, to begin, followed by a *bife de chorizo* with *batatas*, sweet potato crisps. A half bottle of the local wine came, as it often does, in a *pinguino*, a small carafe shaped like a penguin.

The blood sausage was interesting, with a softer texture than any I had tried before, with a hit of spice, but the steak was an epiphany. I had tried Argentinean steak in London and New York where great store was made of flying it in in vacuum packs to maintain freshness. Here it was the real deal, served juicy and rare.

It is tougher, too, than most steaks served in America and Europe. Aging allows the fibers of the meat to break down, which makes the meat more tender and creates a different flavor.

Tenderness is a much overrated attribute. I have heard too many people say, "The steak was so tender you could cut it with a spoon." When was steak ever meant to be cut with a spoon? A good steak should not be as tough as old boots, but you should put in as much work eating the flesh as the animal did building it. If you want soft food, go eat an ice cream.

This was an excellent steak and, when the bill came, the four pounds or so for the whole meal made it taste extrasweet.

After a much-needed afternoon nap to sleep off my lunch and jet lag, I headed out again, this time to the glamorous area of Recoleta, with its elegant restaurants, bars, and ritzy townhouses. My notes told me a small bar, called El Sanjuanino, was considered the best in the city for empanadas.

Very different from the Galician empanada I love so much in Spain, these little pasties are filled with meat, cheese, fish, or a combination. They are obviously popular, as the place was filled with well-heeled people having a predinner drink and snack. I squeezed myself into a seat at the bar and ordered a selection of empanadas with the local Quilmes beer. They were a perfect combination and did just fine by me as a light supper. I could have stayed for more, but I was still bleary-eyed so headed back to the apartment and to bed.

My only contact in Buenos Aires was Fernando Cwilich Gil, a man I had met at the London Bar Show. Unfortunately, he was flying out of town, but had managed to arrange for me to have dinner with his uncle and aunt the next evening.

I woke up late and spent the day clearing my head with a marathon walk through Puerto Madero, the new port development with its expensive restaurants and bars. There was little to attract me to any of them and instead, I followed a group of workmen obviously taking a lunch break and found myself alongside the main canal feeding into the port, where I spotted a row of vans selling Buenos Aires' favorite street food, *bondiola* and *choripán*, which they were preparing on flaming grills. I went for a *bondiola* and was presented with thick slices of beef in a crunchy roll, which I was invited to lace with chili and chimichurri from small bowls on a table next to the van. The meat was even tougher, but worth it, as each bite let out incredible flavor.

The effort required did rather exhaust me and I needed little else to eat until that evening, when I joined Martin and Liljana Sanchez Gil at

La Brigada, perhaps the most famous of the Buenos Aires *parilladas*, or steak restaurants, deep in the heart of San Telmo.

"I am sorry for the ridiculously early hour for supper," Martin said by way of introduction. "I wouldn't normally even consider eating until ten." He explained that, before my arrival, they had committed to attend a party and so had to fit in supper beforehand even though, as Martin explained, eating so early was "going to play havoc with my digestion."

The Argentineans take meat very, very seriously and, Martin, with Latin-American machismo, took control of the ordering without a glimpse at the menu. He summoned the waiter with whom he had a long discussion about the cut of beef he wanted, exactly how long it should be cooked, and what dishes were to precede and accompany it.

First, we were presented with some provolone.

"You can tell how good a restaurant is going to be by the quality of its cheese," Martin said, wagging his finger at me to emphasize the point.

This was followed by goat sweetbreads and chitterlings fried to a beautiful crisp and sprinkled with salt. I was instructed to add five drops of lemon, no more, no less, before I was allowed to dive in. Finally, the main event, the *bife*, was a hunk cut across the grain to give the most flavor. It was one of the greatest steaks I had tried. Martin chewed more slowly, and with consideration, before looking up and saying, "Passable."

Just as they take their meat seriously, Argentineans take their wine seriously. Martin had ordered a spectacular Malbec from the Salta region, whose spicy damson notes served to bring out all the flavors of the meat.

Martin and Liljana invited me to join them at the party, so, an hour or so after supper, I found myself in a strange part of the city attending a party for two local artists. A famous local singer was setting up to perform and, for the next hour, she sang her heart out. And just as in Mexico, every song contained the words "*mi corazón*" at least once. In sixty minutes, the poor love had her heart stolen, stamped on, stabbed, and broken in any number of painful ways.

Martin and Liljana appeared at my side and asked me if I wanted a lift home. It was two in the morning. How the hell did that happen? I gave a girlish shriek and declared that I was going to be late for the taxi I had booked in time for my early morning flight to Brazil.

• • •

I had only been in the city a few days and had barely scratched the surface because of my tight schedule. I had not even begun to think of trips to places outside the city like Mendoza or Salta. Argentina was yet another country I would have to revisit.

I was rapidly coming to the conclusion that *Eat My Globe* could become a full-time job. Now, there's an idea.

Chapter 21
BRAZIL: THERE MUST BE SOME KIND OF WAY OUT OF HERE

When I dreamed up *Eat My Globe*, I had envisioned a trip filled with smiling faces, tables overburdened with food, and local lasses with a loose grasp of morality offering me their tastiest, er, tidbits. I did not expect to be prodded in the chest with a gun by a pizza-faced Brazilian airport guard.

The journey began badly, with a flight from Buenos Aires on Brazil's flying gulag, TAM. We landed at São Paolo and were told by the stewards to stay on board if we were continuing on to Salvador. So, I stayed put.

Another voice came through the speakers telling us to disembark and clear customs and immigration here. So, I got up to leave.

Yet another announcement told us that we should remain seated and would clear customs and immigration in Salvador. So, I sat down again.

After about fifteen minutes, we were finally told to get off the plane and clear immigration and customs in São Paolo. So, I got off the plane.

When I asked where I should go, the staff just shrugged their shoulders.

I found my way to the baggage claim area, collected Big Red, lugged him through customs, and towards a door marked "Transit." I found myself outside the airport with no signposts and not a clue to where I should be heading.

I tried to get back inside, but was stopped by a security guard and told to join a line of people about a mile long. I tried to explain that I had a connection, at which point the guard, who looked all of thirteen, pinned me to the wall with his rifle and started barking at me in Portuguese.

A charming introduction to a country I had only added to my itinerary because friends in London told me how lovely the people were. Others who had been on my flight were in the same predicament. One, an old lady, was sobbing almost hysterically; another, carrying a small child, was screaming at the guards to let her through. It was a scene right from hell.

I found a member of staff who spoke English and explained our predicament. He looked at my ticket and asked, "Why did you get off the plane?" Only immense self-control and the sight of the guard with the itchy trigger finger kept me from decking him there and then. We should have stayed on board after all; our connecting flight was about to leave, with or without us. Everyone had to sprint to our gate where we arrived just as they were about to shut the doors.

It was, of course, the same plane and I was in the same seat next to the same man who had flown with me from Argentina.

"How did you get on so quickly?" I asked him as I sat down, sweat pouring from my brow.

"I do this flight all the time," he smiled. "I always stay put. The staff are stupid. You got up before I could say anything."

I wanted to give Brazil a chance, so I sat back and tried to calm down for the short flight to Salvador.

At least my rental car was there when I arrived and, as I drove through Barra, the port area of Salvador, I began to think that this might just turn out all right. I felt even better when I saw my guesthouse which, while basic, was beautiful with blue tiled walls, spacious rooms, and wide balconies. Best of all, it was a few minutes' walk from the beach.

I changed into my shorts immediately and headed out to explore, my strolling backpack over my shoulder.

"You are not going out with that bag, are you?" the man behind the reception asked.

"Well, er, yes," I replied.

"I wouldn't advise it," he added. "Just take enough cash for dinner and keep your camera hidden. There have been quite a few muggings recently."

Once I went outside, I understood what he meant. I know fear breeds paranoia and I don't consider myself a nervous tourist, but in Salvador, I never really felt entirely safe. Not once in all my time there. I felt as if every eye was watching me and every person was viewing me as a potential mark or victim. It may have been unfair, but it was a feeling that never really escaped me. It was indeed lovely, and lined with men selling coconuts from which they swiped the tops off with machetes before inserting a straw through which you sucked up the chilled liquid inside.

I dipped into a beachfront restaurant for supper, which consisted of deep fried salt cod cakes, tough meat, rice, and French fries washed down with a Brahma beer, and headed back to my hotel, slightly dispirited about the thought of spending the next five nights looking like a walking dollar sign.

After a good night's sleep, however, I decided I was going to make a better go of it and started with a superb breakfast, one of the selling points of the guesthouse: fresh fruits, semolina cakes, guava juice, warm bread, and strong tea.

I felt better already and struck up a conversation with a young Chilean woman called Macarena, sitting at the table next to me. She told me that in the Pelhorino, the old town, there was going to be a party that evening with drum bands and dancing. She did not want to go on her own, so, despite my own aversion to matters dance related, I agreed to join her.

After breakfast, I set out to explore, without bag, of course. I must have walked about ten miles. From the beach area, through the town and down to the Old Town I had been chatting about at breakfast.

I disliked it intensely. The buildings were in appalling states of disrepair and the Pelhorino itself was a depressingly ugly tourist trap with a hustle on every corner.

I fought my way through the street peddlers and hustling cab drivers to the Elevador Lacerda, a huge elevator, which links the top of the city with the lower city. At the bottom was a market where you can sit and watch young men from the local projects performing Capoeira, a distinctive form of martial arts developed by slaves under the guise of native dance. It is hypnotic and impressive as, indeed, was the performers' ability to pry money out of the bystanders.

Around the edges of the market were stalls selling *acaraje*, small balls of black bean paste filled with peanuts or shrimp and deep fried in *dênde,* the local palm oil. I bought a small bag from one vendor, try-ing hard not to inhale the frankly noxious smells from the cooking oil. I took one bite and left the rest on the table next to where I was sitting for someone more desperate than I was. If I had the choice, I would have hightailed it out of Salvador less than two days into my stay.

The evening was better. Not that the town itself ever held any great allure for me, but that night, when I arrived to meet with Macarena for the evening, I found that we had been joined by four others from the guesthouse. They were a good crowd and having far more fun in Brazil than I was. Being with them lifted my spirits.

It promised to be a fun evening as we headed up to the old town and joined the party. It was a hell of an event, with live bands playing, drums sounding, and deafening noise wherever you turned. Soon after we arrived, our group was adopted by a young local, Elton, who took us under his wing in the hope of getting a few dollars at the end of the evening for watching our backs. He was a good guy and led us to a large church in front of which a band was playing reggaeton, an irresistible combination of reggae and samba music.

On the steps of the church, a packed crowd was swaying rhythmi-cally, and we fought our way through to a prime vantage point and joined them, as we sucked down cans of cold beer we had bought from local vendors. As the clock struck midnight, Elton suggested that it was a good time to be heading back to the relatively safe enclave of Barra and helped us all squeeze into a cab after we had gratefully pressed a few notes into his hand.

Having not had time to eat, all of us were starving and headed down to a seafront restaurant where we shared a *moqueca,* a large seafood stew made with coconut milk, peppers, tomatoes, and lots of garlic. It came served in a traditional *capixaba* clay pot and bubbled fiercely from the residual heat for minutes after it was placed in the table. We washed it down with far too many caipirinhas, a lethal cocktail of cachaca, Bra-zilan rum, lime juice, and sugar, before finally staggering back to the guesthouse at around three in the morning.

I wish I could say that this evening of fun changed my view of Salvador, but it didn't. It may have been the fact that I had no more than three hours sleep each night because my room was bedbug central, or it may have been that I had at least three people try to pick my pocket as I walked along the seafront in broad daylight. It may also have been the fact that the food was actively grim. I may not have done it justice, but there appeared little to do justice to.

For whatever reason, when it came time to leave Salvador, I did so willingly. I posted about my experiences on a food Web site and someone replied saying that, on his visit to Brazil, he felt like "fish food in a shark tank." I know exactly what he meant.

I had a twelve-hour layover in São Paolo before my flight to San Francisco.

When it came time to board, I practically ran on to my plane to the United States. As we took off, I leaned over my neighbor and gave Brazil a very recognizable hand signal through the window.

Chapter 22
SAN FRANCISCO: AN APOLOGY

San Francisco was not one of my go-to cities but, as a place to rest my weary bones for a few days after the rigors of Brazil, I thought it would suit me down to the ground. It is very attractive, beautifully situated, and in close proximity to some of the best wine producers in the country. On top of which it has an excellent dining scene, with restaurants ranging from the dirt cheap Mexican taquerias of the Mission District to the dim sum served in one of, if not the biggest, Chinese communities outside mainland China. And its high-end restaurants compare with any other major city's.

It should have made a perfect addition to *Eat My Globe*. The fact that it didn't was entirely my fault. San Francisco was all there ready to enjoy. I was not. This leg of the journey, particularly the trips from Buenos Aires to Salvador to San Francisco had taken their toll and my body felt like it was close to shutting down.

When I arrived at my hotel and threw Big Red on the bed, my body began to shake, I felt horribly nauseated, and my eyelids began to flutter in what I was convinced were the early signs of a stroke, seldom a good sign.

So, really, this chapter is by way of an apology.

An apology to local wine expert, Melanie Wong, who invited me to a smart party in a stunning loft apartment where great food and wine was served and interesting people held intelligent conversations while I snored loudly on the nearest sofa.

An apology to my good friend, Alexandra Eisler, who spent considerable time driving me around the city and across to Oakland in an SUV that looked like she stole it from the set of *The A-Team*, in search of good things to eat only to have me announce testily that the West Coast was "all fur coat and no knickers" to anyone who would listen, and plenty who didn't want to.

An apology to Deborah Morales, my saintly coordinator from Airtreks.com, who had organized, reorganized, and reorganized again, all of my flights around the world with endless good humor and not a word of complaint. She invited me to have drinks and supper with her and a colleague as a thank-you for spending the equivalent of the GNP of a small African nation with them on my tickets. After two glasses of wine, I had to cry off and return to my hotel at eight, and watch *Smallville* on television while eating a ten-dollar minipack of Pringles.

An apology to the good people who run Alfred's, one of my favorite steak houses in the whole of the United States, where I downed four martinis in an hour, barely touched a perfectly cooked steak, then spent a good couple of hours haranguing people at the bar.

In fact, let's make it a general apology to the whole of San Francisco. I am sure it doesn't really care that I didn't do it justice, but I do. And I promise, when I come back next time, I will do better.

I really am most terribly sorry.

Chapter 23
GIVING THANKS IN SANTA CRUZ

One of the very first invitations I received when I posted about my planned trip on the Internet came from a woman named Tana Butler, inviting me to join her and her extended family for Thanksgiving in Santa Cruz, California. I had no idea who she was, but her posts on food Web sites were often very funny, always painfully honest, and accompanied by photographs that made my own attempts look like the holiday snapshots they were.

She also shared my innate ability to piss people off, bearing in mind that there are many on these sites who will get up extra early, make a nice picnic, get in their car, and drive half a day's journey out of their way just to find a reason to be pissed off at someone they have never met, and probably never will meet.

I took the plunge and wrote back saying I would be delighted to join her for Thanksgiving and, over the next six months, we swapped regular e-mails so, by the time it came for me to pick up my rental car and make the short drive from San Francisco down to Santa Cruz, I already felt like I knew her and knew I would like her.

I did not just like Tana, I adored her. Sharp-witted, funny, vulnerable, open-hearted, generous, and spirited, Tana is best described, in the nicest way possible of course, as being mad as a bag of ferrets.

From the moment she walked into the lobby of my anonymous hotel and greeted me for the first time, in person, with the words—"I hope you are feeling strong, honey, you have a twenty-five-pound turkey to carry"—I knew that she had not been kidding when she promised me an eventful Thanksgiving in Santa Cruz. But then, Santa Cruz is perfect for people like Tana.

The west of just about every country attracts the oddballs, kooks, crazies, waifs, strays, and those people who don't fit in anywhere else. In Santa Cruz, you can't help but think that it is filled with all the people who didn't even fit in in San Francisco and Los Angeles. It is gloriously, shamelessly mad and filled with the abundant energy that only comes from people who don't care what other people think of them.

After a brief visit to the Santa Cruz Farmers Market, we headed off to pick up the turkey. It was a big old bugger of a bird, shaming even the colossal ones that used to give their lives for the clan Majumdar's Christmas festivities. Even more impressively, Tana informed me that we would be having two of them, then reeled off all the other dishes that she and her friends were preparing for the meal. I made a mental note not to bother with the free breakfast of multicolored cereal in a Styrofoam bowl at my hotel, as I heaved the turkey into the trunk of her car, then climbed into the passenger seat.

Tana turned to me and said, "I am worried about taking you to my house. It's not at all fancy."

I made an overexaggerated gesture of examining myself in the mirror, turned to her and replied, "I think it will be just fine. As far as I can tell, I have not suddenly turned into the Queen Mother."

Tana let out what I soon began to recognize as her trademark laugh, deep, rich, and genuine. Her home was, as I suspected, lovely. More than fine, it had a large garden, beautiful views of the hills, and littered with toys discarded by her irrepressible grandson, Logan.

For the next couple days, Tana made her home my home. As we pottered around the kitchen preparing food for Thanksgiving with Louis Prima as our soundtrack, her husband, Bob, kept me topped up with wine and beer, and Logan gave me regular updates on the battles between the plastic figurines of knights and superheroes he was overseeing in the yard.

On my first night, we enjoyed the simplest supper imaginable: roast chicken and mashed potatoes. Logan threw a tea towel over his small arm, bowed deeply in waiterly fashion and served a dollop of potato to each of us as Bob carved the chicken into big slices. It tasted as good as anything I had eaten and I said so, not caring how silly that might seem.

"It's because you are eating it with family," Bob said and he was right.

I had eight hours of uninterrupted sleep that night for the first time since my return from Brazil. So, by the time Bob picked me up the next morning, I was busy tapping away at my computer. Tana, too, had been up since the early hours, fussing over her turkey, making her signature deviled eggs, and getting up to her elbows in stuffing.

"I don't think the turkey is going to cook in time," she wailed, "the oven isn't working properly."

The oven was, of course, working properly and the bird looked like it was doing perfectly well without her, turning a glistening bronze as it cooked. I did what any self-respecting man does when there is lots to be done. I opened a bottle of wine and poured myself a large glass, despite the fact it was barely past eleven in the morning, and sat back in a comfortable chair to watch the fun. Of course, when called upon, I did a little bit of chopping here and a little bit of mixing there. But, for the most part, I just sat, drank, stole deviled eggs when no one was looking, and enjoyed the slightly chaotic spectacle.

By the time the turkey emerged from the oven, it did Tana credit, a gorgeous golden fowl with crispy skin, juices bubbling away merrily just under the surface. Tana had roasted the bird on top of its giblets to add extra flavor to the gravy, and began to discard them.

"What the hell are you doing?" I squealed in a high-pitched voice that would have troubled the neighborhood dogs. "They're the best bits."

Tana did not look convinced but reprieved the offally bits from going into the garbage and segregated them on a plate for Bob and me to nibble on while she got everything ready to transport to the location of our dinner. We loaded the car and headed to her friend's stunning home to find about thirty other people there ahead of us, already sipping champagne and laying out plates on a long table.

The amount of food was staggering. Our bird soon joined another on the table, where mounds of salads, pristine white mashed potatoes, creamy dips, cheeses, smoked hams, sauces, cakes, and pies were already arrayed. It was what Baba calls "a three-Zantac meal" and I was ready to dive straight in.

Before the meal, however, our host took the opportunity to make a toast giving thanks for all the people who were there, friends, family, and even the bald, half-Welsh, half-Bengali in the corner trying to pull a bit of skin off the turkey without anyone noticing. It would have been easy to remain a stranger among such obviously close friends and to feel intimidated and uncomfortable, but that was not going to be allowed, and I immediately became part of this extended family.

It was a uniquely Santa Cruz occasion. Everybody seemed to be related to everybody else in some labyrinthine way that I never quite got to the bottom of. The women all referred to each other as "goddesses" without any hint of irony and, at the end of the meal, guitars appeared and people began to sing songs that I suspect were about butterflies and saving whales.

Tana was entirely in her element making sure that everyone had enough to eat and drink, taking photographs, punctuating conversations with that laugh of hers and, at the end of the evening, gathering a group to sing a charming lullaby sending Logan to sleep before Bob carried him out to the car for the trip home.

In the middle of it all, I sucked on the bone of a turkey wing and made a promise to myself that I would return to Santa Cruz for Thanksgiving every year, whether they wanted me or not.

Some things in this life are a matter of trust.

I had had no idea what to expect before I arrived but had adored my first Thanksgiving. I had eaten spectacular home-cooked food in the company of a host of new friends and, best of all, I'd met an extraordinary woman named Tana Butler whose strengths and weaknesses, passions and prejudices, successes and failings are dealt with more honestly than just about anyone else I have ever met. She is a truly human being and my new friend. That was definitely worth giving thanks for.

It's a short drive from Santa Cruz north to Berkeley, but the two cities could not be further apart. If Santa Cruz were a residential home for oddballs, then Berkeley is what becomes of oddballs when they make lots of money and settle down.

There is nothing wrong with that, of course; this is no longer the sixties, and people have to grow up, but somehow the city felt neutered, as if wealth and security had replaced its radicalism with dog-grooming parlors and cupcake shops. I wanted to like it because it was the lifelong home of my friend Alexandra Eisler and her family, but I was disappointed by the achingly trendy shops and overly stylish people.

Alexandra had invited me to join her, her husband Tim, and some friends for a trip to Napa wine country the day after my arrival to sample wines from Hendry Ranch, one of the valley's most famous wineries. Tim and his friends regularly bought grapes from Hendry Ranch winery to make their own wines. Because of that, Dr. Hendry, the owner, was happy to let us visit and indeed to give us a tour of the winery himself.

Hendry Ranch, Tim explained, was a special vineyard, one of those that supplied Cabernet Sauvignon grapes for Robert Mondavi's legendary wine, Opus One.

He was right. Hendry Ranch is quite a place and Dr. Hendry is quite a person, a serious, quiet winemaker who brought the scientific discipline of his other life as a developer of electron accelerators to bear on the heartfelt way he makes wine. Every inch of the vineyard is mapped out, not just with the type of grape, but also with which clone of that type and the root stock. Inside the winery, too, his attention to detail came though as he explained to us which barrels they used and why. I have been on tours of many wineries, but this one was one of the most informative and enjoyable, and Dr. Hendry one of the best hosts.

After the tour, we made our way to the tasting room and laid out our picnic. Dr. Hendry joined us and opened up a selection of his wines for us to try. They are beautifully made wines, but are also huge wines with high levels of alcohol. They may be perfect for the tastes of those brought up on them in the New World of winemaking, but they swamp the palates of those of us brought up on the subtle, arguably more elegant wines of Europe. They were certainly not the reprehensible fruit bombs I had experienced in Australia or in other parts of the United States, but they were just not for my palate. I was definitely in the minority. As I made polite noises, the others were genuinely enthusiastic and ended up buying cases before we left. Horses, as they say, for courses.

My final day in Berkeley was also my final day in the United States. It seemed fitting, then, that my last meal should be at one of its most famous restaurants, Chez Panisse. Thanks to Alexandra's efforts, I had been able to secure not only a table but also two willing dining companions.

In the late 1980s, when I first began to eat out regularly, a reservation at a well-known or well-reviewed place would fill me with nerves and excitement. My very first visit to London's legendary restaurant Le Gavroche was preceded by three nights of sleepless tossing and turning as I thought about the meal to come, a state of unrest I had last experienced when I got tickets to see the Clash in 1979 (the fact that I had sent my mother to stand in line for them among all the punk rockers while I was at school made it even sweeter). Then, a table at a newly opened place still gave me a frisson of pleasure as I waited for the menu and the meal ahead.

Inevitably, as I dined out more often, the levels of excitement died down, dampened by as many bad meals as good. Now, it would have taken something pretty special on the dining front to give me the shivers of my youth.

Getting a reservation at Chez Panisse did, however, give me a genuine thrill. It is an iconic restaurant and, since Alice Waters opened its doors in 1971, it has become one of the most-visited restaurants on any food traveler's itinerary in California. I was looking forward to my meal immensely.

I had something else to look forward to first, however, as Alexandra had invited me for a predinner dinner with her and her family at their house, not far from the restaurant. An oil slick had fouled the bay not long before my visit, because of which crab fishing in area had been suspended. So, Alexandra's uncle Tom had driven down from the upper reaches of northern California with an icebox stuffed to capacity with freshly boiled beauties, which were piled on the table ready for us to attack.

With a sprinkle of Meyer lemon juice, some warm bread, and mayonnaise to dip the flesh into, they did not last long and, just as I was sucking the sweet meat from a claw, which I am not proud to admit I may have stolen from the plate of Alexandra's seven-year-old daughter, she told me it was probably time for her to give me a lift to the restaurant.

My companions for the evening were already waiting for me and looking forward to the meal as much as I was. I had been fortunate enough to have been given a tour of the kitchen that morning by one of the pastry chefs, and had seen the ingredients for our supper being delivered, which served to raise the level of expectation. After all that anticipation, it is a shame to have to say that the meal was not just a disappointment; it was shamefully bad. Chez Panisse bases its meals on a set menu. You get what you are given, which means the success of your meal depends on two things, the quality of ingredients and the quality of the execution.

The ingredients had looked good enough when I saw them being delivered earlier in the day, so heaven can only guess at what they did to them in the kitchen. My heart went out to a plate of leeks, beets, and pancetta that looked like Jackson Pollock had heaved on the plate. It was followed by lamb smothered in a sauce so salty that I could feel my blood pressure rise as I took my first bite, and vegetables so mushy I wanted to look in the kitchen to see if the old cook from my elementary school had been flown in especially for the occasion.

With a desultory cheese course and a bland dessert, our meal at Chez Panisse ended. We each handed over more than one hundred dollars with almost as little enthusiasm as had been shown in the service.

It was a disappointing end to the trip but, after one of my companions dropped me off at the motel, I began to make my notes. Berkeley may not have come up with the goods on this trip, the memorable crab dinner aside, but I had definitely had an unforgettable two months on the road with more food than it should have been possible, and was probably sensible, to eat.

I had been to four countries and more than twenty cities. I had met old friends and made many new ones. I had experienced the down-home charms of Texas and New Orleans, and the urban glitz of Manhattan. I had experienced the outstanding hospitality of the West Coast and the frightening indifference of Brazil.

Headed back to the United Kingdom to spend Christmas with my family and to have a much-needed break; I had another fifteen countries to visit. They definitely would be challenged to surpass the tastes and memories I had experienced so far.

God Bless the Americas.

Chapter 24
THREE MEN AND A STILL

"Of course, I am not bloody all right. I am throwing up blood. In which universe is that considered being all right?"

Admittedly, I was not at my best as I was driven in the early hours of the morning, across the island of Islay to their tiny accident and emergency room but, looking back on it, I was being more than a little harsh on my new friend, John. Even if the fact that I had spent the last nine hours emptying my guts should have given him an inkling that all was not well with me, tummywise.

I am getting ahead of myself.

Of all the people with whom I came into contact as I ate my globe, it seems strange that one of my favorites should be one of the first people I met after announcing my resignation at work, who also happens to live across the city from me, John Glaser. A quietly spoken but intensely passionate American, John is turning the arcane world of Scotch whisky on its head by stealth, hard work, and creativity.

I first met him when I wandered into my favorite bar in search of a martini and found him in the middle of a tasting for his company, Compass Box Whisky, with my friend and cocktail guru, Nick Strangeway. I was invited to join in and soon was sticking my nose into John's business as we sampled a variety of his whiskies with names like Oak Cross and Peat Monster. These, John explained, were *pure malts*, that is, blends of whiskies made from combining only single malt whisky as opposed to the malt and grain mixes of what are known as *blended whiskies*.

It can be confusing stuff, but John's enthusiasm for debunking the mythic nature of Scotch is catching and I knew I was going to like him when he announced, "Making whisky is like making pornography. Both need good wood."

John invited me to visit him at his offices, so that he could explain more about his company and what he was doing. I imagined heather-filled moors, rolling hills, and babbling brooks, until I looked at his card and saw that I'd be visiting an industrial park in Chiswick. It turned out to be a hugely enjoyable day and, at the end of my visit, as we sat over a meal in the leafy courtyard of a local restaurant, John suggested that I should add a visit to Scotland to my itinerary. He would put me in touch with distilleries where I might be able to wangle a special tour.

A couple of days later, an e-mail filled with lots of useful information and useful contacts popped up in my inbox. Halfway down the e-mail was a line, which read, "Kilchoman—brand-new distillery on Islay. Running a weekly whisky-making academy." That was it for me. The chance to spend a week making whisky was good enough, but to do so at a brand-new distillery was too good to miss.

Islay is also home to my favorite whiskies. Islay whisky is unique. The dense taste of peat cutting through the almost soapy smell of the Scotch after it has been cut with a little water is unmistakable. Countless meals have come to their natural conclusion with the gentle sigh of the stopper being plopped from a bottle of Laphroaig or Lagavulin.

Only days after I had returned from the United States, I was booked for the Kilchoman course in December. Both John and Nick had made time in their hectic schedules to join me for the week, which is how the three of us were to be found standing in the still room of Kilchoman on a cold December morning, the day after a rather frightening short hop from Glasgow to Islay's tiny airport.

Anthony Wills created the distillery in 2005, joining seven other world-famous distilleries on the island. Since spirit needs to age in barrels for at least three years before it can be called whisky, and needs even more time than that to take on the distinctive hue from the oak, their first release would not be available until at least 2010. We would be helping Master Distiller Malcolm Rennie make the new spirit, a sort of protoscotch, the result of the second part of the distillation process just before barreling.

The process itself sounds simple enough, but is a painstaking combination of short bursts of action coupled with long hours of watching and waiting for the result. I have to admit that, being a man of little patience, the watching and waiting drove me around the bend, but it appeared not to bother Malcolm and his colleague, Gavin, in the slightest, as they filled their time with endless cups of tea, slices of cake, and amiable bickering. The call to action, however, is a different matter and they soon had us hard at work.

Whisky is made (now listen carefully, this is an expert talking, I have a certificate to prove it and everything) when barley is malted (heated to create extra starches), steeped in water three times (to create moisture and start germination), dried (to stop germination) over peat (in the case of Islay Whisky), mashed to produce a weak beerlike liquid then distilled twice, the second to produce the fine, pure liquid that is then barreled to age into Scotch whisky. This process is quite simple in theory, but allows for endless variations, which give every Scotch whisky distillery its unique characteristics.

Malcolm and Gavin took great glee in giving us all the choice tasks, prime among them shoveling the grain from the malting floor to the mash tun, a job that took the three of us the best part of a morning and resulted in frayed tempers, aching backs, and the creation of some very imaginative swear words as we got in each other's way and generally created havoc.

At the end of our morning's labor, the two professionals came in to see if our efforts had passed muster.

"Aye, you've no done bad," said Gavin, casting an appraising glance at a floor cleaned of even the smallest grain.

"How often does this have to be done?" John asked, his brow beaded with perspiration.

"Every other day," said Malcolm.

I looked at them with newfound respect for having to do three times a week a task that had resulted in blistered hands, clothes wringing with sweat, and had brought us three close to physical violence.

"That's why," Gavin said with a wicked gleam in his eye, "we use yon machine over there. It makes it a lot easier." He pointed to a shiny mechanical tool in the corner.

Only the intervention of John and Nick prevented me from trying to re-create Bannochburn there on the malting floor with a large shovel and Gavin's head.

Over the period of the week, we turned up diligently every morning to be given our tasks, but were pleased to find out that our afternoons were free, giving us time to explore. Before we set off for Islay, I had conjured visions of hostelries where stout yeomen served mugs of foaming local beer, plates of freshly steamed seafood, and grilled meats from local cattle and pigs. Unfortunately, with the exception of a very decent breakfast at the guesthouse, the rest of the food on Islay rated between miserably bad to inedible. For a place that produces some of the best oysters and beef in the country, precious little of it appeared on local menus, which were filled instead with offerings of lasagna or chicken tikka masala or clumsy attempts at high-end cooking by which prime ingredients were swamped in sauces of no discernable provenance.

Raw ingredients produced on Islay fetch such a pretty penny on the mainland, in London and, indeed, throughout Europe, that local people often cannot afford to eat the things they produce. We were also told that the locals simply don't like a lot of the local produce and were not prepared to pay extra to have fresh, delicious ingredients when they could purchase cheap frozen foods from their corner shop.

On one of our afternoons away from the distillery, Nick suggested we head off to visit Islay Oysters, a farm whose bivalves are sought after all over Europe as some of the very best.

Which brings me back to the opening of the chapter. Oysters and I have had a troubled relationship. We used to be madly in love, and I could and would devour dozens of the things at a sitting. Then, we had a falling out. A major row caused by a dodgy one at a meal with a client during a trade fair. I did not heed the lesson and, like an ex-girlfriend whom you know is bad for you, I have occasionally tried to sneak oysters back into my diet with the inevitable results. On one occasion, dining with the Great Salami at J Sheekey, London's most famous seafood restaurant, I gave in to a request to share the Assiette de Fruit de Mer. I tucked into the oysters primarily because, when I suggested I should avoid them, the Great Salami made loud chicken noises, a barb that no brother can leave unchallenged even if he is well into his forties. The result was bad and I had two days off work to reconsider my position on the oyster.

Nick used an altogether more subtle approach—yummy noises and lots of them. As he downed at least half a dozen in less than five minutes he made noises that suggested he was either close to death or orgasm.

"Go on," he beseeched. "You are never going to find one as fresh as this. Ever."

He was right. These were as good as oysters are going to get. Washed over twice a day by the cold-water tides, they made me forget all that had gone before. Lady Oyster sucked me back in one more time.

They were lovely. A beautifully plump specimen was taken from the water in front of me, cut open, and sliced free from its shell. Meaty and delicious, it tasted slightly of the sea and went down with a single pleasing gulp. Damn me, I had forgotten how good they were and, to top it off, I felt fine.

Hallelujah, I was cured. A new, oyster-filled world opened up in front of me. Raw oysters, deep fried oysters, oyster po'boys, oysters Rockefeller. It was a miracle.

Cue mad rush in the wee small hours of the next morning, to the little building the Islay folk like to call their local hospital, and my less-than-friendly response to John's genuine question of concern.

After listening to the doctor tell me to drink lots of liquid and the suggestion that, "I probably would keep away from oysters from now on," I was driven home and sheepishly headed back to bed for the next day.

While I slept, John and Nick spent the afternoon visiting other famous distilleries on the island, Laphroaig, Lagavulin, and Ardbeg. Because of John's reputation in the industry, they were treated royally and sampled tastes from some exceptional barrels, which they drank in as heartily as they did the astonishing scenery in which the distilleries sit.

The next day, our last, I was feeling a little better and managed to force down a light breakfast of cereal, eggs (two), bacon, sausages, black pudding, tomatoes, mushrooms, and toast. Being good sorts, John and Nick suggested we revisit the distilleries so I could get see them, too.

First, though, we had to head back and say our farewells to the good people of Kilchoman and to take a short multiple-choice test to see if we had taken in any of the information we had been given during the week. It ill behooves me to say who came out with top marks, particularly as John, in an act of incredible but unsurprising generosity, picked up the tab for the whole trip. So, all I will say is that the industry professionals did not fare well and I, well, I rock.

Then, we tasted the new spirit. It is an odd experience, like looking at the photograph of someone you knew well when he was a child. All the elements that make up his character are there, but undeveloped. The new spirit is clear, the distinctive color comes from time spent in the barrel and, in many cases, from the legal addition of spirit caramel. The hint of flavors to come are there, too, but overpowered by the alcohol, which will reduce over the period of aging.

The Kilchoman new spirit had all the hallmarks of a very decent Scotch whisky in the making. We were each given a small bottle as a sample of our efforts. Suffice to say that none of them made it on to the plane back to London the next day.

The other distilleries were stunning buildings stunningly situated between the rolling hills and the shores of the roaring sea. I sat on a grassy bank to have my picture taken against signs painted on the sides of the distillery, Laphroaig or Lagavulin, names that alone would make any Scotch enthusiast a little teary-eyed. Because of my friends' enthusiasm, I was given the opportunity to drink the sauce at source.

That night, we sat in front of a flickering fire in our guesthouse and cracked open a few bottles from the distilleries we visited. As I sipped, Nick and John talked shop about the subtle differences between the distilleries we had visited and the Scotch we were trying. For once, instead of being desperate to hear my own voice, I listened to two of the most respected men in the industry share their knowledge. I learned a lot.

In fact, I learned a lot that whole week. I learned how my favorite whisky is made. I learned all about good wood and I learned that I should probably keep away from oysters forever.

Most of all, however, I learned that my regular nighttime drop of the good stuff will never taste quite the same again.

Chapter 25
IMMER ESSEN IN MÜNCHEN

I was halfway through my journey and absolutely exhausted. I had gained about ten pounds in weight, and my bones had started to give a rather alarming crack when I heaved Big Red onto my shoulders each morning.

I had known this would happen, perhaps because more than one person had looked at me when I told them about my trip and said, "What, at your age?" before rolling his eyes. However, I had not expected to be quite so weary-to-my-bones tired. As soon as I got back from Islay, my body rebelled. Before the journey, I had never stayed in bed much after six in the morning. Now, I found it hard to drag myself out before midday.

I needed the rest, and allowed myself the luxury of waking up whenever I wanted, walking around my apartment unshaven, dressed only in a pair of sweatpants I found at the bottom of the laundry basket.

I was shaken from my torpor by the arrival of tickets for the next stage of the journey to Southeast Asia and India. I had to get back to work. There was accommodation to be booked and people to contact. I had another fifteen countries to visit and all that gorging was not going to organize itself.

Before I headed out on the next four-month leg of the trip, however, I had planned a couple of side trips, long weekends to Germany and Iceland.

For reasons I have never quite fathomed, the Great Salami and I had begun a tradition of a road trip to Germany every year. I love Germany, the people, and the food but we had decided to make our annual visit, not in leafy green spring or colorful Oktoberfest autumn, but in January. So, the first week of the New Year, we arrived at Munich's impressive airport, bags in hand, ready to hit a few beer halls.

A short break with the Great Salami is never easy. He is the organizer supreme and extreme. The shortest trip is planned like a military excursion. He even fashioned his own guidebook by cutting out appropriate pages from all the others and combined them with information he had printed from the Internet. The moment we arrived at Munich airport for our three days, the Great Salami pointed us straight towards its own beer hall, our first impressive-size brew, and a local speciality, *Grammel Schmalz*, basically a dish of fat laced with chunks of ham and fried onions. It works incredibly well with the local beer.

The people of Munich are Bavarians, not Germans, as many are keen to remind you, and do things with considerable gusto. Munich has the highest standard of living in all Germany, and opportunities to enjoy oneself are everywhere, from cafés, bars, and restaurants to galleries, museums, and parks. It remains a truly lovely city thanks, in most part, to its forefathers, who had the good sense to preserve the original plans for every building so it could be rebuilt exactly as it was before their destruction in World War II.

However, we were not there to sightsee. The Great Salami's schedule said two things at the top in big letters: beer and meat. In Bavaria, the sausage is almost a religion, from the Weisswurst, upon which the light of the noonday sun must never be allowed to shine to the Schweinswurst, which slips down all too well with a frighteningly dark Dunkel Bier. Their beer just is strong stuff, but because of the *Reinheitsgebot*, a series of ancient purity laws governing the brewing of beer, it is not as prone to give you a hangover as other beers stuffed with chemicals. That is, of course, unless you plan to drink an awful lot of it, which we planned to do.

There is nowhere better to drink a lot of beer than Munich, where the joys of beer and meat come together in perfect harmony in that greatest of all Bavarian institutions, the beer hall. Perhaps the most famous is the Hofbrauhaus, where drinkers from many nations flock to be served strong drinks and frighteningly large portions of hearty food by women dressed in dirndls, a traditional costume. All the while, you are being serenaded by men in leather shorts pumping out oompah music on battered brass instruments.

As ever when we arrive in a new town, we became a bit overexcited and managed to work our way around about five of the best halls before early evening, and found ourselves walking through the streets of Munich swaying ever so slightly in the rapidly chilling evening air.

Our evening had not ended. Earlier in the year, at the London Bar Show, I had been lucky enough to meet Stefan Berg, one of the leading cocktail mixers in Germany. He lives in Munich, and told me to get in touch when we arrived. So, while our daytime had been about beer, the evening was about spirits, as Stefan set out to prove that Munich was up with the very best when it came to cocktails. I was incredibly impressed not only by the range of bars in Munich but by the exceptional quality of the mixing.

Being a good German boy, Stefan also made sure that we stopped off at the Ratskeller for some food to soak it all up and deftly ordered plates of bread topped with thick spicy pates, mounds of mashed potatoes and, of course, lots more wurst. Despite that very necessary break between drinks, by two in the morning, both the Great Salami and I were reeling and headed off on uncertain feet towards our hotel.

I woke up five or so hours later to the sound of the Great Salami drinking a bottle of water and quietly moaning in pain. It took me a good fifteen minutes before I could persuade myself to open my eyes and, when I did, I regretted it immediately, as shards of sunlight pierced my brain like needles. I squealed like a small child and dived back under the covers, making my all-too-frequent pledge that I would never drink again.

And I didn't. Well, not that day, anyway. Nor did the Great Salami. Instead, we spent our day walking around one of the most beautiful cities in Europe, watching people enjoy their weekend. Like so many Bavarian activities, much of the weekend centers around food and much of the food is found around the bustling Viktualienmarkt, where the locals come to buy their weekly groceries and enjoy a plate of Weisswurst.

Sacred to the people of Munich, Weisswurst is meant to be eaten only as a snack between breakfast and lunch. As a fresh, not smoked, sausage, it could not be kept until the next day without spoiling. It is a glorious thing made from veal, bacon, and seasonings like lemon, mace, and parsley in a clear pork skin casing. The locals like to eat their special sausage in a special way, splitting the skins and sucking out the insides which they eat with *Breze*, a pretzel-like bread, another of their passions. It is not as easy as it looks and our attempts to delicately prise the flesh from the skins received cold looks from some of the neighboring tables in one of the small market cafés.

For that evening's meal, the Great Salami had selected another legendary beer hall, the Altes Hackerhaus. Here, as in all beer houses, the menu is predicated on one thing: pork. There are other items on the menu, but you come here for pig in many forms. I chose a plate of *Spanferkel*, suckling pig with creamy, slow-cooked flesh hiding its light under a bushel of crackly skin. The Great Salami selected perhaps the most challenging dish of all, the *Schweinshaxn*, pork knuckle with the same crackly skin but tougher meat, coming as it does from an older animal.

As if hunks of meat the size of basketballs were not alarming enough, they came with potatoes, which Germans eat by the sackloads, and a baseball-size dumpling made—oh, what a surprise—from potatoes. It's an impossible task. We both polished off our meat, down to the bones, but the dumplings remained untouched and sat there viewing us contemptuously for our paltry appetites. We did not even have room for strudel after the meal, which every other man, woman, and child in the place was eating and ladling extra cream on top of. What kind of girlie men were we?

Shamefacedly, we paid our bill and slunk back to the hotel where we spent the night comparing stomach gurgles and mainlining Zantac until the early hours.

For at least ten years, Isabelle Fuchs had the considerable misfortune to visit me at trade fairs as I tried to sell her gift books. She was surprisingly affable about the whole thing and, over the years, even bought a few from me. When she heard about *Eat My Globe* and our trip to Munich, she offered to spend a day showing us around. Originally from across the border in Austria, Isabelle loves Munich, which showed, as she strolled with us through the English Garden, the beautiful green lung of the city and one of the biggest parks in Europe. It also showed as she took us to her favorite beer hall and introduced us to a Schnitt, a double-strength shot of beer served in small measures with an enormous head of foam.

It showed as she sat across from us at supper and ladled spoonfuls of *Saures Lüngerl*, a stew made from calf's lung, onto our plates and smiled as we nodded in delicious agreement that the addition of vinegar to the sauce cut through the fatty meat perfectly. And it showed when she looked at us with an equal measure of disappointment as we pushed our plates away at the end of the meal and said, "But you have not touched your bread dumplings."

Chapter 26
ICELAND: ROTTEN SHARK, ROTTEN WEATHER

Iceland **was** cold. That should not have been a surprise, since the name is a bit of a giveaway. But the sheer ferocity of the chill still came as a shock to my system as I sat shivering in a car in the parking lot of Reykjavik Airport.

If possible, Iceland has an even worse reputation for food than Britain, and would not have been on my itinerary but for an intervention by my friend Magaret "Magga" Kristiansdottir, the manager of one of my favorite bars, which she ran with ruthless Nordic efficiency. At the end of many evenings, I found myself chatting to her over a well-made cocktail.

The day I handed in my notice, I popped in to tell her my news. She gave me a supportive hug and said, "Come to Iceland. You can eat sheep's head."

Now, if anyone else had made that suggestion, I would have told him that I would rather put my John Thomas in a vise. But, coming from Magga after a martini, it struck me as a good idea, which is how I found myself in Reykjavik wondering if my testicles would ever descend from my torso again. The cold did not bother Magga or her best friend, Erla Guðrún, who was busy rummaging around for cigarettes in the glove compartment of her battered old Nissan, as I sat hoping my nose would be the first thing to fall off.

When we finally got going, they pointed the car away from Reykjavik towards the tiny town of Stokkseyri, which Magga promised me was one of her favorite places in the whole of Iceland. The ride there proved to be a hair-raising rollercoaster chase up hills and down slopes in increasingly thick snow until we pulled up in front of a small, picture-book-pretty restaurant called Fjorubordid.

Magga explained that the restaurant was famous for one dish, bowls of crayfish called "village lobster," dressed only in melted butter and served in various portion sizes with bowls of sweet new potatoes.

If the cold had nearly caused me to have a heart attack, then the prices of the drinks almost finished me off. The small beer I ordered was ten pounds and a bottle of wine that I would turn up my nose at in the local supermarket was going to come in at forty pounds. I would have snorted beer through my nose in disgust, but it was too expensive to waste. The girls explained to me that the high prices of the alcohol in Iceland came about for two reasons. The first is obvious: It is a tiny country with a population of only about three hundred thousand, so just about everything must be imported. The other reason was the prohibitive policies of successive Icelandic governments that had only allowed the overturn of prohibition laws within the last twenty years.

Whatever the reason, I stopped chugging and carefully nursed the remaining precious liquid until our food arrived. When it came, the delicious smell alone was enough to make us fall on our plates and rip the shells off the small, incredibly sweet seafood, giggling happily as butter ran down our chins. They were as good as any seafood I ate on the trip and, when Erla declared that she could not possibly finish her bowl, I dived in before anyone could say, "Locals hold back."

Erla had decided to decamp for three days to her boyfriend's place, and leave her entire flat back in Reykjavik to me. After so many acts of kindness on the trip so far, I should not have been surprised, but have to admit that, cold and tired as I was, such an unexpected act of generosity made me appreciate my luck. I fell asleep, counting my blessings.

The next morning, a thick layer of snow lay across the city. Pleased that I had brought a thick pair of socks and my nonslip walking shoes, I headed out to meet Magga.

Reykjavik is a small but buzzing town, neat as a hospital bed. The people, too, seemed very content with their lot on that Saturday morning as they wandered around stylish modern shops and myriad coffee bars. Magga, however, wanted to take me for a taste of real Iceland, which she suggested, a little strangely, could be found at the local bus station.

I followed along, trudging through ever thicker snowdrifts until we came to the local bus stop where, standing at the corner, was a brightly lit café with a larger-than-life-size photo on the wall of the owner proudly holding a plate of food. Magga instructed me to sit down and went off to order, returning with a broad smile and a tray containing a bottle of lurid orange drink, a can of malt tonic, and half a sheep's head on a plate.

"It's called a *Swidd*," she announced matter-of-factly, blissfully unaware that I was engaged in a staring contest with the one remaining eye in the sheep's head and that I was losing. "You drink Christmas ale with it," she added as she opened the bottle of orange pop, mixed it with half the can of malt drink, and handed me the glass containing the murky result.

I took one sip and quickly pushed it to one side turning my attention to the sheep's head. With an encouraging nod from Magga, I tore a chunk off the jowl. It was nowhere near as bad as I expected.

Fatty and with a slightly charred taste from where, I was told, they singe the fur off before boiling. I didn't even balk when Magga suggested that I eat the eye, which popped in my mouth like a meaty little candy.

Magga, however was in her element. After we had removed most of the flesh from the skull, she picked the whole thing up, prised open the jaw-bone, and began to chomp on the tongue.

"It's the best bit," she mumbled, globs of fatty lamb littering her face. All this and she could mix a martini, too.

Magga munched happily for half an hour until the bones were picked clean. Then, she wiped her chin on a napkin and told me she had something important to do, heading off into the snow leaving me alone with the fleshless grinning skull of our lunch.

I went off in search of another Icelandic obsession, the hot dog. First brought to the island by visiting American troops, it was given its own very different and delicious Icelandic twist. Bæjarins Beztu Pylsur, the most famous stand on the island, sported a picture of Mr. William Jefferson Clinton indulging in more than one of them, a good, if hardly unique sign. It's a good sausage, smothered in a spicy remoulade sauce and topped with crunchy fried onions. I can see why they appeal to people and presidents alike.

Even with one of the highest standards of living in the world, Iceland remains a hard place to live in the twenty-first century because of the weather. God only knows what it was like in times past when, for huge chunks of the year, it was isolated from the rest of humanity. As a result, Icelanders developed a food culture that is considered to be one of the most challenging anywhere.

I learned all about this on my last evening as Erla took over the reins on a short driving tour around the city, including a visit to the presidential residence. Erla announced proudly that, in Iceland, everyone has the constitutional right to make an appointment to see the president if he or she has something he wishes to discuss.

I was delighted to see that the only security was a small sign saying, "Please Don't Pass this Point if You Don't Have an Appointment."

Just try that at the White House or 10 Downing Street.

Erla's main aim, however, was to explain to me all about the *Thorrablot*, which she translated as "Thor's Feast." During the harsh winters, fresh food was almost impossible to find, and the people lived off the fish and meat they had caught during the warmer months and preserved by smoking or pickling. At the end of January, in the depths of midwinter, a sacrificial feast was held in honor of Thor, for which people came together to eat, drink, and sing.

When the Vikings were converted to Christianity, the festival was banned, but it experienced a revival during the nineteenth and twentieth centuries, as Iceland struggled for independence from the Danes. Now it is a regular part of the calendar, and shops are filled with traditional foods for the feast. I wanted to take some back for the Great Salami, so Erla pulled her car into a large market and took me to a section devoted to *Thorrablot* goodies.

It's challenging stuff, all right. Sour ram's testicles, roast puffin, and seal flipper obviously caught my attention, as did *Blodmor*, the local version of blood sausage. But the one thing I was especially looking for was *hakarl*, rotten shark meat.

Even after encountering the legendary durian fruit in Asia, I count hakarl the foulest smelling food. It has a stench like urine, which explains why many tourists, including me, believed the folktale that part of the curing process involved people peeing over it.

Quite how they came up with the notion of burying shark meat for three months to get rid of the poisonous uremic acid in the flesh (which the shark evolved for flotation), I am not sure. However, the result is chunks of dried, horribly pungent white flesh meant to be downed in one go with a shot of Brenivin, the local sesame-based hooch. It is undoubtedly the single most unpleasant thing I have ever put in my mouth, worse than rat or dog and much worse than cod sperm sushi.

Nonetheless, I bought a small tub to take home, along with a bottle of the Brenivin and some blood sausage and presented them proudly to the Great Salami.

A year later, they remained untouched and unopened, sitting threateningly at the back of the fridge.

PART IV

THAILAND, MALAYSIA, VIETNAM, PHILIPPINES, AND INDIA

7

Chapter 27
THAILAND: SAWADEE

My first meal in Thailand could not have been more simple and delicious: a plate of fried rice, cooked in front of me at a street stall, and served for less than the price of a daily paper in the United States. This favorable impression stayed with me until I left Thailand a week later, after a few days in Bangkok. It was a feeling that also grew from the warmth of the Thai people. Energetic and passionate, they are among the most genuine and gentle people in the world. I never lost the impression that they were sincere when they greeted me in the traditional way, as the receptionist at my hotel had done, with *"Sawadee ka,"* which means hello.

Thailand has its problems, of course, particularly in Bangkok, with traffic and pollution to make even China take notice, a chaotic transport system, even with the relatively new Skytrain and, worst of all, the widespread poverty and the attendant vices of drugs and prostitution. Yet, I can't help thinking that many of Thailand's problems are caused by foreigners, the expats who still treat the country and particularly the cities as playgrounds where just about anything goes and the visitors who flood in to take advantage of loopholes in the laws against sexual tourism.

My guesthouse was in Sukhumvit, close to great shops, bars, and restaurants and endless opportunities for eating. Unfortunately, Sukhumvit is also where Bangkok's dark side rears its head. I had made a reservation for an introduction to royal Thai cuisine at Ban Kanitha, a well-recommended restaurant close to my accommodation.

The cooking flavors meant business. Raw prawn were "cooked" in a sauce of limes, chili, and fish sauce and presented in a salad of bean sprouts; soft-shell crabs were fried to give each bite a pleasing crunch.

Even a dish of classic phad Thai was better than any I had tried outside Thailand.

My evening's pleasure was only slightly lessened by the sight of two paunchy drunken British expats, barking at the gentle manager.

"Don't make it too bloody spicy. You did that last time even though I told you not to. If you make it too bloody spicy, we won't pay for it. Got that?"

The manager, of course, just smiled beatifically. I felt ashamed of the representatives from my country.

On the walk home, I took a detour through one on Bangkok's infamous streets of girlie bars, Soi Cowboy, and came close to bringing my supper back up at the sight of fat, old, ugly European men groping girls young enough to be their daughters, none of whom looked as if they wanted to be groped by anyone let alone these corpulent, lecherous Neanderthals.

A few of the girls called out to me.

"Come, buy me lady drink." "You want massage?"

Their lips formed thin smiles but their eyes were blank. It was my first experience of Thailand's seedier side and it made me angry. I went to sleep with the sounds of Sukhumvit filtering through my window and those small, sad smiles of the small, sad girls filtering through my jet-lagged dreams.

The next day, I marked three Bangkok landmarks on my map, all of which promised plenty of chances to eat. Chatuchak market was great fun and already bustling when I arrived at eight thirty in the morning. After a couple plates of passable spring rolls, I followed my nose to some of the best fried chicken in the world. I am a sucker for fried chicken, and this example came with a sauce so fiery I had to diffuse the heat with umpteen glasses of fresh juice from an adjoining stall.

Crunchy food is a bit of an obsession for the male members of the clan Majumdar. When I was a child, when my mother roasted a chicken, she and my sister would help themselves to the plump breasts while the four men would fight over the bones and the crispy skin, which we would reduce to nothing but a pile of sawdust. My mother would have been proud of my efforts on this day, as was the owner of the stall who nodded approvingly as I left nothing but a few shards of bone at the end of my meal.

With the humidity now almost unbearable, I found my way to one of Bangkok's staggering shopping malls, Siam Paragon, which claims to be the largest in the world. It is a claim hard to argue given that it has three major luxury car dealerships on its third floor.

All shopping malls in Bangkok have food courts, similar to the high-end Japanese food halls in department stores. The selection of bars and self-service restaurants would satisfy the needs of a small town. An army of chefs prepare food fresh to order and you pay with a prepaid card specific to that mall. I returned again and again filling my tray with bowls of tom yam soup, crab cakes, and belly pork with glass noodles for the price of a lunchtime sandwich back home.

I wanted to fit in some sightseeing, so the next day I used Bangkok's efficient boat service to criss-cross Bangkok's river from Wat Pho to Wat Arun, back to the Golden Temple, ending up at the Royal Palace. When I arrived, much of the palace was cordoned off and thronged with people dressed in black. I had not really kept up with news, so I made my way to an information booth to find out what was going on.

Princess Galyani Vadhana, the sister of the King of Thailand, had died a few days before my arrival and the whole country was in mourning. The Thais are monarchists and there are severe penalties for showing disrespect to the King. Simple acts like standing for the national anthem in a cinema are universally followed. The dignified displays of mourning and affection for the deceased princess were genuinely moving.

Since I could not see the Royal Palace, I dug out my map and realized that I was only a short ride in a tuk-tuk, Bangkok's frightening but cheap auto rickshaw, from another, less salubrious Bangkok landmark, Khaosan Road. Made famous most recently as the starting point for Alex Garland's book *The Beach*, Khaosan Road is the unofficial center of the backpacking universe. It is pretty much a given that every young person traveling the region will pass through there at least once.

I, too, passed through there once and at great speed. It's an unpleasant place, filled with cheap cafés selling banana pancakes to teenagers who want to travel but don't want to eat any of that nasty foreign food. The kids have all gone native, the nice clothes their parents had bought for them for the journey tossed aside within about thirty seconds of getting off the plane and swapped for the nearest pair of Thai fisherman's pants. Quite frankly, they look silly.

Making sure to station themselves at the front of each café were the travel Nazis, young white men with dreadlocks and lots of meaningful tattoos whose self-appointed task is to guide naïve young folk through the pitfalls of travel, whether they want any advice or not. I have met an awful lot of them on the road. You can tell them nothing about anything that they have not done before, more cheaply and more authentically. They look at you with contempt for taking out your *Lonely Planet* or *Rough Guide,* and God help you if you have a *Frommer's.* "For American tourists, mate. For American tourists."

Khaosan Road was not for me. I hopped on the nearest tuk-tuk and got to my chosen spot for lunch, Chote Chitr, a small restaurant with a big reputation. Its walls are covered with both national and international reviews raving about the simplicity and freshness of the food. When I arrived, a handful of tables were occupied by local office workers and I was able to slide in to a table near the kitchen where I could watch the food being prepared. After ordering a cold Singha beer, I asked the owner to choose for me as I do when, quite frankly, I don't know what the hell I am doing.

I was presented with three beautiful dishes: a salad of banana blossom served with seafood, chicken, and spiked with the sharpness of tamarind; *mee krob,* a dish of fried, crispy vermicelli mixed with chicken and soured with Thai citrus fruit; and a fiery red curry made with slices of duck, Thai basil, and lime leaves.

That evening, my last, I wanted to try of another of Thailand's classic dishes, the green curry. The versions I had tried in the United Kingdom had always left me thinking that there had to be more to this popular dish than a lurid green sauce and chunks of chicken. With the help of the receptionist at my guesthouse, I found my way to another small street market and sat in front of an elderly woman as she prepared my supper. Behind her another woman was grinding the ingredients for the sauce, the scent of chilies, shallots, garlic, and galangal (also called blue ginger, an earthy, citrusy root) filling the air as she pounded them in a mortar and pestle. The cook tossed chicken in a wok with a little oil before adding the sauce to spit away its rawness for a few minutes. She poured in two ladles of coconut milk and allowed it to sit bubbling away for a few moments before spooning it into a large bowl, which she placed in front of me with a plate of rice and some limes. The tastes were incredible. Sparky with lime, fiery with chili, and savory with garlic and shrimp paste. I cleaned the bowl to the last drop.

It was exactly the kind of meal I had hoped to eat in Thailand. Exactly the sort of meal I had hoped for when I first set out on the journey. The chance to find out what these famous dishes, so often served in the West, but neutered by bad ingredients and lack of soul, taste like when they are made properly and with care.

I could not have asked for a more perfect end to my short visit to this remarkable city.

My time in Bangkok was up, so I made my way back to the guest-house to pack and took the opportunity to have an early night before my crack-of-dawn trip to Chiang Mai.

I got little sleep. The malaria pills were still causing me nausea and as I sat on the edge of the bed reading the notes which came in the packet of pills I was alarmed to find they were also the medicine of choice for people with syphilis. I made a mental note that when I got my repeat prescription for Africa I would ask the doctor to write in very large letters: FOR MALARIA. NOT FOR THE CLAP.

Chiang Mai had been an afterthought, a late addition when I realized I had some days to spare before flying to Malaysia.

Although relatively small, its numbers are swelled by a large expat community from the West who come here to eke out their pensions, and by thousands of travelers who are also making the most their budgets on the way to Laos, Cambodia, or the hill tribes of Thailand itself.

Being on the tourist trail, it did mean that the possibilities of good food were harder to find, with lots of cafés offering meals for homesick British, German, Dutch, and Australians and as much Western food on offer as northern Thai.

One meal of note did provide a bowl of Chiang Mai's signature dish, *khao soi,* a thin curry soup served with side dishes of cabbage, chili, fish sauce, limes, and shallots so you can flavor it according to taste, another simple yet entirely delicious dish.

However, despite the lack of food treats, it proved a very welcome place to spend three days. It has a famous night market thronged with stalls selling everything from fake DVDs to fabulously expensive silks. It is the center for the teaching of Thai massage and every road is littered with shops offering everything from a simple foot rub to a two-hour full-body massage. Outside each shop, the masseuses, all women, sit and chat until a potential customer passes, at which point they sing-song out in unison, "Massage, you want massage?"

There are obviously some places offering a happy ending to the experience, but on the whole, it is good natured, cheap, and fun. Unfortunately for me, when I went to have a foot rub, they took off my shoes and socks, took one look at my gout-riddled toe with its large bunion and squealed, "Have weird foot. Must charge more."

Just as well I didn't ask for the full massage.

Chapter 28
CALL ME ISHMAEL

"Darling, it's too spicy, too spicy." Chef Ismail Ahmad picked up the plate of fish heads from the table and handed it back to one of the chefs with a shake of his head. "You see, darling," he said turning back to me. "If it is too spicy, all you get is the heat and none of the flavor."

I was standing in the kitchen of Restaurant Rebung in the Bangsar area of Kuala Lumpur. I had been invited to spend a day with Chef Ismail as he and his team prepared a buffet of over forty dishes taken from the nearly four hundred in the chef's traditional Malay repertoire.

Standing next to me as we watched this force of nature at work was Lex Ster, an irrepressible nineteen-year-old blogger who had offered to show me around her home city. Lex had told me about Rebung and about Chef Ismail, one of Malaysia's most well-loved chefs and known as a guardian of traditional cuisine. I couldn't figure out what she was talking about for a while because, as a teen she spoke mainly in text speak, and had not yet developed the ability to breathe between words. Her English was impeccable, however.

Lex had taken me on an eating tour through Jalan Petaling, Kuala Lumpur's impressive Chinatown and now, we were at one of her favorite places for chicken rice.

I was eating on my own that night and had asked her for some suggestions. She replied, "Rebungisawesomethechefisreallyfamoushere-anditservesthebesttraditionalmalayfoodinthecity.LOL☺." Or something like that.

She also decided at this point that she should start calling me Uncle. "Anothermalaytraditionforanolderman.LOL☺," she smiled, knowing that she had destroyed my self-image as a vibrant independent traveler.

I took her at her word about Rebung, however, and used Kuala Lumpur's shabby public transport to find my way up to Bangsar for supper on my first evening in the city. Arriving just as they were opening, I was shown to a table inside and given a menu. There was no mention of a buffet, so I ordered a plate of *kway teo bandung*, a soupy noodle dish, which, although pleasant, gave me little reason to think the journey from my hotel had been worthwhile.

"Darling. What are you eating?" a friendly voice boomed out.

I looked up to see Chef Ismail smiling at me, his eyes shining through thick spectacles.

"Didn't you want to try the buffet? It's famous, darling."

He beckoned me to follow him to the outside terrace where, by now, a huge selection of dishes had been laid out just out of my view. My heart sank. I was full and, as he gave me the tour of the plates, it all looked and smelled so good, I knew I would have gone for it given the choice.

"Don't worry, darling," he said, pouring me a bowl of clear chicken broth. "Have this and come talk to me."

As we chatted, I told him about my trip.

"Well, darling, you must come back on Saturday, and you can spend the day with us in the kitchen."

It was too good an offer to turn down.

After giving me a bear hug, he returned to the kitchen and I finished my broth, each delicious drop tasted like it was doing me good, and set off back to the hotel.

I was only staying one night in Kuala Lumpur before heading up to Penang to visit some of the famous hawkers' markets there before they closed for Chinese New Year. Then I would be back in Kuala Lumpur and could take up my invitation at Rebung.

Malaysian food is a magnificent combination of its immigrant history. Authentic Chinese exists next to a fusion of Chinese-Malay food; excellent North Indian tandoor cooking alongside a uniquely Malay take called *nasi kandar*—which I sought out as soon as I arrived in Penang. The name originates from the Malay word for balance, *kandar*, because peddlers would carry pots of curries balanced on poles on their shoulders. Now, street stalls have taken their place with trays of rice, curries, fried chicken, and seafood from which you choose, having them spooned over the rice so the sauces combine to a rich amalgam, all to be mopped up, of course, with a freshly cooked roti. It is gloriously messy, but deliciously good fun as you eat with the right hand, clearing the plate and licking your fingers as clean as possible.

That evening, I headed to one of Penang's many food courts to make sure I sampled some of the local Chinese specialties before everything closed down. Already, they were gearing up for the big day with red banners everywhere and men in dragon suits frightening the kids.

I visited a handful of stalls and came back to my seat with a mixture of Malay, Chinese, and local Nyonya dishes: Chinese *char kway teo*, flat rice noodles stir-fried with vegetables and seafood, was normally cooked in pork fat, but increasingly, because of a large Muslim population, oil is now used; a bowl of *Assam laksa*, noodle soup, topped with chunks of fish and soured with tamarind; and *popiah*, a fresh spring roll, spread with hoisin sauce and filled with egg and bean sprouts. All very different and representing some of the many cultures of Malaysia, but they sat together as happily in my stomach as they did on the plate.

I was exhausted and anticipated a good night's sleep. Instead, I spent the night being bitten by bedbugs and had to change my room twice until I found a mattress that was not infested. In the morning, I counted over one hundred fifty bites, and one, on the side of my head, had swelled up until I resembled Martin Lawrence. That is not a good thing, just in case you were wondering. To make matters worse, when I headed out covered in cream to stop the incessant itching of my spots, I realized that I had my dates wrong and that most of the shops and restaurants were already shut. Things looked bleak.

I found a Malay Indian mamak that was open and had a breakfast of *roti canai*, a Malaysian staple brought over by immigrant workers from India. Flat breads made with egg, flour, and *ghee*, clarified butter. They are only eaten in the morning, with a bowl full of delicious thin lentil dahl. Incredibly addictive, I ordered four of them before I felt full.

Although many of the shops and restaurants were shut, I found plenty of things to distract me during the next two days, including a hike up to the top of Penang Hill, or Bukit Bendera as it is now known, the sight of one of the first hill stations of the British Empire. There I spent a day being pampered at one of the hotel spas on Batu Ferringhi, the wide sweep of glorious beaches to the north of Penang Island.

During the evening, however, it was more difficult to pass the time and, after I had eaten in one of the few open places, I would head back to my hotel to write, hoping that I would not get eaten myself.

I was pleased to return to Kuala Lumpur, where Lex joined me on my visit to Rebung. When we arrived on Saturday morning, things were already getting underway and Alfred, Chef Ismail's restaurant manager, was busy organizing the chefs.

Rebung's kitchen is laid out in traditional Malay home style, with sides open to the air and large steel woks placed on burners. Compared to much Chinese cooking, traditional Malay food does relatively little stir-frying, relying on long slow cooking to bring out the flavor of preserved ingredients like salted fish and dried beef. They use plenty of fresh stuff, too, with large bowls of raw vegetables to crunch on and salads made of banana flower hearts. Fresh cooked specialties are eggplant covered in fiery sambal, fresh fish grilled on banana leaf or rubbed with turmeric and fried in palm oil, and beef and chicken cooked in fiery sauces.

Unlike many other celebrity chefs, Chef Ismail actually spent time in the kitchen, tasting and commenting on every dish.

"More salt, darlings. More salt."

By midday, people had begun to arrive and Chef Ismail, happy with what was happening in the kitchen, moved to the front of the house to greet the guests.

Seemingly everywhere at once, Ismail was greeting guests as they arrived, making sure to flirt shamelessly with the elderly ladies, ladling out bowls of soup to take to each table, and bringing plates of new dishes hot from the kitchen.

"Try this, darlings, do you like it? Okay, let's put some on the buffet."

It was enormous fun and more like attending a large family dinner party than going to a restaurant.

"That's the way I want it, darling," he told us. "This is food my grandmother used to cook. It's family food."

After hours of watching the food being prepared, I wanted to eat it, especially since I had missed out on it at my previous visit. We joined the line at the buffet and loaded our plates with fresh popiah, curries, and salads, all to be eaten with our right hands.

"Ihadbreakfastalreadybutthisissogoodlcouldjustkeepeating.LOL☺," Lex mumbled through her umpteenth spring roll. I knew exactly what she meant.

"Thanksforaskingmealong☺," she smiled.

"No problems, love. What are uncles for?"

Chapter 29
HANOI: CROUCHING DOWN FOR PHO WITH UNCLE HO

In cities around the world, I have developed a sixth sense for avoiding the thousands of cars on the roads. When I arrived in Hanoi, I had to recalibrate my strategy to deal with the hundreds of thousands of bikes and motor scooters that filled the roads twenty-four hours per day. I am happy to share with you my very successful technique for staying alive in Vietnam: Never be ashamed to use a local as a human shield.

The locals have built-in instincts about when to cross a busy road and at what speed. If they get it wrong, at least they get hit before you. I am not proud to admit that, if it is between me and an old lady in the road survival stakes, granny's going down.

My quirky guesthouse in the Old Quarter of the city, with its small roads and offshoot alleyways, appeared to be the Vietnamese equivalent of Boys Town, with half the male teenage population still asleep on blankets on the floor of the reception. I left Big Red, and went straight out for something to eat, immediately bringing into play the survival technique discussed, as scooters shot on either side of me on my walk along the alleyway towards Hoan Kiem Lake in search of breakfast.

Vietnamese food has become increasingly popular in the West in the last twenty years. In part, it is due to emigration of large numbers during and after the Vietnam War, which brought sizable expat communities to America, France, the United Kingdom, and, particularly, Australia. The light, clear flavors of Vietnamese food, combined with its use of fresh ingredients and little fat, fits well with the Western obsession for healthy eating.

Arguably the most famous dish of all is *pho*, a noodle soup, which is good any time of the day, but a must for breakfast. Cooked noodles are placed in a bowl with slivers of meat or seafood, sprinkled with spring onions, and fresh red chili, and topped off with ladles of hot beef or chicken broth. In the Old Quarter that morning, the air was already filled with the smell of *pho* being prepared. Using the trusted rule that the best and safest street food is to be found at the busiest places, I selected a crowded spot, pulled up a small plastic stool, and pointed to a woman with a bowl of beef soup indicating that I wanted the same.

Less than a minute later, I was presented with a steaming bowl filled to the brim and topped off with a freshly cracked egg softly poaching in the hot broth. Every spoonful had layers of flavor and texture. I spiked the broth with a chili paste sitting on the wooden counter and added a dash of fish sauce for salt. It was delicious and I knew that, for my few days here, breakfast would be taken care of.

Hanoi is a major stop on the tourist trail, the streets filled with back-packers on their way to or from Thailand, or traveling south through Vietnam by train, many of them hardly stopping long enough to appreciate what Hanoi has to offer. This may be because no one would ever call Hanoi an attractive city. It suffers the problems of so many other cities in developing countries—pollution, dirt, poverty, and decaying infrastructure. These are worse in Hanoi because the strict Communist regime has neither the finances nor the inclination to do anything about them, but the city still has plenty to offer and is made enjoyable by the sheer energy of its locals. The Hanoi people appeared reserved or even cold at first but, over time, were as welcoming as any others.

I spent the day in search of Vietnam's most famous son, Ho Chi Minh, to this day revered in the country as its greatest hero and liberator. Known to everyone as Uncle Ho, his body was mummified against his wishes, and housed in true Communist-leader style in a mausoleum in the Ba Dinh Square.

After failing to see the mummified bodies of Mao and Lenin in Beijing and Moscow, I was determined to see Uncle Ho, and made my way around the square to the entrance guarded by young soldiers who looked barely old enough to carry toy guns, let alone real ones. I joined a surprisingly small line, handed over my camera and bag, and filed respectfully along in front of the body. He was in better shape than I imagined, perhaps due to the fact that he apparently goes on a two-month holiday to China every year for a bit of a wash and brushup. The quiet tears of the older people in the line made for an unexpectedly moving experience.

On my journey from the airport to the Old Quarter, I had shared a cab with a young man from England named Darren; we had agreed to meet later for a drink. By his own admission, he was not that experienced when it came to food, but was willing to try anything and, over the next couple of days before he had to join his own travel party, he became my wingman as we went in search of great things to eat.

All over the Old Quarter, signs were posted offering *bia hoi* (beer) for sale. The three main Hanoi breweries make their bottled beers as well as barrels of fresh beer with no preservatives. The beer won't last more than a day, so is sold for a few pennies a glass at shops all over the city, where you hunker down on small plastic stools to sip the refreshing brew. After a few glasses, Darren and I felt like we could conquer the world and agreed that, the next day, we would find our way to La Mat, also known as Snake Village, in order to eat our slithering friends.

Viewed through the bleary goggles of *bia hoi*, the idea of eating snake had sounded good to us. But, the next morning, when Darren arrived at my hotel to meet me, he was a lot less certain, as indeed was I. We took a cab for the short journey out of the city, and down a small side street to be suddenly surrounded by a posse of men on scooters, each employed by a different snake restaurant, all screaming at the driver to bring us to his establishment.

When the driver finally disgorged us, we were almost immediately surrounded by people trying to persuade us to eat in their restaurants. For once, I was not ashamed to admit that I was having second thoughts.

"I don't fancy this much, mate," I looked across at Darren who looked back with a grateful look in his eye.

"Me, neither."

We walked around the neighborhood for a while, trying to convince ourselves that we had done the right thing by resisting the serpent, especially when we saw the shops filled with snake medicine and wines. We found another cab to take us back to the city, where we shared a last beer, but inside I felt lousy. I had set out to go everywhere, eat everything, and had turned down this unique opportunity because some nasty men on bikes shouted a bit. I felt like a fraud.

• • •

The next day, I had booked myself into a cooking school at the ultra-smart Metropole Hotel, remnant of French Colonial times, where Graham Greene had lived when writing *The Quiet American*. It was a fabulous day of cooking. The young woman chef, Thuong Thuong, who led the course, first took us on a tour of the Cho' 19–12 market, famous for the quality of its fruit and vegetables and the freshness of its fish and meat. Then, at the hotel, our teacher showed us how to make fresh salads using the hearts of banana flowers, whole fried fish, and the small, delicate spring rolls for which Vietnamese cuisine is famous.

Afterward, we decamped to the hotel restaurant and helped ourselves to the buffet, a collection of nearly one hundred dishes made in small portions to maintain freshness. I sat with my fellow students and enjoyed the meal, but kept thinking back to my failure at La Mat and that somewhere there was a snake with my name on it.

I scheduled my tour to Halong Bay for my last day in the city, and when I awakened, still having snake on my mind I decided I had to go and right my wrong. I girded my loins and caught another cab, this time making sure he dropped me off about a ten-minute walk from La Mat so that I could scope out a likely candidate, choosing a restaurant called Quoc Tien. It was more sedate than I imagined and the restaurant itself was not the gloomy den of iniquity I had anticipated, but light and airy with a smart terrace.

As for the meal, well, after selecting a cobra from the tank as one would a lobster, I watched as it was killed and its heart placed in a glass with some spirit laced with a little blood, which I drank down in one gulp of burning alcohol. The heart reminded me of an oyster and I remained convinced throughout the meal that I could feel it beating.

The rest, felt more ordinary, thankfully, bits of snake braised, stir-fried, and deep-fried with rice and vegetables.

I hate to say it, but it tasted like . . . Well, you can finish that sentence yourself.

Chapter 30
A FILLER IN MANILA

Few places on my trip surprised me as much and as pleasantly as the Philippines. My expectations of it and the food were low. It is not considered cheap or safe for travelers, and it is not on the tourist trail of Southeast Asia, because its government has neglected to promote how beautiful and varied this country of more than seven thousand islands is. Nor has the government promoted the range and quality of the cuisine, so most people assume it consists entirely of *adobo*, the famed dish of pork and vinegar; *lumpia*, the local versions of spring rolls; and *lechon*, barbecue suckling pig. Because I had never been there, my impressions of the country were formed from Western media horror stories of crime, corruption, and crippling poverty.

Only the intervention of my Filipino aunt Evelyn, in New York, changed my mind and itinerary, and I decided to bypass Cambodia and Laos to head to the Philippines instead.

Evelyn reassured me that Manila was worth a visit, and that the food had great variety. Most important, she would be in the country at the same time.

"You have lots of cousins there. I will make sure they look after you."

I was sure they would. Few people ever say no to Auntie Evelyn.

A terrific food writer named Robyn Eckhardt, who runs a Web site called Eating Asia, had given me some helpful hints about Malaysia, and, in passing, had mentioned that she thought Filipino food was one of the undiscovered treasures of Asia. That was enough for me. Manila it was, and I am delighted I made that decision, because my visit was one of the highlights of the whole trip.

There is no doubting that Manila has many problems. The traffic is chaotic and going even the shortest distance takes much planning and, of course, with the traffic comes the problem of noise and pollution made worse by the stultifying humidity. Poverty, and the uneven distribution of wealth, is readily apparent in the shantytowns clustered by the airport runways, which give way to the luxury hotels and private houses, all in secure compounds. With poverty comes its unhappy bedfellows of drugs and prostitution, and the area around my business hotel in Makati was surrounded by girlie bars and massage parlors all catering to the recreational desires of, primarily, fat Europeans.

Despite these problems, common to virtually all developing nations, there is much to recommend the place. The people are among the friendliest anywhere and swamp you with their hospitality and goodwill. The cheery greetings of the hotel staff were genuine and they volunteered hand-drawn notes to show me where to find the best food. The drivers of Manila's plentiful and cheap taxis were, after a gentle bout of haggling, trustworthy, and another useful source of information; and stall holders, restaurant staff, and shop workers could not do enough to help.

Then there is the beauty of the country. Not Manila, which is as ugly as a rejected set for *Bladerunner,* but head a few hours outside or to the far reaches of one of the islands and the scenery is glorious.

Most of all, for me, the food was good, amazingly varied, and the enthusiasm for it—including that of my relatives—bordered on psychotic obsession. I had not encountered this level of passion for food since Mexico. Given the fact that the two countries were both ruled by the Spanish and many governors of the Philippines came from Mexico, this makes sense. And it made me feel right at home.

There appears to be no such thing as a short meal or a small meal and, when Filipinos eat, they also like to talk. Filipinos talk about anything and have an opinion on everything. Even when they don't know what they are talking about, it never seems to hamper them. It is more important to have an opinion and to express it than for an opinion to have any basis in fact.

Filipinos are most opinionated about food, as I found out during my first meal with my cousin, Carlo Tadiar, at a restaurant called Abe. Laconic, with a dry wit, Carlo had a slight American twang to his English, as many Filipinos do, a legacy of the era of American so-called protection after the Spanish left the country. The shopping mall in which the restaurant was situated was another legacy and the Filipinos love malls so much that, at times, you would think you were in Kansas, not Manila.

Editor of a popular men's lifestyle magazine in the Philippines, Carlo talked to me while also ordering food and shouting into his cell phone in Tagalog, the local language, at the same time. Between conversations, he managed to take me through the mounds of food that kept appearing on the table.

Delicious and deeply savory, each dish was packed with astonishing textures and flavors. *Kare-kare,* a slow-cooked stew of oxtail was cooked so the bones released their gelatin and thickened the sauce. Chunks of *bangus* fish were "cooked" in lemon juice and palm vinegar and topped with chili. Roast chickens were stuffed with Filipino rice and dried fruit. *Lechon,* the legendary suckling pig, was served with a sauce made from the pig's liver; *camaru,* a bowl of crunchy, deep-fried crickets, with sharp raw onions. Finally, something called a *Bicol Express* was an arse-threateningly hot dish of pork, coconut milk, and fiery green chilies.

It was all wonderful, the sort of food that raises jaded taste buds from torpor like Lazarus from the dead. Sharp, clean flavors, savory, delicious stews—and a crunch factor that Filipinos demand from at least one dish every meal. Hence the love of deep frying. I adored it.

As I dived headlong into bowl after bowl of food, Carlo explained what was planned for me during my visit. I grunted as if I understood as he listed my itinerary, but I wasn't really listening. I was too busy focusing on the food in front of me to make sure that he, and our two dining companions, did not take my fair share of anything. He could just as easily have told me that I was about to be tortured on live television the next day and I would have given him the same nod of enthusiastic agreement as I pierced another piece of suckling pig with my fork.

It would be fair to say that my first meal in the Philippines was a great success. If this was how good it was going to be, I could hardly wait for the next few days. It got even better.

On Thursday, Carlo picked me up in a car and announced that we were heading out of Manila on the two-hour drive to the city of Angeles in the Pampanga region. He had decided to include an article about my trip in his magazine and to combine it with a meeting of minds between me and a famous local artist and gourmet cook, Claude Tayag. As the tower blocks and slums of Manila faded into the background and we entered rural areas, and saw fields of rice being harvested and rolling hills and mountains in the distance, I saw why Aunt Evelyn had told me she thought it was one of the most beautiful countries in the world.

One of the best cooks in the country, Claude had agreed to prepare a meal for us at his home, which Carlo told me was worth seeing, constructed entirely by Claude himself from remnants of local churches and farmhouses. The house, a *bale dutung*, or "house of wood" was extraordinary, and so was Claude. A true polymath, Claude Tayag is a painter, sculptor, writer, musician, and cook. He had laid every plank of wood in the house and made every stick of furniture, all in a traditional Filipino style with the living quarters elevated and the side panels removable so that air could flow through on humid summer days. He led us out onto a large deck overlooking a garden in which stood half a dozen of his sculptures, made from old ploughshares, and seated us around a table, which he had also made, to begin the meal.

I sat in rapt attention as Claude and his wife brought out dish after dish, explaining how each was prepared: A salad of crunchy paco ferns served with pickled quail eggs had a duck egg dressing. It was followed by *bulanglang*, a seafood stew with guava and fresh prawns with heads so large that Claude instructed us to rip them off, to allow the fat to dribble into the soup as a thickener. Fried hito fish came next wrapped in mustard leaves with *balo balo*, a condiment of fermented rice, which Claude makes and sells under his own label, followed by another version of *kare-kare* stew, this time with fish. Most simple and most delicious of all, adding the necessary crunch, a bowl of *bagnet*, deep fried belly pork.

And there was rice, too, of course. No meal in the Philippines happens without rice. I was staggered by the range of flavors, colors, and textures in this meal—one of the very best I have ever eaten.

After a dessert of white salad that was made of sweet corn kernels in caribou milk, Claude shepherded us towards his car for the short drive into the city so that I could taste perhaps the most quintessentially Filipino dish of all—*sisig*. Created in his hometown of Angeles, *sisig* is made up of leftover bits of pig, cheek, nose, and ear, chopped fine with chili, and cooked in a hot plate to form a crunchy layer on the bottom. Served communally so that people can fight over the crispy bits as they talk, it is a dish that every Filipino loves to have with a cold beer.

It was the perfect way to end what had been one of the very best days of *Eat My Globe*.

Over the next few days, I set out to explore, sometimes alone and sometimes in the company of yet another cousin, Ethan, a huge teddy bear of a man with a deep laugh that peppered his conversation. I liked him immediately.

"Man, I hear you have been doing some good eating? Heh, heh, heh," he boomed at me in his baritone voice. "Let's see if we can't do even better. Heh, heh, heh."

And we certainly tried. We tried *lechon*, the famous dish of whole roasted pig, at Salcedo, the weekend market for middle-class Manilans.

"It's from the Cebu region," he told me knowingly. "They don't serve it with the liver sauce." They say if you need sauce there is something wrong with your *lechon*, which is just what my friend John King said of the barbecue we ate in Texas.

We tried *sinigang*, the Filipino equivalent of Jewish chicken soup. Soured with tamarind, it is flavored with pork, beef, or seafood—in our case, with a huge hunk of corned beef simmered in the broth.

"It has to be sour, man or it's not *sinigang*. Heh, heh, heh," Ethan advised as he slurped up another mouthful.

We tried crispy *pata*, braised pork hung up to dry for up to twenty-four hours, then cut into chunks and deep fried.

We tried pork skewers. "My favorite," Ethan said joining a long line for them at the market, from which he emerged brandishing four meaty skewers. "One's never enough," he said, without any argument from me.

He really was a man after my own heart attack.

Thanks to Aunt Evelyn and my newfound cousins, I had enjoyed my time in Manila more than I could have possibly imagined. So, I was delighted when she joined us for a last meal, painstakingly prepared by Carlo at the enormous family home. For our main course, we had perhaps the most well-known dish of all, *adobo*, pork and chicken marinated in chilies and vinegar, for many Filipinos, the ultimate comfort food.

Ten of us sat around the table and ate, drank, and talked for over five hours, until the small hours of the morning. We talked mainly about food and how things should be done properly, and how so many young people now took shortcuts. Everyone shook their heads mournfully. I felt totally at home.

I could not have been happier. I had discovered a new cuisine and one that could not have been more suited to my taste for hot, sour, and crunchy and, best of all, I had discovered a new family, a family who shared my own obsession for food.

My next stop was to discover my old family.

I was off to India.

Chapter 31
INDIA: CRAZY BEAUTIFUL

It is hard to know where to start with India. Do I start with the negatives? The fact that nothing you have experienced ever prepares you for India? For the assault to every sense, the noise, the pollution, the poverty, the filth-strewn streets, the bewildering number of people, and the shattering of every value you ever held as normal?

Do I start with the country's lunacy, which ranges from the engagingly eccentric—a neon sign outside a bank in Bangalore reads: 24 HOUR ATM (EXCEPT BETWEEN THE HOURS OF MIDNIGHT AND 6AM), or the horrifying levels of disease and poverty? Do I start with the fact that India is easily the hardest country on earth to deal with, harder even than China? It is a country often so profoundly irritating that I suggested to one Indian official that they replace the Ashoka Chakra on the flag of the Republic of India with an image of a single buttock, just to warn people how half-assed things can be.

Or should I start with the positives? With the fact that India seems unstoppable? Not just tapping at the glass ceiling placed upon developing nations by developed ones, but head butting it with increasing ferocity. It could soon be the most populous nation on earth. It could soon overtake many countries in the West in terms of its GNP. It is already at the forefront of medical and technological development and, for better or for worse, it is already the biggest purchaser of weaponry.

What about the awe that India inspires in its history, its architecture, its vastness, and its explosions of colors?

Perhaps, as the book title suggests, I should start with the food, which cannot be bettered anywhere in the world for its variety and range and quality. Of course, the term *Indian food* is nonsensical, like saying

European food without acknowledging the difference between Finnish and Spanish. There are twenty-eight states and seven union territories in the Republic of India, ranging from Kashmir in the North, to Tamil Nadu in the South, from Maharashtra in the West, to Bengal in the East. Each has its own distinct cuisine born out of the geography and political history of the region. In the North, Mogul invaders brought grilling and the subtlety of cream and almonds; in the Southwest, the cooking of Goa shows the Portuguese influences of garlic, chilies, tomatoes, and vinegar.

It is no easy matter knowing where to start with India. But, then, it is no easy place for me to know where to start with me being Indian. If indeed, that's what I am.

So, instead, let me start with Baba, my father, Pratip Majumdar. Baba first moved to Britain in the mid-1950s, primarily to complete his medical training as an orthopedic surgeon, but also to escape his father's expectations that he would join the family homeopathic practice back in Calcutta.

My grandfather was, by all accounts, brilliant and well respected, a member of the Indian Communist party and part of the intelligentsia that pushed for independence from Great Britain after World War II. However, his relationship with my father was uneasy, punctuated by long periods of noncommunication, which meant my father infrequently returned to India. It also meant that I never met my grandfather.

I take very much after my father. He is his own man, suffers fools not at all, and, while he is intensely loyal to those he considers friends, he cuts those who cross him out of his life like a malignant tumor. I have many reasons to be grateful for his strength, generosity, and support over the years, but the unwelcome side effect of his fallout with his own father has been a profound lack of my sense of identity.

I joke that I am half Welsh, half Bengali, but in reality I have always felt half non-Welsh, half non-Bengali. Not particularly comfortable or welcome in either camp, I speak neither language at all and while my glistening olive skin may be a sure-fire hit with the ladies (who snorted?), it has led to me being called "Paki" in Rotherham (which is both racist and geographically incorrect) and "half-caste" in India.

Five weeks in India promised to be interesting, not just for the food.

Delhi is to India what Washington is to the United States, not a desperately exciting city, but as the administrative heart, it makes a decent starting point and reasonably sane place to begin an introduction to the most insane country in the world.

It is a place where my taxi took me to three hotels other than the one I had requested, trying to persuade me that mine was closed. When I did finally get to my hotel, the staff denied all knowledge of my reservation, but, after I ultimately persuaded them to give me a room, I walked in to find a card on the bed that read: DEAR SIMON MAJUMDAR: We hope you enjoy your stay.

The morning after my arrival, I decided to spend a few hours sightseeing. I only had two full days in the capital before heading to Mumbai, so I flagged down one of the infamous yellow-and-black auto rickshaws. Thousands of these buzz around the streets of the capital, in fact, in every city in India, like angry hornets. They are great fun, extraordinarily dangerous. Above all, they are cheap and, as you haggle with the driver to agree a fare, you do have to keep reminding yourself that the amount you are arguing over is loose change that you would not stop to pick up if you dropped it on the streets of London or New York.

I spent the morning looking at the Red Fort, the center of Mogul ruler Shah Jahan's capital, which takes its name from the miles of red brick that form its outer wall. In previous years, nearly every visitor was a foreigner, but now, while still packed to the rafters, more tourists seem to be locals, a sign of India's burgeoning middle class.

It is a hugely impressive place, but I was more moved by my next stop, the home of a woman many still consider the mother of modern India, Indira Gandhi. Since her assassination in 1984, the simple but dignified bungalow she called home has become a museum to her life and a shrine to her legacy. At the rear of the house, in a neat garden is the path along which she walked to meet the man who turned out to be her assassin. It has been covered in glass to protect her last steps in the gravel and the point at which she fell.

By now, I was starving and had my auto rickshaw drop me off in the heart of Old Delhi.

The romantic notion that street food always tastes better than food in restaurants is, of course, complete and utter rubbish. Just because you eat food prepared for you by some toothless old granny while standing at a street corner does not give it any more intrinsic quality and, of course, you add to it the Russian roulette element of not knowing if you will make it back to your accommodation before your arse explodes.

I often met travelers along the way who offered up their encounters with dysentery as some sort of badge of honor.

"Oh, yeah, I only eat on the streets. It's where the real people eat," they would proffer.

"That's why they all die at fifty," was an obvious reply.

In other countries on the trip, I had, of course, eaten food from roadside stalls—in China, Malaysia, Vietnam, and Thailand. I had taken great care to head to places crowded with locals with the view that a high turnover would mean fresher food and less chance of me spending the night heaving into the porcelain. So far, I had been lucky, but I was less inclined to take the risk in India, for two reasons. The first being that the locals here seem to have stomachs that can cope with anything, anything at all from the fieriest chilies to germs that would have biological terrorists shaking their heads in disbelief. The second is that, of all of the Asian countries I visited, the standard of hygiene in India is easily the worst. Old ingredients covered in flies cooked in oil days old served on plates washed in the same murky water for the whole day.

With my level of misfortune, I just knew there was a meal there with my name on it. So, I had done my research to find restaurants and cafés that had good reputations with both locals and visitors, trusting that they would ensure at least a modicum of cleanliness.

Karim's in Old Delhi was such a place and, as I sat down at one of the communal tables, the smells coming from the kitchen reminded me of why a world tour could not leave India off the list. The unmistakeable whiff of ghee, onions, and spices set my heart rate racing.

As I looked at the menu, a young man sitting opposite me began chatting to me, introduced himself as Sunit, and turned to the menu board on the wall, saying, "They are famous for their mutton dishes here, but try the butter chicken. It's excellent."

Butter and chicken together, I liked the sound of those odds. So, when the waiter arrived, we both ordered the same and Sunit added a side dish of mutton kebabs, which he insisted I should share.

We both received large bowls of chicken in a gravy made primarily with tomatoes. On the top was a wicked-looking slick of melted ghee (clarified butter), and to the side, a sliver of green chili. It was every bit as good as Sunit claimed and, like him, I ate with my hands, gnawing the chicken bones to sawdust and mopping up the sauce with fresh paratha bread, occasionally taking big bites from our side dish of kebabs.

When food this good is put in front of you, you can forgive India anything.

At the end of the meal, having been told about my trip, Sunit insisted on paying for the meal, an incredibly generous gesture which, although it had happened many times before on the trip, never failed to make me feel all fuzzy inside. I only hoped that the butter chicken would not.

On my final day in Delhi, I decided that it was time to have one of my occasional blowouts and spend my entire daily allowance in one high-end restaurant as a counterpoint to the cheap and homely places that were my normal destination. After a morning of sightseeing, including a visit to the moving memorial to Mahatma Gandhi, I had my auto rickshaw drop me off in front of the Sheraton Hotel where my chosen restaurant, Bukhara, was situated. Regularly featured on lists of the best restaurants in the world, they serve some of the best cooking from India's Northwest Frontier, where intense flavors from tandoor-grilled meats and creamy, slow-cooked dahls combine to an intensely robust effect. It is no surprise that Bill Clinton was a fan, as well as Vladimir Putin, who insisted on eating here every time he visited Delhi.

A waiter appeared and wrapped a bib around my neck, explaining that, since I had ordered the house specialty of tandoori chicken, I would need it to protect my clothing. When a platter containing the whole bird was brought out of the kitchen, its fragrant odors preceded it, and I was slobbering before it hit the table.

Tandoori chicken appears on the menus of every Indian restaurant in the world and, in principle, it is one of the simpler dishes to make. Marinate chicken in yogurt and spices and grill it. However, like all things seemingly simple, getting it right is more difficult than it looks. Too much marinating makes the meat spongy, too little and it dries out. At Bukhara, it was perfect. This is not a dish to nibble at politely. You vacuum it up, chomping loudly with no thought for the mess you are making on the table, your hands, or your clothes. Thank God they gave me the bib.

The chicken was so good that I almost forgot to turn my attention to their other signature dish, the Bukhara dahl, a version of Makhani dahl traditionally made by allowing Urad lentils to cook in milk overnight in the embers of the cooling tandoor. To it are added onions and garlic, spices, and enough butter that each serving should come with its own defibrillator. It is so good that the handful of fluffy paratha breads with it scarcely seemed enough. As in Thailand, I found myself picking up the bowl to lick it clean. I would have gotten away with it, too, if it had not been for those pesky waiters. Returning to collect the plate, he said, "You have a stain on your face, sir."

I turned to the mirror by my seat to see my reflection with its telltale ring of sauce around my mouth from the lip of the bowl.

"Don't worry, sir," he said calmly as he handed me a hot towel. "It happens a lot."

I am sure it does. And I was pretty sure it would happen to me if I went there again.

Chapter 32
MUMBAI THE UNSTOPPABLE

Delhi may be the capital of India, but it is Mumbai to which everyone looks to lead the way. With well over sixteen million people and seemingly as many cars, the sights, sounds, noise, and smells of Mumbai make it India to the power of ten.

Where Delhi seemed, by comparison, sedate and a little staid, Mumbai crackles with raw energy. It seeps out of every open sewer and explodes with every parping horn from the black-and-yellow taxis that churn out enough pollution to make your eyes weep the moment you set foot on the decaying streets. While Delhi is a useful stopover on the way to somewhere else, Mumbai is that somewhere else. No trip to India would be complete without a visit there. It feels like riding on the world's highest rollercoaster without a harness.

There is, of course, much to deplore about India's cities in general and this one in particular—the gut-wrenching poverty and the crumbling buildings and roads seem to suggest that, when the British left, they took all their tools with them. The stench that fills the air from the filth-strewn streets and clogged gutters makes even the most seasoned traveler gag and cover his mouth and nose. It is a challenge to every Western value and an assault to every sense.

Nonetheless, Mumbai is truly one of the world's great cities, and it doesn't really care if you approve or not. You get the feeling that, if you were to mess with Mumbai, Mumbai would just turn around and kick your ass.

Nowhere is this more apparent than when it comes to food. Mumbai has a reputation as the best city in which to eat in India, perhaps in the whole of Asia, and the staggering variety is made possible by the influx of people from every corner of the subcontinent.

The coastal location made Mumbai the Gateway to India, where you will find Muslim sitting with Parsi, Bengali sitting with Jain, and Tamil sitting with native Maharashtrian for meals ranging from local favorites of *phav bhaji*, the curry-in-a-bun snack, or *bhel puri*, to hot Parsi *dhansaks* with their lentil gravies, Bengali sweets, tandoor-grilled rolls and kebabs, seafood cookery from the southwest Konkan Coast, or creamy korma from the North. All can be washed down with juices from fresh fruits and sugar cane or a long cold beer, as your taste and religion dictate.

Mumbai is not great for sightseeing. Once you have looked at the deeply unimpressive Gateway to India and sailed out on a rickety old ferry to the Elephanta Islands, you have more or less done Mumbai. That leaves plenty of time to explore what Mumbai is really about—visits to Crawford Market or Chor Bazaar produce eye-popping sights that both astonish and disgust; on trips to Chowpatty Beach, you can watch Mumbaikars at play and doing what they do best—eat.

Mumbai's location means that it has great seafood. Its proximity to Gujarat means it has sensational vegetarian food. Entire streets are dedicated to food stalls, small snack shops, midlevel eateries, and high-end restaurants, covering every taste and budget.

I had just a few days there and knew that I was not going to able to try everything, but I had a plan. My hotel was just around the corner from a true local institution, Vithal Bhelwala, where they have served one of Mumbai's signature snacks, *bhel puri*, for generations. Puffed rice mixed with a combination of *sev* (sticks of fried flour), onions, potatoes, to-matoes, and chili, *bhel puri* can be dressed with chutneys of tamarind or coriander. Vithal offers twenty-five different versions including one, I noticed on the menu, made with cornflakes and called a Western Bhel. It's a great introduction to the area and, after two large platefuls of their Special Dry Bhel, I was ready to walk it off on the way to the location I had in mind for supper.

My budget didn't quite stretch to the high-end restaurants, like the famous Konkan Kitchen, for its southwest seafood, so I headed to a small recommended restaurant, Apoorva. Like so many neighborhood places in India, Apoorva didn't appear desperately welcoming at first, being mainly a place for working men to come for a drink and some food after work. Lighting was dim and the only air-conditioning a rattling fan above each table. The food was fantastic, with a classic dish of *prawn gassi*, a small dish of sweet shrimp cooked in a spicy sauce of coconut milk soured with the juice from a *kokum*, a native fruit renowned for its medicinal properties. They place a knife and a spoon on the table for you, but in India, people usually use their hands.

Eating with your hands has many benefits. You can combine the ubiquitous mound of rice with the sauce of whichever dish you are eating so that each grain gets a proper coating. Everything also just tastes better. Don't ask me why, it just does. My cutlery remained untouched as I scooped fingers full of spicy rice to my lips and spooned up the sauce with a crispy *appam*, a bowl shaped pancake made of fermented rice flour.

I asked the waiter what was in the sauce.

In the United States, if you are silly enough to ask such a question they can easily spend as much time describing a dish as the chef did cooking it. "It's an infusion of milk from a cow named Doris from Johnson State Farm, with Meyer lemons from the second branch from the top, mixed with cilantro picked at midnight while we all sang "76 Trombones" from *The Music Man*. The chef used his right hand while preparing the dish and laced the final emulsion with two tears shed while thinking of his mother."

"It's a gravy," my waiter responded.

"Yes, but what's in it?" I pressed and he headed off to ask someone who might know.

Returning, he proudly announced with a slight bow, "It's a red gravy," and went off to serve other tables.

If I ever get to wait tables at Jean-Georges, I am going to use that as my stock response.

The next day, I set out to visit two of Mumbai's most famous shopping districts, Crawford Market and Chor Bazaar. The scurry of a rat over my open-toed sandals persuaded me that a good pair of solid walking boots might be a better option, so I returned to my hotel to change.

By this time in the trip, I was beginning to be a bit tired of markets, but India's markets are something else. The stench makes their Chinese equivalents seem like a visit to a perfume factory and, when I saw a cage-laden truck full of white-feathered chickens, most dead but some still struggling as they were dragged out and quickly dispatched with a rusty knife by a bored-looking worker, I decided that I would probably do something vegetarian for breakfast.

Phav bhaji is traditionally a lunchtime dish or an evening snack, but a nearby stall was already serving this classic of the region, Maharashtra, to market porters who had been working for hours. Basically, it is a mix of potatoes, chili, tomatoes, and peppers mashed together on a large metal hot plate until it forms a thick spicy gravy, then served on a bun. It is laden with fat and the soft, white bun is the stuff of Atkins' nightmares, but it was enough to set me up for a good few hours' walking.

By midmorning, the city was in full flow and I dodged traffic to head to the Maidan, the much-needed parkland lungs of the city. It was filled with crowds of men playing cricket. Much more than a sport in India, cricket truly is India's one unifying religion. Star players are worshipped as deities or reviled like demons, depending on their performance, and the crowds attending cricket matches would make Joel Osteen jealous. Every spare inch of newsprint or minute of the airtime is dedicated to talk shows about the successes, or more often the failures, of India's national side. Even away from the parks, any spare stretch of street can be turned into a pitch with makeshift stumps and bats. As you walk, you need to be constantly vigilant as the words "Ball, ball, ball!" are shrieked to warn of an impending missile coming your way.

I mooched for four hours before hitting my next target for lunch— Ideal Corner, a small restaurant on two levels that served steaming bowls of the classic Parsi speciality, mutton *dhansak*, in which chunks of goat are cooked with lentils and spices. As nearly always with meat dishes in India, the meat comes on the bone, for two reasons. One is the extra flavor that the slow cooking of the bones releases into the sauce. Secondly, cooking on the bone acts as a natural timer. When the meat begins to fall from the bone, the dish is done. The combination of spices, lentils, and sauce enriched with gelatin from the bones in mutton *dhansak* is stunning, and I received nods of approval from the owner as I picked up each bone and sucked it clean before adding it to a pile at the side of my plate.

On my last night, I planned to head to one of Mumbai's many excellent upscale restaurants after a visit to Chowpatty Beach, a stretch of sand at the top of Marine Drive. Deserted during the day, it was already kicking into action when I arrived in early evening. Itinerant astrologers, ear cleaners, and hawkers fought for my attention while crowds descended on the snack stalls selling *bhel puri*, scooping it into their mouths with the help of the flat, fried bread. There was plenty of action, but I wasn't tempted.

My sightseeing done, I hopped in a cab and took the short journey down Colaba Causeway to the only legally sanctioned street stall in Mumbai, Bade Miyan, considered one of the best in the whole city. Even if I did not know the direction, I would have found my way there because of the alluring smells and the crowd. The streets around the stall were packed with customers and cars were double parked as people came to eat or to get food to go.

Young men with official badges wandered around handing out the short menu, and I stopped one and ordered a mutton roll. He dived again into the throng and reappeared a few moments later with a small parcel containing my presupper snack.

Heading in the direction of my dinner, I unwrapped my kebab as a nice little preappetizer appetizer, took a bite and stopped dead in my tracks. It wasn't just good, it was sensational. So good in fact, that I stood rooted to the spot until I had finished every last shred of it. All thoughts of my planned supper gone, I turned on my heels, headed back to Bade Miyan, and spent the next two hours there working my way through the menu until I realized it was past midnight.

The taste of those kebabs stayed with me until I arrived back at the hotel. In fact, if I close my eyes, the taste stays with me still. But that is true of so much about Mumbai. It stays with you and, despite its savagely unforgiving elements, you leave thinking that you have barely scratched the surface of the city and its food.

After Mumbai, I carved a space in my schedule to take some time to recharge my batteries, catch up on some much-needed sleep, and even to read a book rather than worry about writing one. I wanted to eat well, of course, but I didn't have any plans.

For my vacation, I chose Goa, the former Portuguese colony on the southwest side of the subcontinent that only became part of India in 1962. The north of the state is overdeveloped with resorts and now overcrowded with tourists from all over the world—primarily the United Kingdom and, increasingly, Russia. It was not for me. The south, however, remains relatively unspoiled and I chose a basic but pleasant-looking resort in Cavelossim.

The difference was apparent the moment I left the airport. Goa is quieter, obviously, but anywhere would seem quiet after Mumbai. More than that, the whole pace of life was much gentler. The Portuguese legacy still remains in the faces of the people, the names on the shops and buildings I passed en route to the hotel. It is also in the architecture, with as many church steeples on show as temples.

The hotel was charming and suited me perfectly. It was moments' walk from the beach and I quickly changed into a rather fetching pair of three-quarter-length shorts and some flip-flops and headed out to see what was going on.

The beach was the stuff of a holiday brochure photographer's dreams. Stretching for miles in either direction, the sweeping sands, waving palms, and blue seas were broken only by the occasional beach shack serving food to the few people around at that time. I flipped off my flops, and spent the next hour walking on the hot sands before choosing a shack at random and sitting down for my first meal.

As with so much in Goa, the food too takes its lead from the Portuguese legacy, who introduced, among other things, chili, tomatoes, and garlic to the cuisine. They also ate pork, which the primarily Roman Catholic population of Goa had little problem with eating, but which is untouched by Muslims and Hindus in the rest of India. All these ingredients come together in the signature dish of the region, pork vindaloo, taking its name from its two key ingredients, vinegar and garlic.

Few dishes in the canon of Indian food are more misunderstood than vindaloo. This beautiful dish has become debased, all about the heat, all about making the experience as close as possible to eating broken glass. A proper vindaloo is certainly fiery. The pork marinates for a long time in chilies, but there is so much more to it than that. In the best, chunks of pork shoulder are left overnight in a mix of palm vinegar, ground spices, including cloves, chilies, and lots of garlic, and then slow-cooked without added water until the meat is tender and the sauce a thick gravy with immense depth and layers of flavor.

When well done, as it was at my chosen beach shack, vindaloo is one of the best Indian dishes of all, and I sat spooning hunks of flesh into my mouth with a large paratha, with the sound of the waves lapping in front of me.

My experiences of vindaloo have not always been so pleasant. In 1993, I was emerging from the breakup of my marriage and it had taken more than a year to get back in the game again. Finally, I met someone and we began to date.

On our third date, we decided that, after the evening meal, she would be coming to stay with me at my flat in Harrow. We arranged to meet at a local Indian restaurant. I arrived first, as I always do, and ordered a beer. She arrived twenty minutes later and I could not help but notice that she was carrying a very large bag, one that could easily have shielded a small car from the rain.

I said nothing as she struggled with this heavy load but helped her place it under the table while we ordered our dishes, among them a vindaloo (ah, you knew there was a point to this, didn't you?). Our meal arrived, and it was quite good, too. As we began eating, I raised the subject of the bag.

"Er, that's quite a big bag for a weekend stay."

Working industriously on a piece of tandoori chicken, she replied.

"Well, I was thinking if I am going to stay over, I should probably bring over a few clothes and take some space in your cupboards and drawers."

I have to admit that my response was less than gallant. What I should have said was, "Darling, I am sure in time that would be perfect, but I think it is a little early in our relationship. Perhaps we can discuss it later?"

What came out of mouth, joined by spittles of naan bread, was, "You're mental. We've only been out twice and you want to move in? No bleeding way."

She was a little upset by this and began to cry. She stood up, grabbed her leviathan of a bag, and began to drag it towards the door of the restaurant.

"F*cking bastard," she blubbed, between tears.

Then, she paused, reached for the large bowl of vindaloo, and deftly poured it over my head so the oily slick on top and the sauce dribbled down my hair and onto my suit. As I sat with curry dribbling down my linen jacket, she headed towards the door with all the dignity she could muster.

I cleaned up as best I could, aware that I was the center of attention. I got the bill, paid for the meal, and got up to leave. As I approached the door, one table of young men, on a night out and the worse for wear, began to applaud. Soon all the tables in the small restaurant had joined them and I walked home with the burn of chili on my skin and the sound of a standing ovation in my ears.

Vindaloo has never quite tasted the same ever since.

• • •

My time in Goa was exactly what I needed. Each day, I would head out for a breakfast of fresh fruits and curd from the market stalls in Cavelossim before taking long, luxurious, barefoot walks along the beach until I felt it was time to have something else to eat. Each morning, as I walked, I would watch the local fishermen beach their small boats, haul out their catch of local fish and other seafood, and take them straight to the beach shacks to be prepared almost immediately for waiting diners. I can't recall too many times when I have had seafood this fresh and for relatively little money. Lunch each day consisted of large crayfish or local lobster simply grilled and doused with limes picked from the trees behind the shacks or quickly stir-fried and served in a sauce made of coconut milk and fresh green chilies.

I spent afternoons by the pool sleeping or chatting with the other guests, mostly couples who had been returning to the same resort for years. To my delight they soon included me in their group as we congregated by the bar every night to drink rather too much of the locally made spirits with names like "Blue Ship Gin" and "Honeybee Whisky." Then we had supper at a local restaurant, which made the best chicken tikka I have ever eaten in my life, alive with spices and sparkling with drops of lemon juice sprinkled on it just before serving.

Towards the end of my stay, Serrafino, the owner of the hotel, invited me to join him at a meeting of local businessmen and guesthouse owners who had created a forum for responsible tourism. Although the area around Cavelossim seemed like a paradise, under the surface many problems were making themselves more and more apparent, particularly, he explained with the influx of new tourists from Russia.

"They see Goa as a brothel," he explained sharing with me the horrific figures for sexual tourism, drug-related crime, and the sexual abuse of children. The all-inclusive resorts, he told me, were owned by major international companies, which meant that little money found its way into the local community.

At the end of the meeting, an owner of one of the local guesthouses provided supper for us all with a seafood *thali*. Served in the traditional manner on banana leaves, *thali* is a mound of rice surrounded by ten or so small portions of different dishes, including fried clams, shark cooked with *kokum* juice, and squid cooked simply with spinach. It was a simple meal shared with local people, and the talking went on until nearly midnight as we ate under the stars in the garden of the local church where we had gathered. It seemed like the perfect full stop to my time in Goa and, as I drove back with Serrafino, I told him I hoped that tourism would not ruin one of the most beautiful places I had visited on the trip.

"The trouble is," he sighed, "we want people to come and see how beautiful Goa is. We want them to meet our people, eat our food and, of course, spend money in our community. But the very action of them coming changes forever what we want them to see."

It is the great dichotomy of tourism, of course, but, with people like Serrafino, perhaps Goa might be able to strike that balance. I hope so.

After two months on the road and nearly a month in this toughest of all countries, I was exhausted. On top of which, I really was heading off to the land of my fathers, now.

Next stop, Kolkata.

Chapter 33
KOLKATA: LAND OF MY FATHERS

Kolkata is like an ex-girlfriend who you know is bad for you, but about whom you cannot stop thinking. She has always let you down and treated you badly, and you have promised yourself hundreds of times that you are not going to spend any more time in her company. But, then, just as you think you are finally over her, she does something so utterly alluring, so impossibly irresistible, you find yourself falling in love again.

That is my Kolkata, the land of my fathers. Kolkata is not easy-access India. It is not like Rajasthan, which is India with training wheels. Koklata is not as easy to navigate as Mumbai, and it does not have the beauty of the South's beaches and palms, nor does it have the awe-inspiring mountain ranges of the North.

Kolkata is a challenge to everything that you think you know to be right and proper. The sheer volume of people, some fifteen million and rising, all of whom seem to be on the streets all the time; the stultifying humidity which, even in the spring, can have you and your clothes dripping with sweat within thirty seconds; and pollution, which can have you and your clothes turning a lovely shade of gray in the same time.

It is impossible to understate the scale of the depravation and degradation under which large sections of the population in Kolkata live, clinging to life by a thread by whatever means it takes; foraging through piles of festering garbage in search of scraps to eat; hustling for work on the streets selling anything they have to offer, including themselves; and begging, which is always persistent and often aggressive.

It is little wonder that few if any foreigners mark the city as a tourist destination, a great shame because Kolkata, the Kolkata I have encountered is also a magical place, a city filled with unexpected beauty, immense intelligence and passion, astonishing sights, and some of the best food in India.

My father grew up in Kolkata, and regaled us with stories of it when we were children, stories of flying fighting kites from the roof of his home, of playing games in the compound that housed all the different branches of the family, of servants climbing trees to fetch the juiciest lemons to make cooling drinks, and of Brahmin cooks producing meals of great simplicity but stunning flavors using few ingredients and even fewer spices. Because of this family history, I still have strong emotional ties to Kolkata, a city that never fails to astonish, whether it is your first time there or, like me, the latest of many.

I thought about all this as my companion grabbed hold of my arm for support as we fought our way through downtown Kolkata, avoiding the crumbling paving stones, pools of stagnant water, mounds of stinking rubbish, and the attentions of just about everyone to my very white, very redheaded friend, Vanessa Sly. Vanessa's eyes were popping out of her head and she had a look on her face that said, "What the f*ck is a nice middle-class Michigan girl like me doing here?" She looked like she wanted to be almost anywhere else in the world. Even Michigan.

Responsible for purchasing tea for Zingerman's Deli, Vanessa had met me when I visited Ann Arbor on my American leg of the trip. When I had mentioned that my upcoming trip to India would include visits to Kolkata and Darjeeling, Vanessa asked if I would mind having a companion. I was only too pleased to agree but, as we walked, I am sure she was regretting her decision.

As we headed in search of the offices of a contact of hers, she was beginning to see Kolkata in all its glory.

"Loooook!" She grabbed at my shirt sleeve and pointed at a woman washing both her clothes and her small, naked child in the same puddle of dirty water.

"You are going to see a lot more of that, I am afraid," I said, concerned that she would find it all a bit hard to take.

"No, that," she pointed again, more firmly.

Behind the woman, on the pavement were two small monkeys who were going at it like, well, monkeys. I made a note to myself to remember the sight, not that the image of two monkeys shagging on the streets of the downtown area of one of the largest cities in Asia is one you forget in a hurry.

Finally, we found the address we were searching for and were ushered into the quiet, air-conditioned rooms of Ashok Gandotra, one of the most prominent tea traders in Kokata. We had met with Ashok the previous morning in the genteel environs of the Tollygunge Club, one of the oldest, most exclusive private clubs in India. Over tea, he had given us both a brief introduction to Darjeeling tea, which, unsurprisingly, he considered the best in the world, before inviting us to join him for a tasting.

As we arrived, a range of teas was already being allowed to brew in boiling water, and they were soon laid out in a line with spoons and spittoons to clear our mouths. Ashok explained the selections: First- and second-flush single-estate leaf teas from some of the finest gardens in Darjeeling; leaf teas from other countries so we could make comparisons; blended teas that used whole leaf, broken leaf, fanning (basically leftovers after sorting), and dust. Each blend, he explained was designed for the tastes of different countries: Thick, strong teas for the Middle East, consistent but mediocre blends for the United Kingdom, where, he explained we drink a huge volume of tea, but not of great quality. He was most disparaging about the tea that's drunk in the United States, where, in my own unscientific experience, it would easier to find Bigfoot than a decent cup of tea.

"They basically just want a neutral liquid they can drink cold with ice," he said slurping from a bowl marked "U.S. Blend." "It could be anything, it just has to be brown and wet."

This was Vanessa's show, and I stood back as the two experts tasted together, sucking up tea from tablespoons from each bowl, rolling it around in their mouths to release the flavor before spitting out.

"It is not just the taste that makes a good tea," Ashok explained, holding up a bowl to the light. "There is color and brightness."

First-flush tea, harvested at the end of March, is a greener, more astringent tea with a pale color. Generally considered to be weaker than the *second flush*, picked in May, which has more depth of both flavor and color, first flush has nonetheless developed a large following for its ability to refresh. By comparison, the teas produced from broken leaves or fannings were duller to the eye and the palate.

After the tasting was over, I wanted Vanessa to get her first real taste of Bengali food. Before independence from Britain, Bengal was one of the largest states in India. Now it is split into two, West Bengal, where Kolkata is located, and East Bengal, which became East Pakistan and, afterward, the beautiful but blighted nation of Bangladesh.

Bengal in general and Kolkata in particular is known as the literary and political heart of India. It was the capital before Delhi and, in India, there is a saying, "What Kolkata thinks today, India will think tomorrow."

Kolkata remains one of the safest places in India, and Bengalis are among the friendliest people in the world. The food, too, is unique. Unlike much of India, where the food can be characterized by strong tastes and pungent spicing, Bengali food, or more accurately, Kolkatan food is subtle and understated, using few spices to complement their cooking of ingredients. Turmeric, mustard oil and powder, ginger, and fresh chilies are commonly used with the bony river fish that Kolkatans love.

In fact, Kolkatans obsess about food, and from these roots my own obsession comes. (With respect, I never thought it came from Wales.) The people of Kolkata spend most of their waking lives talking about food, from their simple breakfast of *luchi*, the local version of puri, which are stuffed with potatoes or chickpeas before being dipped in sour tamarind water; to prelunch snacks of *shingra*, the local version of a samosa, stuffed with cauliflower; to lunch, taken on the hoof or in a restaurant; to supper with their family; to a late-night snack of spicy fish rolls.

When they are not eating, they are arguing about eating or talking about past meals, even if those meals were years in the past. They all sounded very familiar.

Kewpie's Kitchen was the real deal, just like sitting in the front room of a traditional Bengali home. We chose from a *thali* and, while we waited, sipped on an Aampora *shorbat* made from mangoes, black salt, and cumin seeds for the sour-sweet tastes that Bengalis love. When the meal came, I began to forgive Kolkata everything, as I used the fresh puri bread to help the various plates of vegetarian foods from plate to lips. *Lao*, a gourd, was slow-cooked simply with nigella seeds and melted creamily in the mouth. Bowls of *shukta*, a mixture of hard and soft vegetables, were cooked, again with very few spices, in this case the Bengali version of five spice, *panch phoron*, a mixture of fennel seeds, black mustard seed, fenugreek seed, cumin seeds, and nigella seeds.

There was eggplant dipped in chickpea flour and deep fried until crispy and little balls of steamed eggplant in a sauce made with *doi*, Bengali yogurt. Best of all there was LSD—*life-saving dahl*, the Bengali equivalent of Jewish chicken soup made with red lentils and, compared to many versions of this Indian staple, very thin.

I was as delighted by Vanessa's reaction to the meal as I was by the meal itself. For those who have only been exposed to curry-house slop, food in India can be both a revelation and a challenge with its unusual textures and spicing, but Vanessa not only cleaned her plate, she did it without cutlery, using her hands like a local.

When my father returned to India for a short while in the late 1950s, he took with him his young Welsh bride. The family were wary of a marriage outside the caste but took to my mother primarily because she developed an immediate and deep passion for Bengali food, allowing them to rationalize that "She must be a reincarnated Brahmin."

As I watched Vanessa scoop up her lunch with perfect technique, I could not help thinking my family would have approved.

Kolkata was, I am told by Baba, once a very beautiful city, once known as the Paris of the Orient, with wide avenues, tree-lined streets, and clean-flowing rivers. It is hard to picture now, as you dodge traffic and dead animals. Beneath the chaos, elements of the glory remain, and the next day, I took Vanessa on a quick tour to show her the Maidan, Kolkata's own expanse of parkland, and the Victoria Memorial, a towering, impressive tribute to the late Empress of India.

Kolkata's New Market is one of the most frightening places I have ever visited, not because of the sights and the smells, which are challenging enough, but because the moment anyone, particularly a foreigner walks into the market, he or she is surrounded by scores of touts begging you to come to the shops they represent. They are not just persistent but aggressive and often physically abusive.

Vanessa, of course, was a target from the moment she set foot in the place. Her red hair was acting like a homing beacon for every salesman in the place, who began to follow us and then to grab at us, trying to drag us towards their shops; in the end, I had to become aggressive back. Even when we sought a haven in one shop, the others waited outside. It is an experience that shames an otherwise extraordinarily friendly city.

We were both a little shaken, and needed something to restore our good faith in the people of Kolkata at this point, so I suggested we head to another institution to indulge in desserts and other sweets, the greatest of all Bengali treasures. When it comes to sweets, the passion of the Bengali goes beyond obsession and becomes almost feral. Never, ever try to come between a Bengali and his rightful ration of sweets.

These concoctions can be challenging to the uninitiated, however. The textures of delicacies made mainly from milk can be unpleasant on the tongue the first few times, and the levels of sugar probably explain why the levels of diabetes in Kolkata are higher than anywhere else in the country. However, these treats are incredibly addictive and at K.C. Das are produced at the highest quality. Preeminent in the pantheon of sweets is *mishti doi*, a simple combination of yogurt, cream, and different flavors.

Two other favorites are *gulab jamun*, which are popular all over India and made of milk solids mixed with cream, then served in a rose-water-flavored syrup, and my mother's own personal favorite, *rasgulla*, made from cheese rolled with semolina, then poached in syrup. These dishes originated in the neighboring state of Orissa, but were brought to Bengal by Brahmins employed as cooks by wealthy families like my father's. K.C. Das was one of the first places to sell them commercially and even now, some one hundred thirty years after it first opened, they remain as popular as ever.

We would be heading back to Kolkata for a few days at the end of our time in India, and I hoped then to have a chance to connect with some of my father's family. But, after a long, wearying day, it was time to head back to the guesthouse and pack our bags for the journey up to Darjeeling and the Goomtee Estate Tea Gardens.

Chapter 34
THE DARJEELING EXPRESS

Darjeeling **produces** the finest black teas in the world, as it has since the British first experimented with the growing of bushes and fermenting of leaves there in the middle of the nineteenth century. Now, there are more than eighty different gardens that help slake the world's taste for this most refreshing of brews.

I am a self-confessed tea nut. I drink cups and cups of it a day from the first cup to help prise my eyes open in the morning, to the midafternoon cup with a digestive biscuit to my postdinner quencher.

I can't do coffee. It is one of the few things that will empty my stomach quicker than watching a porno starring Andrew Lloyd Webber. For simplicity's sake, I tell people I am allergic to it, but I think it is more psychosomatic and stems back to a sneaky, childhood slurp from a strong cup of coffee that had been left by an adult, which resulted in release at both ends and a subsequent and total aversion to all matters bean related.

Like many Brits, my love of tea and, indeed, my knowledge of tea, had once been limited to the strong, dark brew beloved of construction workers all over the country. Give me a large mug, preferably with a humorous motto on the side, filled with a threateningly dark brown liquid and I am happy as a clam.

Vanessa had developed a passion for tea as she worked at the Zingerman's deli, and could talk with experts like an expert. She had made all the arrangements for us to head up to the Goomtee Estate in the hills some two hours from the town of Darjeeling itself. It was also nearly four hours from the nearest airport, Bhagdogra, which meant a long and perilous climb from the flats up towards the mountains before we reached our accommodation.

There was rubble on the roads, we were told, from recent riots in favor of the separation of the region from West Bengal to become its own state of Ghorkaland. On every spare wall, graffiti had been daubed supporting their claims: GHORKALAND IS OUR DEMAND.

By the time we pulled into the estate and settled into the guesthouse, it was already dark and, because the air was much thinner at the altitude of four thousand feet, it was cold enough to have us running to put on sweaters and jackets.

Goomtee comes from the Nepalese word for "turning point," and the garden, set in a fork in the road, has been owned by the same family since the 1950s, when it was bought from the British by Mahbir Prasad. Its reputation for producing some of the finest teas in Darjeeling made it the perfect place to watch the process of production from picking to packing.

Our stay at the guesthouse included all of our meals and, of course, innumerable cups of tea made from the leaves harvested in the gardens. As we sat down to enjoy our first pot, served in the British way with milk and a tray of biscuits, Vanessa became slightly alarmed when I took the tea cozy from the pot and placed it over my head. I don't see it as particularly peculiar behavior. I have always done it and so have many of you, if you are honest. It seems a perfectly sensible way to recycle the luxurious warmth from the pot. However, I do sometimes forget that I have done it, and open the front door of my apartment to the mail carrier or various deliverymen while wearing a tea cozy shaped like a kitten on my head.

The tea was bright, fresh tasting, and inordinately refreshing.

In the Goomtee Guesthouse a permanent staff of five people was dedicated to our care, since we were the only guests. If we wanted tea or a snack, we only had to ask. After our hikes around the tea gardens and the factory, there was precious little else left to do but read, eat, and sleep, a welcome relief after my last hectic couple of months.

The cook at Goomtee had a great reputation and the food he prepared for us every day was simple but memorable. He used few ingredients to stunning effect and produced dishes from all parts of India, and even some from Nepal and Tibet, close neighbors of this part of India. Food came in a never-ending succession to the table until we held our hands up in submission and went to sleep it off or walk it off in the manicured grounds.

Breakfasts were small steamed rice cakes called *idli*, served with a fiery sauce known as *sambar*. Lunch, the biggest meal of the day, could be Tibetan steamed dumplings called *momo*, served with fresh salads, more Bengali dahl, rice of course and vegetables fried in chickpea-flour batter. Best of all, for supper, the staff would bring out plates laden down with *shingra*, the Bengali samosa stuffed with spicy cauliflower.

Fortunately, we also got lots of exercise. Vanessa had timed our trip to coincide with the first harvest of the first flush from the Goomtee Estate and, very early the morning after our arrival, we were summoned into the impressive and slightly frightening presence of the estate manager, Mahesh Maharshi, who had run the garden with an iron fist for more than thirty-five years.

"You see," he boomed, making us cower slightly in our chairs on the other side of the desk (he prefaced every sentence with this loud phrase). "You see. I have instructed the section supervisors that we should begin harvesting today. But," he warned, "it is looking like rain and we may have to cancel until tomorrow."

We headed out with him to the gardens armed with knobby walking sticks he had insisted we would need to help us on the uneven roads. The supervisors were gathering to be given their instructions, and the pickers arriving from the homes the estate provided them on the grounds. As Mahesh began issuing his instructions, the gray clouds in the sky began to shed their loads, at first in a gentle drizzle, then with increasing ferocity as the winds grew in strength.

"You see," Mahesh exclaimed pointing upwards, "we can't pick in this, it will damage the leaves and make a bad end result." He sent the workers back to their houses with strict instructions to be ready if the weather changed, and sent us off with Michael, one of the factory managers, for a tour of the factory.

The processing of tea is surprisingly complicated. The collected leaves are withered, dried to remove as much moisture as possible, rolled to break up the buds into the recognizable strands we know as *tea*, fermented or oxidized to change the color to black and to increase the release of flavor. Finally, before packing, it is dried once more over blowers of hot air. As in many factories that I visited, levels of hygiene here and throughout the garden were high and I found myself donning another pair of boots and a set of overalls before entering. Interesting though it may have been, I had seen enough factories on this tour to last me a lifetime and was pleased when we were finally able to head back to the guesthouse and catch up on some much-needed sleep.

Fortunately, the next morning was bright and clear. At quarter to seven at the meeting point, groups of pickers, mostly female immigrants from neighboring Nepal, were being sent to designated gardens with a yield target to harvest during the day.

I asked why all the pickers were women.

"You see," Mahesh explained, "women have smaller hands and are better able to pick the stems with two buds; we need to make good tea without damaging them."

We went with Michael to walk through the gardens, which were set against the snow-topped hills, the sun breaking through the thin cloud cover, to watch the picking. The women were already hard at work filling the baskets, which were attached to their backs by cloth draped over their heads. They stopped picking as we approached, intrigued by Vanessa's fiery red hair and pale skin, and even more by her smooth hands.

The workers deftly snapped buds from the waist-high bushes, and tossed them over their shoulders into the baskets, which can each hold nearly two and a quarter pounds of tea. Every picker has a targeted amount and quality of buds that they harvest, and the details of every basket are recorded in huge, handwritten ledgers back in the estate office. The work is tough, that was obvious, but compared with many other jobs in that impoverished region, with its high unemployment, the workers in tea gardens consider themselves fortunate with schools, hospitals, meals, and housing provided by their employer.

"We work very hard," Michael explained, "but workers are treated well and stay here for a long time." He, too, had been with Goomtee for more than thirty-five years.

Our time with them, however, was up and, after our tour, we headed to Darjeeling itself, a couple hours farther up the mountains. The journey was even more terrifying than the one to Goomtee. I was only too pleased that we had not taken the famous Toy Train, Darjeeling's narrow-gauge railroad, which meanders for several bone-shaking hours from top to bottom of the mountains every day.

Darjeeling is pleasant, but, after the tranquility of Goomtee, coming to a town predicated on serving tourists, who use it as base before heading to Nepal, was an unpleasant return to the real world. The food was unpleasant, too, neutered to offend as few travelers as possible. As fresh and exciting as the food had been on the estate, it was dull and uninspiring in the city. Some passable *momo*, Tibetan dumplings, were fine for one meal, but the food in most restaurants would not have passed muster at a buffet in the United States, let alone in India.

Rather than eating, we joined the tourists, visiting the markets, and even getting up at three in the morning to climb into a jeep and join a parade of cars hurtling to the top of Tiger Hill, where, after about two hours waiting in near freezing conditions, we watched the sun rise over the ridges of the Himalayas. It wasn't enough to make me warm to the town, and I was not sorry when it came time to head back down to the airport and to Kolkata.

When I checked my e-mail, I was thrilled to see that I had received a note from two of my relatives, Baba's middle and older sisters, inviting me to visit them on our last day in Kolkata. Baba had not been back to India for thirty years. As with so many in the Indian diaspora, he had always meant to return but, with the passing of each year and then the death of my mother, it became increasingly unlikely. As he had said to me in a phone conversation before I left on this stage of the journey, "Britain is my country; India hasn't been my country for fifty years." As a result, he had lost touch with his siblings, and wondered what reception I would receive. I need not have worried; they were, after all, Majumdars by blood.

I warned Vanessa that food would be involved, but she wouldn't listen as she shoveled the delicious breakfast of *channa masala*, spiced chickpeas, and *luchi*, puffed bread, down her throat in the guesthouse that morning.

"Sure, sure," she said, as I dodged a volley of bespittled bread from her mouth.

At the first port of call, my father's elder sister hugged us both, then led us into their apartment, where my uncle was already seated at a table heaving with food.

"We thought you would have taken breakfast already, so we just did some snacks," she said pointing apologetically at plates of spiced potatoes, mutton cutlets, and a pile of balloonlike puri breads.

Rather relishing Vanessa's obvious discomfort at the sight of so much food, I said, "Vanessa loves Bengali sweets, too."

"I'll send someone out to get some," said my aunt, hollering into the kitchen for the maid to run out.

We somehow managed to work our way through most of the

Visas

IT IS THE RESPONSIBILITY OF THE PASSPORT BEARER
TO OBTAIN NECESSARY VISAS

Given leave to enter the United
Kingdom for an indefinite period.

IMMIGRATION OFFICER
* (035)
-7 JUL 1978
HEATHROW

IMMIGRATION OFFICER
(386)
EMBARKED
5 OCT 1978
HEATHROW (2)

5 JAN 1979

6

spread, including the desserts, with some effort, before my aunt announced, "We have a taxi coming to take you to your middle aunt. She just phoned, I told her Vanessa likes sweets, so she has just sent someone out to get some."

Vanessa gave me a withering look, but it was worth it to see her face turn almost as green as the top she was wearing. True to form, when we arrived at our next port of call, bowls of *mishti doi* and *rasgulla* had been laid out, and my aunt stood over us as we force-fed ourselves spoons of creamy yogurt from the store below my aunt's house.

"Much better than K.C. Das," she said, nodding approvingly.

By the time we left, we were both feeling decidedly puny and headed back to the guesthouse to sleep it off before it was time for Vanessa to get to the airport for her long journey home. I was not leaving until the next morning, which gave me time on my own to reflect on my visit to the land of my fathers.

Had I actually discovered anything? Not really. I felt no more Indian than I had before I arrived, but I was pretty certain that it would be a long time before I headed back to India again. It's just too crazy for a half-Welsh half-Bengali to cope with.

PART V

SOUTH AFRICA, MOZAMBIQUE, SENEGAL, MOROCCO, SPAIN, TURKEY, AND ITALY

Chapter 35
SOUTH AFRICA: IT'S MY PARTY AND I'LL BRAAI IF I WANT TO

"Steaks should be juicy. They should be thick and they should be saucy."

I certainly wasn't going to disagree with Emil Den Dulk. For one thing, he was well over six feet tall and built like a linebacker. For another, he was wielding a wicked-looking cleaver, using it to carve two-inch-thick steaks from a twenty-five-pound strip of sirloin, ordered specially for the occasion of my first ever South African *braai*, or barbecue.

Outside, Emil Senior, his father, was busy stoking the flames of the barbecue grill pit and adding more wood to the fire. Back inside the kitchen, his mother, Sonette, was fussing over the traditional accompaniments. Neal McCleave, a friend of mine for more than twenty years, turned to me, glass of wine in hand, and said, "It doesn't get too much better than this," pointing to where the sun was dipping behind the mountains on the horizon.

I had been delighted to get an e-mail from Neal asking if he could join me on my trip to South Africa and Mozambique. The pleasures of solo travel and the joys of dining alone in bars and restaurants filled with groups of friends and loving couples enjoying each other's company had lost their appeal. Despite making new friends along the way, I had experienced prolonged bouts of real loneliness in Southeast Asia and India, exacerbated by the exhaustion of being on the road for nearly a year. I was not going to pass up the opportunity to spend two weeks in the company of a good friend.

Neal likes his food but doesn't share my obsession with it and often deflates my long-winded descriptions of elaborate meals with a curt, "Just start wearing a dress and get over it." His own favorite food story involves coming home from school one day and finding his father munching happily on a cheese sandwich that Neal knew for a fact had been in the garbage bin twenty-four hours before.

After India, I'd spent three short days in London, before heading out on the road again to Cape Town, the first part of the last leg of the journey. Neal was joining me two days later. I don't know of a more beautifully situated city in the world than Cape Town. With Table Mountain towering over one side and the waters of the ocean lapping on the other, Cape Town can make South Africans go a bit teary when it is mentioned. I spent two enjoyable days wandering around the shops of Long Street and the marinas of the impressively restored waterfront.

I was less impressed with the food in those two days, however, with most of the options being ersatz versions of European and American restaurants, supplemented by cheap and cheerful food for the huge number of backpackers who use Cape Town as an easy access point for their exploration of Southern Africa. It says a lot that the best thing I ate was a *boerwors*, a spicy South African sausage, served from a nighttime stall on Long Street. It was tasty enough, but hardly the basis of an entire cuisine.

Cape Town, like all of South Africa, has its problems. Apartheid may have gone, but the white, black, and colored South Africans are still separated by huge levels of mistrust, and the even more powerful forces of economics, which mean that the black population still fills the majority of menial roles and live in the townships of District 6, and the white population still controls the majority of the wealth.

Despite this, South Africans have an almost insatiable passion for life and for enjoying themselves and few people I met on the trip displayed that more than Emil Den Dulk. I had been given Emil's contact by my friend John Glaser of Compass Box Whisky, and had first met him the night before when he had picked up Neal and me at the end of a boat trip to the infamous island prison, Robben Island. After a tour of the somber buildings of the jail and a glimpse at the tiny cell in which Nelson Mandela had been held for so many years, both Neal and I had been silent and deep in thought on the return journey.

Emil announced that he had tickets for the Taste of Cape Town food festival, and drove us to one of the most beautiful parts of the city, where local restaurants had set up stalls to serve two or three of their signature dishes. For several hours, we wandered from stall to stall with Emil and his friends eating everything on offer and sampling South

African wines, before heading back to the city and the more genteel environment of Bascule, a bar with the biggest selection of whisky in the Southern Hemisphere.

Some of the food, from Cape Town's famous restaurants, like La Colombe, had been good, very good in fact, and some had been ordinary, but I couldn't help thinking that it was a pale reflection of what I might be getting back in London or any other major city. I wanted to find something truly South African and, as Emil poured me a couple of fingers of peaty malt whisky, I told him so.

"Well," he said, smiling back at me, "you're certainly going to get that tomorrow. We're going to have a braai for you out at the farm."

That was just what I wanted to hear. The braai is at the very heart of South African culture, even more so than a barbie for our Australian chums. It is not just a meal, it's a way of life, and the center of most South African celebrations.

"There'll be a lot of food," Emil warned us. "Don't have too big a lunch."

We took him at his word and were waiting, ravenous and ready when he picked us up late the following afternoon. We had even prepared for the braai with some preemptive exercise by attempting to climb Table Mountain, a feat which I failed to achieve, in no small part thanks to the rather stupid combination of a huge hangover, malaria medication, and a large fried breakfast, much of which ended up in a puddle on South Africa's beloved rock.

Emil's parents run one of the most prestigious wineries in South Africa, De Toren. In the heart of the Stellenbosch wine region, it is set in sixty-five acres of the most beautiful land imaginable, with views of the Cape Fold mountain ranges in the distance on one side of their house and the Indian Ocean in the distance on the other. The wines from their estate are well respected, particularly the Fusion V made from the same five grapes as Bordeaux, and it wasn't long after we arrived that Emil Senior opened several bottles from different years for us to try, and Emil Junior began to build the barbecue using wood from pruned vines. Soon, he had a roaring fire going, and had started to prepare the sirloin steaks he had carved by coating them with a dry rub. A large South African sausage, a *boerwors* was formed into a spiral and skewered, so it would hold together over the coals.

Emil produced a dish of small round bundles of meat wrapped in fat.

"They're called *skilpadjies*. It means 'little tortoise' in Afrikaans." They were made of minced lamb's liver mixed with coriander leaf, then wrapped in fat before being roasted.

There are a lot of rules and rituals for a braai. The preparation of the grill and the cooking of the meat is men's work. In fact, it is one man's work and, while the designated griller, the *tong master*, takes charge, the other men stand around drinking, offering sage words of advice about the size of the flames and the position of the meat on the grill. Women provide the traditional accompaniments to the meat: cheese sandwiches, grilled on the fire to be eaten while the meat is prepared; and *meili pap*, a porridge made of ground maize and served with a sauce made from tomatoes and chili.

Sonette introduced me to an Afrikaans word, *lekker*. She said it as she sniffed the air filled with the smells of cooking. "It's going to be *lekker*. It means lovely or tasty."

When it all came together, we gathered around the family dining table and joined hands to say grace before sitting down to one of the biggest meals I've ever had. The steaks were every bit as good as I had anticipated, with a nice spicy crust formed by the rub giving way to a flood of juices as I cut through the flesh. The meat was fresh, not aged, reminding me of the steaks in Argentina rather than the ones in the United States, and the *meili pap* proved to be the perfect starch to soak up the juices as well as innumerable glasses of wine Emil Senior kept pouring us.

Above all, I shall remember the hospitality of the Den Dulks. Neal leaned over to me as he was ripping apart his dessert, a *koeksister*, a dense, syrup-coated doughnut, and said, "It's hard to believe we had not even met these people twenty-four hours ago and now we are sitting in their winery eating their food and drinking their wines." By now I knew that, when it came to sharing their food, people could be incredibly generous.

Emil Senior topped up my glass with more of that excellent Fusion V and I looked at Neal, and said, "Welcome to my world, mate. Welcome to my world."

Neal's world, however, is the Internet and he is good at it, having risen to a high level with a service provider in London. In a booze-addled moment of generosity he had offered to organize and pay for the two of us to spend a few days of rest and relaxation at one of Mozambique's secluded beach lodges and, after two more days touring the stunning wine country around Cape Town, we caught an early morning flight to Maputo, the capital.

Cape Town had not felt like Africa. It was developed and prosperous. Maputo felt like Africa from the moment we landed, the strong military presence at the airport, the chaos of clearing immigration and the inevitable battle for a taxi to our hotel. There, too, things were a shambles, and we entered our room to find that it had only one bed and that it was occupied by a large naked man watching football and scratching his gonads.

"Welcome to Africa," Neal gave me a thin smile and stomped off back down to the reception.

He had that look of the consumer crusader about him I had seen many times over the years, so I waited with the bags while he went to give the staff what-for. Eventually, after two more changes, we finally found ourselves in a room with air-conditioning, two beds, and a working television. The staff obviously got their revenge, because the next morning, Neal looked like he might not make it through to lunchtime. We had eaten in the hotel the night before, supplementing a few local beers with a plate of mystery meat, which was now making its way out of both ends of Neal.

He battled on and we ordered a taxi for a guided tour of the city, which is hideously ugly and reminded me of Salvador, Brazil. No surprise, really; both are former Portuguese colonies. Just as with Salvador, a visitor does not feel particularly safe and, as our driver deposited us at each point of interest to have a few minutes' walk around, he watched carefully to see that we were not separated from our wallets or worse.

There's not a lot to see, a crumbling old fort, a train station, a tin house built by Mr. Eiffel of Parisian tower fame, and, probably most interesting of all, a seafood market where bowls of huge Mozambique prawns were for sale, plump specimens you could take to the cafés and stalls next to the market to be prepared fresh for you.

I wanted something a little more relaxed, however, and asked the driver to take us along the coast to Costa do Sol, a remnant of colonial days and still considered the best fish restaurant in the city. Neal was still looking a bit green, so, in support, I chose a young Portuguese wine to match the color of his face and a plate of fried squid to begin with. Looking queasy, he persevered. Then, the main course arrived: twenty-four of those astounding prawns, grilled simply and doused in butter.

They were staggeringly good, meaty, and sweet, and I ripped the shells from the flesh before rolling them in melted butter.

Neal's prawns looked just as good, and tasted even better when he finally declared he could eat no more without being sick. He allowed me to polish them off and wiped the juices from both plates with a slice of bread, as he suffered my loud, exaggerated yummy noises. There are few things more enjoyable in life than a mate having a bad time.

After considerable research, Neal had decided we were going to spend a few days at Guludo Beach Lodge, a small resort predicated on responsible tourism, which employed most of its staff from local villages and was built from local materials. A five-hour jeep ride from Pemba in the north of the country, our accommodation consisted of *bandas,* which opened up almost directly onto the powdery, white sands of the beach. There was no electricity, with light coming only from oil lamps. For the three nights we were there, we drifted to sleep and were awakened by the sounds of the aqua blue sea lapping gently nearby.

The food was good, though limited by what could be collected from Pemba, a day's drive away, as well as what was brought to the kitchen from the beach by local fishermen. Meals were served under the stars at tables set back from the beach and Neal, who traveled light, had not packed more than one joke, came out with the same line every night, "Shall we go to our special table, darling?"

It was good to have a few days when food was not the center of my every waking thought. I did as little as possible, swaying gently in a hammock for hours on end while catching up with some reading. My only exercise came when Neal and I visited the local village, and were followed everywhere by a gaggle of beautiful, inquisitive children keen to see the movies and pictures of them we would take on our cameras. I could not resist, and was soon playing the Pied Piper, running around the narrow dusty streets of the town with half the juvenile population in tow, squealing and giggling with delight.

When it came time to leave the lodge and head back to Johannesburg, we were slightly deflated. We had both needed the change of pace of the lodge. I was heading on to the next stage of the journey and Neal back to work. I was sorry to see him go, but it was time to head our own ways and I was off to Senegal.

Chapter 36
SENEGAL: TERANGA

In the local Wolof language, *teranga* means welcome, and is not just a greeting but a state of mind, the expression of the hospitality of the nation's inhabitants.

It obviously doesn't apply to weary travelers on around-the-world trips, however, because the welcome I received on my arrival in Dakar was not, I suspect, one that Senegalese tourism would ever wish to advertise.

My friend Isabelle Fuchs, in Munich, had been married to a man from Senegal, and had promised me that the food there was good and that her ex-husband, Keba, and his family would look after me, introducing me to all the local foodie specialties. I am a trusting sort and know better than to question the Germans. I duly added Senegal to the list, envisioning communal meals, women in multicolored garb furiously pounding spices, and maybe the chance to get my hands bloody in the slaughter of something that once bleated.

Thirty seconds after walking out of the airport terminal, I wished I had never heard of the place, and was fully prepared to turn around and spend every penny in my account to get on any plane going anywhere. Even back to China.

It started well enough. The plane from Jo'burg was on time and, as it was continuing on to the United States, only four of us got off the plane in Dakar. Immigration was a breeze; they even had swish new forms emblazoned with that word, *teranga*. With only a handful of bags to come through, I collected Big Red in ten minutes. Then, to use the technical term, it all went tits up.

Keba was supposed to be there, along with a man he had asked to accompany me during my stay in Senegal. But, as I stepped out of the grim arrivals hall, they were nowhere to be seen. I had a phone number, which I punched into my mobile. After a few rings, it was answered in French.

THEM: "Incomprehensible French gibberish."
ME: "Içi Simon."
THEM: "Encore d'incomprehensible French gibberish."

My schoolboy French did not really help here. Had they wanted to know the way to the Sacre Coeur from the Eiffel Tower or "*les choses nécessaires pour preparer le pétit dejeuner,*" I would have been their man. Unfortunately, that was little use in Dakar airport at midnight looking for someone I had never met before.

If my expected hosts were not there to greet me, plenty of other people wanted to take their place and, suddenly, in a scene not unlike one from a George A. Romero movie, I was surrounded by about thirty heaving bodies, all with arms outstretched. Touts I could deal with. I could "non, merci" the would-be taxi drivers and the people selling phone cards and chewing gum although I really did want to ask the man who proffered an edition of French Scrabble Classique to a weary passenger at midnight what the bloody hell he was thinking.

Others had less professional matters in mind. One person grabbed my arm while another tried to wrest my mobile phone from my hand. Another had already laid dibs to Big Red, on which I was sitting, and was trying to push me off using a short runup and a shoulder charge he must have learned from watching rugby on satellite television.

I heard someone barking loudly, again in French, and looked up to see someone beaming at me through a ring of gold-capped teeth. My savior gave me another beaming smile, then said in a tone less friendly than one would hope for from a welcoming party, "Give me fifty dollars and I will make sure no one hurts you."

Oh, just great. Now I was the bitch of the local mobster. He began to push my luggage trolley over to the side of the car park and turned, beckoning me to follow with a look that said "you're fucked" before flicking open a mobile phone and hollering down the mouthpiece. A good-looking boy like me could fetch top dollar on today's market and I fully expected to be packed off by noon to serve as a love slave to a fat woman in an Arab state with a name that sounds like phlegm.

Just as I had nearly given up all hope of ever seeing my beloved Big Red again, I felt another, altogether gentler, hand on my shoulder and turned to see the wide, engaging grin of a tall man in a black bomber jacket.

"You must be Simon?" he said. "I'm Bath. We've had a lot of trouble getting through security. I hope you haven't had any trouble."

"Trouble?" I wanted to scream at him. "Trouble? I've practically been gang-raped. That man over there, walking away with my bag by the way, is on the phone right now trying to sell me into slavery and, to top it all off someone tried to make me buy the French edition of Scrabble."

However, before I could say a word, he had spoken quietly with my self-appointed bodyguard, who gave in without a fight, and was lifting Big Red onto his shoulders, gesturing for me to follow him to a waiting taxi. There I met Keba, who told me that I was not going to stay with him after all, as he was leaving for Germany the next day. I needed to find a hotel. The fact that it was well past midnight did not seem to faze him at all. The taxi driver took us to a procession of fleapits until we found one that had space and met the requirements of my meager, hastily calculated budget.

I finally crashed in a hotel room that was as tired and worn out as I was by about three thirty in the morning. *Teranga* indeed.

The hotel was only able to manage a poor trickle of brownish water in the morning and weak, flickering lights in the evening, but it had an excellent Internet connection. By morning, I had already fired off a mail to my travel agent begging her to help me get earlier flights to Morocco. Yet, after I joined my guide to Senegal, despite the dubious beginnings, it turned out to be one of the most enjoyable stops of the trip. All thanks to my new friend, Bath (pronounced *Batch*).

Sakhary Sy, or Bath, as he was known to everyone, spoke perfect English littered with Americanisms picked up while acting as a translator for the U.S. military. Bath was also one of the kindest, gentlest people I have ever encountered. About my own age, he lived with his family, including his ninety-seven-year-old father, in a town some twenty miles outside Dakar, and seemed to know everyone in the city. He knew every beggar and panhandler in Dakar by name, often giving a few coins. "Charity is one of the pillars of Islam," he explained.

He sent away hawkers, not with a shout but with a smiling, *"Bene-nyon inshallah"* (next time, if God wills it). He stopped every day at the same shoeshine man, and used his loose change to purchase small song birds, kept in cramped wooden cages, so he could release them into the skies, saying, "Perhaps as they fly away, they will pray for me."

He loved his city and announced to me, slightly incongruously, that it was his 'hood.

I liked him immediately.

On our first morning as he took me on a walking tour, I explained to Bath why I was there.

"Food?" he replied. "Well, I love food, and we have great things to eat here." With that, he turned and headed in the direction of Sadaga, the central market of the city. The market was interesting enough, but the real reason we were there was to try *mafé*, one of the staples of West African cooking.

While the little storefront joint he led me to, Chez Khady, bore a name that reflected the city's French colonial past, the restaurant itself was pure Africa. Communal tables were already heaving as we arrived, paid for our simple meal, and carved out a place for ourselves amid the bustle of men in flowing robes and women in explosions of colorful fabric. When the food arrived, it was incredibly simple, delivered without airs and graces, on a plate of rice served next to a bowl of stew with a pleasing slick of oil on the top.

My first taste put this up there with the braai in South Africa. It was just damn tasty. *Mafé* is beef or goat cooked with chili, onions, tomatoes, and local vegetables, including cassava, until it thickens to form a rich, satisfying stew with a definite kick. Not enough of a kick for Bath, however, who showed me how to mash up the Scotch bonnet pepper served in the stew so it slowly released its juices as you ate. It was a wonderful dish, so deeply savory that I could taste it for hours afterwards.

Dakar turned out, against all my low expectations, to be a pleasingly laid-back city with one or two interesting sights, a charming museum, and many cafés. However, I realized that in a couple days I would have seen everything and would be killing time better spent elsewhere, even with earlier flights to Casablanca.

Bath came up with a plan. The next day, we boarded a ferry for the infamous Isle de Gorée, an island used by the Portuguese, then the French, to house slaves ready for shipping to the Americas.

The Casa de Eclaves looked benign enough in the gentle morning sunlight, until Bath began to explain to me that, in each of the tiny pens in front of us, thirty people were held at a time before being shipped off, never to return. Through the infamous Door of No Return, more than fifteen million Africans were sent to the Americas. More than six million died en route.

We were subdued on the short ferry ride back, but Bath wanted to introduce me to another Senegalese staple, *yassa*, a dish of chicken marinated with chilies, oil, lime juice, and garlic, before being roasted, then served in a sauce soured with palm vinegar and olives. It was another great taste, simply prepared and served but with layers of flavor that again benefited from the mashing up of a Scotch bonnet pepper to add extra heat. The local Gazelle beer that Bath insist we drink with it was also a good accompaniment.

Senegalese food made me feel my journey had not been wasted. For so many developing nations where food is fuel before it is fun, it's simple stuff. Expensive proteins in the form of beef, chicken, fish, or goat are padded with filling carbohydrates of rice, millet, or potatoes. The Senegalese make sure it is never dull. Their preparation involves fresh ingredients, slow cooking, and challenging spicy hot pepper, and they serve it with added doses of hospitality at large tables where guests often eat from one big communal plate.

Bath's dream was for every visitor to love Senegal as much as he did, and suggested we travel to his hometown of Rufisque, where I would see real life away from the capital. He suggested we go by local taxi, private cars which congregated by Independence Square, ready to be hired for the hour-long journey. I was ever so slightly alarmed that our chosen carriage appeared to have no doors, but Bath was not fazed and, joined by three others, we squeezed into the car which sank until it was just clearing the ground. Two of the driver's friends appeared carrying the missing doors and began attaching them to the car with the aid of packing tape, going over and under the car until, satisfied, the driver set off on the journey with us trapped inside a Christmas present on wheels.

Nonetheless, it got us there and, an hour later, after we had waited patiently for the driver to unwrap us, Bath took me to his home to introduce me to his family. His two sisters were busy preparing lunch, one gutting and cleaning fish, the other pulverizing spices in a bowl to create "soul" used to flavor the most famous dish of Senegalese cooking. *Thiebou djenne* means, simply, "fish with rice," but that does not do justice to a fabulous dish in which sweet, bony fish is cooked with vegetables and served with spiced rice that has been allowed to cook until the bottom develops an addictive, crunchy layer.

When mealtime came around, Bath took me into his room, where we ate together from one large plate placed on a small table. The rest of his family sat outside in the courtyard enjoying their own communal meal. The pleasure he took in serving, then eating, the meal was tangible.

"Here, have some sauce," he said ladling a spoonful over a portion of rice for me. "The flavor is the best. Mix some hot sauce with the fish. It brings the sweetness out."

We cleaned the plate down to the last grain of rice and he pushed back his chair with the same huge grin on his face that had been such a welcome sight at the airport.

"Man, my sisters can cook," he said with a satisfied sigh.

Moments like this made the challenges of *Eat My Globe* worthwhile. Here I was, in a house, in the middle of Senegal with a man I had only met a day or so before, sharing a meal prepared by his family.

Later, Bath took me to his favorite bar, where we sat until late in the evening listening to the drum-heavy music that seems to be the soundtrack to life in Senegal, drinking more Gazelle beer and the rather potent rosé that the locals like so much.

As it turned out, Bath was a total player and, in the course of the evening, had added the numbers of many women to the already impressive list he had on his phone. I liked him even more.

He insisted on seeing me to the airport, even though I had to check in at four the next morning. "I don't want you to have the same experience leaving Senegal as you had arriving," he explained over my protests.

As we said goodbye, I fumbled in my pocket and found a handful of loose change that I would not be able to use, handing it to him thinking he could at least use it to buy some of that Gazelle beer he liked so much.

"Thanks. I'll use it to buy some more birds to set free," he said with another big smile. "I'll ask them to pray for you."

With that, he extended his hand to touch knuckles and headed off towards the city.

That was Senegal. That was my new friend, Bath, and that, in the end was the true meaning of *teranga*.

Chapter 37
OFF ON THE ROAD TO MOROCCO

Casablanca, Morocco's capital, gets horrendous press. One guidebook describes it as "unloved and unlovely" and another as being "actively rank." It is not a pretty city. In fact, it is rather ugly and has few tourist attractions, unlike Marrakech or Fez, except for the Hassan II Mosque, which was completed recently and is second in size only to Mecca's in the Islamic world. With an impressive capacity of more than one hundred thousand, the calls to prayer blasted out by its sizeable speakers can be heard all over the city.

I liked Casablanca. It had all the hallmarks of a city that really appeal to me, a city not based on visitors, but full of normal working stiffs getting on with the task of earning their daily crust and then spending the rest of their time figuring out where to have that daily crust.

Despite its lack of appeal to tourists, Casablanca has its own bustling charm and enough food options for even someone with my now-jaded palate to perk up and take notice, and certainly enough to fill the two days I had before catching the train to Marrakech.

Because of its mainly Muslim population, Morocco is a predominantly dry country. The few places that sell beer are as dark and unwelcoming as a Hell's Kitchen sex shop. I decided that a few dry days would not harm me, and found my way to one of the many coffee shops that litter the streets and alleyways of Casablanca.

Serving little besides strong coffee and thick, sweet mint tea, the coffee shop is at the center of Morocco's culture, where men, always men, come to meet and argue over anything and everything. Chairs are always set so they face the street to allow people-watching; I used the coffee shops to catch up, make some notes, and plan where to eat.

I ate very well, too. I caught a cab up to Le Quartier Habous, the new city built by the French in the early twentieth century, and found my way to a strip of butchers specializing in camel meat. The heads of the meats' previous owners were swinging from hooks outside the shops just in case you had any doubts, and at the end of the strip a man behind a large grill was charring large steaks and kebabs. I bought a kebab and doused it in chili sauce. It was the toughest meat I had ever encountered, like old beef, and after chewing furiously on the same piece for over twenty minutes, I discarded the rest and went to look for something a bit softer.

Benis, in the same district, is one of the famous patisseries in Morocco. I bought a box full of sublime pastries, some light and crumbly, others filled with pistachios and cream, and some drowned in honey; all were incredibly addictive. I polished off a box of fifteen as I walked back towards my hotel.

Best of all, on Mohammed V, one of the main roads through the city, a small market sells fruit, vegetables, fresh fish, and meat. On surrounding streets, storefront cafés prepare food bought at the market. At one end, men ran across the street with freshly killed chickens to thread onto rotisserie skewers and, at the other end, the constant whirr of machinery pumped fresh juices into small glasses.

I chose a shop at random and sat on a small bench. Using my schoolboy French, I ordered half a roast chicken with bread. It was a freshly killed chicken, grilled slowly on a spit, until the flesh remained moist and fell from the bones, but the skin was crispy and delicious. It was served with a bowl of olives warmed through with juices from the chicken and mixed with olive oil, lemon juice, and lemon zest. Even with a fresh pomegranate juice, it all cost under two dollars. That's why I liked Casablanca so much: honest food prepared by working people for working people with immense friendliness and hospitality.

As much as I liked Casablanca, I found it hard to warm to Marrakech. It's certainly beautiful: the twisting alleys of the Medina, the explosions of color in the labyrinthine souks, and the well-preserved remnants of its royal past. It should be the perfect place to experience Morocco and Moroccan cuisine at its very best.

There are vast numbers of tourists, mainly French, then Spanish, Germans, a smattering of Brits, and Americans. Obviously, I added to the tourist numbers, so shouldn't complain, but will anyway. Like all cities that depend on the tourist trade, Marrakech seemed neutered and false.

The mayhem of the Jemma El Fna, the main square of the Medina, with its snake charmers, acrobats, dancers, and fortune tellers felt more like a ride in a theme park than a real expression of the character of the city. The bustling streets had all the edge of a well-polished pool ball.

As with the city itself, so with the food, much of which was aimed at extracting cash from the gullible, rather than providing quality or a taste of genuine Moroccan hospitality. There are possibilities of eating well. It took the help of the owner of my charming, well-placed *riad* to help separate the good from the bad.

My stomach had behaved itself on this part of the trip so, returning the favor, I kept well away from the stalls of the night market, where they sell interesting things like sheep's heads and bowls of snails, but where plates are cleaned by dipping them in a bucket of the same water all night. I also gave a wide berth to the fruit stalls offering freshly squeezed hepatitis A in a glass. Instead, I sought out a couple higher-end restaurants, one in the Medina and one in the new town.

Riad Dar Mimouna came highly recommended and, like most *riads*, worked on the basis of set menus giving me the opportunity to try superb royal Moroccan cuisine, including a superb example of a *pastilla*. The sweet, savory combination of the pastry stuffed with chicken and almonds, then dusted with sugar, is not to everyone's taste, but it was one of the highlights of my visit. A classic *tagine* of lamb with prunes and almonds was less surprising but equally well prepared, the bony chunks of lamb giving up a blubbery marrow.

For my last blowout meal in the city, I found the highly recommended Rotisserie de la Paix, situated in the new town built by the French in the 1920s. There was a pleasant shaded garden which in ninety-degree heat was a welcome place to sit and have my first dose of alcohol in Morocco, a half bottle of rosé, for which the country is well known. Top of the line was the royal mixed grill, which offered a colon-challenging plateful of kebabs, sausages, chops, and chicken served with fiery dipping sauces. It was not cheap by local standards. Despite this memorable meal, I was not sad when it came time to leave Marrakech and take the train back to Casablanca. Moroccan trains are wonderfully efficient, and a first-class ticket confirmed a seat in an air-conditioned carriage. As I boarded, I realized I would have traveling companions for the journey and when the Moroccans travel, they bring food and, being one of the most hospitable peoples on earth, when the Moroccans bring food, they share it.

My carriage was full as we pulled out of the station and, within half an hour, everyone was chatting in a mix of Arabic and French. Soon, the food began to appear. Lots of it, loaves of soft bread, cheese, dried fruits, hunks of chicken someone had in a cold bag, and flasks of coffee and sweet tea. My contribution of half a pack of Pringles was shameful, but no one seemed to care, and I was invited to join the party as we all happily stuffed our faces until the train pulled into Casablanca's Voyageur railway station.

I said my farewells, swapping hugs and business cards with my new friends, but I did not have time to linger. I needed to go straight to the station. It was time for a reunion. Together again with the Great Salami. Where better to do that than Spain?

Chapter 38
SPAIN: A HORSEMAN RIDING BY

"Sounds good," was the Great Salami's slightly unconvinced reply whenever I sent him an e-mail extolling the virtues of one of the countries on my visit and whatever dishes I happened to be enjoying. Then he would ask the annoying, but defining, question, "But is it Spain?"

He knows me too well. Wherever I am and whatever I am eating, I will always make comparisons to the food of my favorite country, Spain. It's his favorite, too. We both have been slightly obsessive about Spain since our parents bought a place on the Costa del Sol in the early 1980s, in Fuengirola, a small fishing village turned Sodom and Gomorrah. In the last decades of last century, charter planes of people were disgorged each summer to spend all day getting as red as possible on the beach, and all night as drunk as possible in bars before ending their day's activities with a fight and a much-needed vomit.

Despite this, we fell in love with the town, the country, and the food. The Great Salami and I have punctuated every year with at least two trips to Madrid, our favorite city, and supplemented that with at least a week's touring around various regions of Spain, always, of course, in search of great things to eat and drink. One trip was to the north in search of Galician octopus and Asturian cider. Another, a trip to Zaragoza, where we went and paid homage to Felix Jose Martínez, also known as *El Cortador de Jamón*, the Cutter of Ham. He is recognized as the finest exponent of the delicate art of cutting the *jamón ibérico*, which I mention in the very first lines of this book and which is the finest of food products.

When we finally got to meet Felix, we trembled and giggled like schoolgirls and, after watching him at work, we had pictures taken with him and asked him to sign a menu from his restaurant for his "estimados amigos Dos Hermanos." When I posted about this at length on our blog, one regular reader replied, "You boys really ought to get out less."

He was right, of course, but we didn't care, our passion for Spanish food knew no bounds. On our last Madrid trip, before I set off to eat my globe, we hit more than forty bars in three days, ordering at each one a small shot of beer or wine to have with the vast array of tapas available.

One of the great Spanish creations, sherry has always been one of my favorite tipples. When I was a student of theology, each evening I would sit in the darkened room of my dorm, puffing on a pipe (no snickering at the back), and having important discussions about God with fellow students, all the while sipping on a small glass of Harvey's Bristol Cream. Obviously, I was totally insufferable as I sat there pontificating—I still am when given half a chance—but it was my first introduction to this most underrated of drinks.

As the Majumdar children grew older, our Christmas morning traditions expanded to include the opening of a bottle of crisp, cold *fino* sherry as we waited for a ridiculously large turkey to brown in the oven. Even now, when I taste this delicate, slightly acidic wine, I half expect to turn around and see my mother wrapping sausages in bacon or happily rolling balls of stuffing.

Sherry has a real image problem. Most people have never tried it and think it is a spirit, which it is not, or something that is overly sweet and cloying, which it can be, but that is like saying that all opera involves big, fat women in armor shouting at you in German. Through Andrew Sinclair, a friend who promotes the products of González Byass, one of the great sherry families, I learned about an annual April event called the Feria de Caballos in Jerez. Actually a fair for the local horsemen, it's really an excuse to drink stupid amounts of sherry. González Byass would be able to find some hotel space for us.

By the time April 2008 arrived, I was exhausted but excited. I connected with the Great Salami in Madrid and by late afternoon we were already in our hotel in Jerez de la Frontera ready to indulge in sherry and sherry-related products.

The hotel was by far the nicest I had stayed at in an entire year. After dropping off our bags, we headed out to explore—only to find the town was shut. Not one bar open. This wasn't the Spain we knew and adored.

We were getting desperate. After all, we had been nearly twenty-four hours without *jamón* and the Great Salami was beginning to go cold ham on me. All at once, we spotted a gaggle of well-dressed pensioners heading in the opposite direction. We did an abrupt about-face and followed them, realizing that, when the Feria comes to town, the town itself closes and its bars move to the fairground to set up shop.

As we approached, we could already see the sky lit up by the lights from the fair, but nothing prepared us for the incredible sight as we walked through the main entrance. To call this simply a fair didn't do it justice. It covered an enormous area and was packed with *casetas*, lavish stands representing the bars, clubs, and sherry *bodegas* of Jerez. Music mixed with happy chattering was deafening as tens of thousands of people milled from stand to stand with glasses of sherry in their hands.

We were struck immediately by the good nature of it all and could not help commenting that, if the same event were held in the United Kingdom with all that booze and people wandering around with glasses and dancing, the local police and emergency crews would be working overtime. Here, locals young and old were just hell-bent on having a good time. If someone bumped into you, he apologized; if you were lining up to get to the bar for a drink, they would make way for you. For two boys from South Yorkshire, where touching someone's pint leads to a friendly kicking, it was all a bit disorienting, but not unpleasantly so. We stayed until way past midnight before heading off to bed, although Jerez was still in full swing.

The next day, we had been promised a tour of the vineyards and *bodegas* of González Byass. Founded in 1885, González Byass was a joint venture by the wonderfully named Manuel Maria González Ángel and his English agent, Mr. Byass. Nearly one hundred and thirty years later, it remains in family hands and is one of the most famous names in sherry, particularly for Tio Pepe, named after Manuel's uncle, who was the first to create the fortified wines we now know as *fino*.

Andrew and others in our special tour group looked a little worse for wear after a few days and late nights at the fair. Dark glasses were de rigueur, and there was the slightest air of loin girdage about them. The Great Salami and I, however, were now in fine fettle, and bouncing around in excitement as we were chauffeured out to the enormous vine-yards of Palomino and Pedro Ximinez grapes. With over 2,250 acres, they are an impressive sight, but paled in comparison with the *bodegas*, the wine cellars of González Byass back in Jerez where we were to be given a personal tour by Martin Skelton, the head of the U.K. office.

Each *bodega* or warehouse has its own character, taken from the type of sherry being produced inside. The lofty warehouses of *fino* barrels had that sharp, clean smell of fresh, young sherry. Those housing the Pedro Ximinez are filled with a sweet, almost musty hue. It would be as easy to get as drunk on the aroma as it would be on the wine itself.

Martin Skelton gave us a short history lesson as we walked through the *bodegas*, explaining that sherry really began with the transport of wine to Britain in the 1800s, where it was fortified with brandy to keep it from going off on the long journey. Fino was created almost by acci-dent—when sherry fails to fortify sufficiently, a must develops on the surface of the wine that stops it from developing a deep color.

Sherry is produced by the Solera system which, I realize, sounds like a progressive rock album, but, in fact, refers to the way that barrels are stored and filled: The oldest barrel is partly emptied and then refilled by the next oldest and so on; that the final result is a blend of many ages of sherry.

Obviously, the proof is in the tasting and, after the tour, Martin led us to a room where a complete range of sherry had been laid out for us. I wish that anyone who claims not to like sherry could have sam-pled the variety, from the *fino* which is perfect with the local Andalucian specialty of fried fish, to a range of thirty-year-old wines which would make the perfect complement to chocolate or figs.

As if to prove the versatility of the sherry, Martin then suggested we head back to the Feria and have some lunch, served with Tio Pepe bottled freshly for the event. By three that afternoon, the fair was in full swing again, each *caseta* buzzing with the sounds of sherry-fueled chat-tering. The air was also filled with the haunting sounds of *sevillanas*, a local offshoot of flamenco, which summarizes the courtship between a man and a woman in twelve prescribed steps. Everyone—from small children to grandparents—seemed to know them and everyone seemed to be dancing.

I settled myself down at a table in the lavish González Byass *caseta* for the more important matter at hand, a lunch consisting of large plates of *jamón*, local Manchego cheese and mounds of freshly made *fritura* of fish and seafood, which we washed down with more bottles of Tio Pepe than I or my liver care to remember.

At this point, we were joined by one of the descendants of the original Mr. González, who wanted to share with us the fact that, the day before, more than twenty-five thousand bottles of Tio Pepe had been sold at the fair. A record. As if in celebration, before he left the table, he waved at one of the servers, and the table was suddenly covered again in platefuls of food and bottles of sherry.

The Great Salami picked up a crisp, freshly fried anchovy, popped it in his mouth, and swooshed it down his gullet with a good glug of chilled *fino*. Then he turned to me and mumbled, "Every now and then, just for a moment, life stops kicking you in the ass."

We don't always see eye to eye, but in this case, the Great Salami was bang on the money.

Chapter 39
ISTANBUL: EATING EYTAN'S WAY

T h e   A n g e l Mangal was a Turkish restaurant at the less glamorous end of Upper Street in London's Islington. The grilled meats were
among the best in London, and we could regularly be seen gnawing at
our standard order of special mixed grill with quail and a side order of
sweetbreads, washed down with pungent Turkish wine, which worked
perfectly in context, but tasted like camel urine whenever we were silly
enough to open a bottle at home.

My meals with the Great Salami, however, were never that easy and
we constantly monitored each other's intake so that there could be no
possibility that one could steal more than his fair share: "Have you just
had a sweetbread?" or "That's a big piece. It counts as two."

This simply has become habit in every meal we share. So much so
that, as Jay Rayner, restaurant critic of the *Observer*, wrote, "The Majumdar Brothers have so many rituals they could job share as the Pope." He
opined that the reason for our "your turn/my turn" approach to meals
was that we came from a large Bengali family and, if such methods were
not enforced, there was a strong likelihood that the runts of the litter
might starve.

As you can imagine, the notion that there might ever have been less
than enough food on the table to feed her brood did not go down well
with Gwen Majumdar, and the Great Salami and I both received phone
calls of the "I am more disappointed than angry" variety the moment
the paper hit the stands. I can still hear her announcing with Welsh de-
fiance, "Well, neither of you look like you ever went hungry."

Our routine, however, did have some roots in our childhood, specifically, the times that the Great Salami was allowed into the kitchen on Sunday as lunch was being divvied up. While Auriel, Jeremy, and I would stand watching, noses pressed to the glass panes of the kitchen door, Robin would pull all the choice bits off the roast chicken, fat off the beef, or crackling off the pork and eat them noisily in front of us, before finally allowing us to come to the table. He termed these his treats, and declared them his birthright as the eldest son.

This scarred me deeply, and we now have an unspoken understanding that no one of us gets more than the rest, and any accusation of such a crime is a very, very serious matter in the Majumdar household.

Along with this deep morality that guides our way of eating, there is another, marginally more sane reason we choose to eat our mixed grill this way, which is so that we can compare tastes and critique the same foods at the same time. Was the plump chicken wing, piping hot off the charcoal grill, as good as before? Was the thin lamb cutlet with a ribbon of crispy fat properly seasoned? Were the nuggets of thymus gland cooked so they still retained a little bite? Such things were and are important to us and a good hour or so after the meal is taken up with an in-depth discussion of the performance of the grillmeister.

The owner of the Angel Mangal was a beguilingly taciturn Turk named Mustapha. In the eight years we were regulars, I think I saw him smile once. Even then, it involved the slightest twitch of the lips, and only happened when we were discussing his beloved football team, Besiktas. Then, our restaurant was gone due to the double whammy of increasing rents and food costs. Mustapha went back to Turkey. We tried other places, but they were never quite the same.

"Perhaps," I thought, as I scribbled the word "Istanbul" on my initial list, "I can recapture some of the magic at the source."

In Turkey, my room overlooked the Blue Mosque, glowing in the light of a half moon. It seemed impossibly romantic until I was tossed out of bed a few short hours later by the first Islamic call to prayer. Unable to sleep, I showered and headed down to breakfast, which in Turkey is a delight: warm bread, eggs, cheese dribbled with honey and sprinkled with thyme, olives, cucumbers, and tomatoes all to be eaten with *cay*, or tea, which they seem to like at a ratio of three large lumps of sugar to one thimbleful of liquid.

With one foot in Asia and the other in Europe, Istanbul is one of the world's most vibrant cities. The population estimates seem to vary but one thing is for certain: when Turkey joins the European Union, Istanbul will by far surpass London as the European Union's most populous city.

Every Turk seems to be on the street at the same time, selling stuff, making stuff, or fixing stuff. The noise and smells are a heady combination and can easily overwhelm the incredible sights. A sightseer's dream, Istanbul can fill a week of anybody's time, even if his unhealthy obsession is food rather than antiquities. Besides the Blue Mosque—so lavish a testament to faith with its six minarets, that the ruling sultan had to pay for an extra tower for Mecca, so that this was not seen as a challenge—there is the Hagia Sofya, the greatest church in Christendom when built. After the conquest of Constantinople by the Moors, it became another imposing mosque, and is still one of the largest enclosed spaces on earth.

The Topkapi Palace is the home of generations of ruling families with its elaborate warren of rooms and courtyards, legends of harems, and treasures including the bejeweled Topkapi Dagger. The Spice Markets and the Grand Bazaar display just about everything you can imagine for sale from stalls many of which are hundreds of years old.

I intended to see it all, but I was here for the food and my expectations were high. I knew enough to get away from the touristy Sultanahmet region of the city, and headed into the back streets and towards the river. In most cities, these areas contain choice little holes-in-the-wall, joints, and eateries packed full of locals. For whatever reason, I couldn't find them. The cafés were filled with people who certainly did not seem to be backpackers from Norway, but still offered dried-out kebabs and miserable-looking vegetables all served with the slightly odd double-carb combo of rice and chips.

A favorite pair of shoes was consigned to the trash, worn out as I traipsed from the Old City to the New City in search of something decent to eat. Places with promising displays of meat in the window cooked them into inedible meaty bullets and, whenever I did stumble into a truly local café, I was either ignored or handed a tourist menu that offered fish and chips.

In my first four days in the city, the best thing I ate was a fish sandwich. To be fair, it was not just any fish sandwich but the *balik ekmek*, a local speciality prepared at restaurants underneath the Galata Bridge spanning the Bosphorus between Europe and Asia. It combines freshly grilled mackerel fillet on a soft roll with a good helping of sharp, raw onions, doused with lemon juice, and sprinkled with salt. It is incredibly delicious, but hardly formed the basis for a seven-day visit.

I was desperate and depressed and posted about my plight on the Dos Hermanos blog, resigning myself to spending the rest of my time in Istanbul sightseeing and eating dire food.

Fortunately, for me, Eytan Behmoaras responded.

A thirty-year-old Turk living in London, Eytan was a reader of Dos Hermanos and, dismayed by my post, had taken the time and considerable effort to send a long list of good restaurants to visit, proving to me that Istanbul was worthy and not, as I had rather peevishly suggested, "A place where the ingredients are mediocre and the techniques not good enough to cover that fact up."

Kadikoy, a short ferry ride away, is a fully formed neighborhood in its own right, with shops and a bustling market and a restaurant, Ciya, that Eytan had suggested looked promising and, with the waiter's help, I picked out four items to sample from a wide selection on the counter. At once, I understood what Eytan meant. Each dish placed in front of me was better than anything I had eaten in Turkey. A bowl of lamb stew, soured with local plums, came with whole, braised cloves of garlic. Another dish of eggplant had the intense flavors that only come from long, slow cooking. Best of all was a plate of lamb's intestines stuffed with a mixture of ground lamb and bulgur wheat. It may only have been a sampling, but already, as I mopped up the juices with a slice of warm bread, my perception of the food of Istanbul had changed for the better.

There was a lot more to sample in the area, including fish restaurants offering meals of Black Sea turbot or simple snacks of mussels on sticks. Cafés serving lamajoun, flat bread topped with spiced minced beef to be rolled up and eaten on the hoof, and tubs of fresh yogurt onto which honey was dribbled straight from the comb.

My biggest regret, however, is that I have but one stomach to give, and it was attached to a body that was close to shutdown with a sudden cold. So, I bought myself one last treat of baklava, the frighteningly rich pastry traditionally plumped out with lamb fat, and headed back to bed, where I shivered through the next few calls to prayer.

The next day was my last so, despite the fact that I still felt miserable, I was determined to try more of Eytan's suggestions.

At the heart of the New City, Taksim Square is lined with innumerable stalls selling freshly squeezed orange juice, and Turkey's own unique take on the hamburger. Premade, the sliders sit steaming in glass cabinets, greasy, nasty, and devoid of merit. I loved them, devouring two in about three minutes and sitting there licking my fingers wondering if I could fit in another two before my stomach rebelled.

I did. I regretted it immediately and it added to my secret fear that, in fact, when it comes to food I have no standards. I am just a very greedy person.

To work off the grease, I walked back to the European side of the city, admired the bristle of fishing rods on the Galata Bridge, and settled myself at a table on the terrace of Restaurant Hamdi, overlooking the storied Bosphorus. Theirs are known as the *ne plus ultra* of kebabs in Istanbul, and I can see why. Hand-minced with a frighteningly sharp knife, the lamb is moist with fat and rich in flavor. The service was suitably miserable and the wine suitably rough, so I raised my glass in a silent toast to Mustapha and the Angel Mangal as well as to Eytan, who had saved me from getting an entire city wrong. Thanks to him, Istanbul and I got along just fine.

I am sure Istanbul will be just thrilled to hear it.

Chapter 40
SICILY: AN OFFER I COULDN'T REFUSE IN PALERMO

"She is a cheek," Claudio leant over to me in a conspiratorial manner, hand covering his mouth. "But she has a deek."

It was one of the more unusual introductions I had experienced on the trip, but there was no doubting the veracity of Claudio's grappa-fueled statement. The person sitting opposite me smoking a cigarette had been going for the feminine look, but the tight jeans "she" was wearing sported a package, which suggested there was obviously still work to be done.

Claudio was the owner of a small bed-and-breakfast in Palermo, Sicily. I had arrived well past midnight after a long-delayed flight from Istanbul. My back ached and I had a pain in my foot that I found out later was a stress fracture. I was in a sorry state.

Over breakfast the next morning, Claudio began scribbling down the names of local specialties.

"Ah," he sighed twisting his finger against his cheek a sign for delicious. "Sicily has the best food in Italy, the best meat, the best cheese, the best pasta, and the best wine. You are going to eat well." Because of Sicily's history and its proximity to Africa, it had "nine denominations in one island," which led to a wider range of food than anywhere else in Italy.

Well, he would say that, wouldn't he? I have watched enough movies to know not to argue with a Sicilian and took the notes he offered, folding them into my back pocket as I went to look around the city.

I liked Palermo immediately, although it seems not to have made up its mind about its identity. Massive restorations of historical monuments sit uncomfortably next to gaping holes in the ground and derelict buildings. However, you can forgive the occasional ugliness when a city has so much passion. Palermo crackles with raw energy.

The old town and the market districts of Capo and Ballaro are filled with stalls selling meats, cheeses, fruits and vegetables, and an astonishing variety of fish. Many stalls advertised with signs pierced by the fearsome spike of the swordfish, and owners barked out a list of their wares in a cacophony of sound. To escape the din, I ducked into a local café.

By this time, I was running on fumes. I felt bloated and unfit, jaded, lonely, and depressed. I was ready to go home. It would have taken a very special place to get me excited and reawaken my taste buds. Palermo was it.

I had met many nationalities obsessed with food, but few could stand their ground with Sicilians, for whom food is obviously an offer you can't refuse. From the morning coffee that comes with a rich, buttery pastry, to a midmorning sandwich snack, to long leisurely lunches, afternoon cakes, and mammoth-sized suppers, there seldom seems a moment in the day when Sicilians are not eating or talking about eating.

I ordered a thick, dark hot chocolate and a cannoli, the uniquely Sicilian pastry tube filled to bursting with sweetened ricotta cheese. One was enough for me, but others in the bar were working their way through mounds of them. Feeling more energetic after that huge intake of sugar, I took out Claudio's notes and began to think about a midmorning snack. One thing in particular caught my attention.

A *pani ca meusa* is one of the favorite snacks of every self-respecting Palermo man—slices of calf spleen simmered in lard and served on a soft roll with a good sprinkle of salt and lemon juice. You can have it *single,* which is just spleen or you can have it *married* to a few additional slices of calf's lung.

Claudio had scribbled down the name of one of the best places, a small storefront facing the harbor. As I joined a line of middle-aged Sicilian men outside, I received more than one quizzical look. Service was rapid and, two or three minutes later, I was standing at the counter with a large sandwich in my hand containing the married version. The meat was soft and melting from the long simmering in lard, the salt cut through the offal taste, and the lemon juice lifted the whole thing up a level. The juices had soaked through the roll and the final combination was entirely fabulous.

Of course, I could have eaten another there and then. But, I had lunch to think of and wanted to turn my mind to matters pasta. Sicilians are very specific about their pasta and about their sauces and, as I walked away from the harbor back towards the town center, I referred to Claudio's list again to decide which one of the seemingly dozens of trattorias to visit.

He had written *spaghetti con le sarde* in large letters, and underlined the word *spaghetti* three times to make it clear that this was the only acceptable pasta to have with this sauce made of sardines. I chose a place and ordered as he had instructed me, along with a flask of the local Nero d'Avola wine.

It was a challenging plateful given my breakfast, cannolo, and spleen sandwich, but I managed to polish off a pile of pasta spiked through with garlic and meaty chunks of sardine in a fragrant tomato sauce flavored with local wild fennel. The wine worked perfectly and, after my meal, I sloshed a little of it in the almost empty bowl and wiped the resulting mélange up with a hunk of warm bread.

Tempted to give supper a miss, on my way back to the bed-and-breakfast, I wandered into a small, smart-looking wine bar and spent an hour or so trying the local white wine made from the insolia grape, together with a plate of melting fatty ham, figs, and creamy local goat's cheese.

Claudio was having none of my thoughts of fasting for the evening and invited me to share supper with him and his partner, from Tunisia. She had spent the day making *brik*, a savory filo turnover stuffed with tuna, capers, and fried eggs and, as I emerged from my room, she was placing a towering plate of them on the table. They were delicious, but I could scarcely do them justice given the amount I had eaten throughout the day.

The next morning, Claudio announced that he was not going to give me such a huge breakfast, because we were going on a tour of the local neighborhood, Vuccaria, famous for its fish market, street stalls, and restaurants. Displaying the day's catch was a man serving *polpo*, octopus, which he bought at the harbor every morning and simply boiled in salted water before serving it warm with the head split open, so the insides could form a creamy coating of the meat.

"The 'ead is the best bit," Claudio mumbled as he licked fishy brain matter from his fingers.

As we ate, a friend of Claudio's walked by.

"He is one of the last makers of *bottarga* in Palermo," Claudio added with a pained expression.

I was surprised as I thought that *bottarga,* dried mullet roe used for grating over pasta, was a specialty only of Sardinia. Not so, apparently, as the friend proved, holding up a large slab of fresh fish roe he had just extracted from the belly of its owner.

"He is going to cure it now. It will be ready to sell next week."

We stopped in for a drink at Claudio's favorite bar, filled with gruff old men, cigarettes drooping from their mouths. Claudio ordered two large, cold bottles of Moretti beer and, while I kept watch over them, he ran around the corner returning with a plate filled with fried seafood he had bought from another bar.

"The perfect combination," he added giving me that finger twisted in the cheek movement again.

Finally, as we drained the last of our liter bottles of beer, Claudio announced, "Is time to have some lunch. Follow me."

I did as I was told and waddled after him. We ducked into the tiny entrance of a trattoria called Café Attico.

"The owner, Giovanni, is a good friend and makes the best food in the city," he assured me, as we were shown to a table outside in a busy alleyway.

After a couple bottles of the inky Nero d'Avola were placed in front of us, Giovanni and Claudio got into a heated discussion, which involved lots of hand waving and pointing in my direction. Claudio explained, "He did not think you would like sea urchin. I told him you ate anything."

A large plate of *spaghetti con ricci* was placed in front of each of us, the pasta tossed with a sauce made from the fresh sea urchin. It tasted freshly of the sea and, from where I sat, I could see Giovanni in the kitchen splitting open more of the spiny creatures and adding them to pans of garlic sizzling in olive oil.

Claudio apparently knew everyone in the city. As we ate, we were joined by a parade of his acquaintances, all of who protested they couldn't possibly spare the time for a drink before sitting down and spending the next four hours with us getting horribly pissed. At one point, I was surrounded by seven of them, all hard-faced and all arguing about food as they tucked into the bowls of homemade semifreddo and cannoli that Giovanni had brought to the table along with two bottles of lethal local grappa.

It was at this point that Claudio leaned over and pointed to Valentino, the preop transsexual and Claudio's upstairs neighbor. She had joined us at some point during the meal, a fact I had missed, because I was horribly, horribly inebriated.

"She has invited us to supper. Is okay? Because, as I say, she has a deek," he added as if this might matter to me.

"As long as she can cook, I don't care if she has two of them and can tie them in knots," I replied swaying slightly in my seat.

Giovanni presented us with a bill, which, I suspect, barely covered the cost of the wine we drank, and Claudio and I staggered back to his apartment arms around each other for support.

"You are good man. You should stay for longer," he told me as he fumbled for the key, let us into the apartment, and I stumbled towards my bedroom.

A few hours later, as I was sleeping it off, he rapped hard on my door. Disturbingly, he looked right as rain and breezily announced, "Time for supper with woman with deek."

Whatever her sexual definition, Valentino could certainly cook and had prepared a dish of linguine in a sauce made from veal and thickened with potatoes. It was just what I needed to help soak up the booze, and it was another of those many moments I had experienced on the trip, when I looked around me, at the food in front of me, the people I was with (several more had joined Claudio and me), and thought, "How did a good middle-class British boy like me get a chance to do this?"

I raised my glass and proposed a toast to Valentino, and everyone joined in. I somehow knew that I was not going to get any sleep that night as Claudio stood and plopped the cork from another couple of bottles of wine.

At four in the morning, Claudio insisted on giving me a lift to the airport bus on the back of his scooter which led to the unlikely sight of a Vespa weaving its way unsteadily through the empty streets of Palermo carrying two men, both the worse for wear, one carrying a large red rucksack and holding on for dear life.

As he deposited me at the bus stop, he kissed me on both cheeks. "Ciao, you come back soon. We have more eating to do."

With that, he hopped back on his bike and sped off into the night waving over his shoulder as he headed into the distance. I just said a silent prayer of thanks for the fact I was still alive, and for the opportunity to see Sicily through one of its native sons.

Chapter 41
ALL ROADS LEAD TO ROME

Veni, vidi, vici. At least that's how it should have been when I entered Rome, in triumph. I had been, I had seen, and I had eaten. Rome was the last official stop on the trip before I headed off to meet up with the Great Salami for a wine-sodden end of the adventure, a week back in La Rioja.

I had been to thirty-one countries. I had eaten thousands of meals, met hundreds of people, and completed a task that had not even entered my mind eighteen months before. I should have stormed into Italy's historic capital even more unbearable than ever. I should have stayed in a fine hotel sipping on the best wines, while unutterably attractive Roman girls gave me shoulder rubs, peeled me grapes, and applauded my achievements while whispering in my ear, "You are not a god."

Cut to picture of shambling fortysomething hobbling up five flights of stairs to a tiny room in a grubby hotel, throwing Big Red on the floor, collapsing on the bed, and bursting into tears. At the end of my adventure, I was almost inconsolable. Not that there was anyone there to console me.

I had developed a bone-deep exhaustion. I had not slept the night before on my last night in Sicily, and the headache of my grappa-fueled hangover had kept me awake on the plane. My foot was now beating out constant, and painful, African rhythms. I winced as I pulled off my walking shoes and socks and looked at the bright red swollen lump that was now where my foot used to be.

Most of all, however, I think my tears represented a welling up of all the emotions of the last year and a half. Thoughts first of my mother. My last visit to Rome had been in 1980, my last, reluctant, childhood holiday with my parents, at the age of sixteen.

They had both been in their glory, my father, a successful surgeon, my mother, the local magistrate. In true form, Gwen Majumdar, who had experienced a secure but modest upbringing, was reveling in doing nothing by halves. We stayed in one of the better hotels, ate meals at expensive restaurants, and my father, who remained besotted with my mother from the day they met until the day she died, surprised her with gifts of lavish jewelry.

Now, nearly thirty years later, I was far from my peak and filled with fear. What was going to happen now I had finished? Did I start looking for another job in publishing? I would certainly need the money. Or was this, as so many people had told me along the way, the beginning of a new chapter? I didn't know, I had not even thought about it much during the trip, but now I would have to. Added to all the other things I was experiencing, my worries escaped me in floods of salt water.

After a good blub, I was feeling better, or at least spent. I stripped and had a shower, swallowed a fistful of painkillers to numb the pain in my foot, and took out my guidebook and notes. I may not have been in any shape to conquer Rome, but I was at least going to have a bit of a wander.

It's impossible to do the Eternal City justice when you only have two full days and can't walk terribly well. Not that such impediments could seemingly stop the coach loads of elderly American tourists I encountered at every turn as I hobbled around the town. At the Colosseum, I was battered out of the way by a wave of blue-rinsed women who made their way to the front of the line using their walkers as an excuse and a handy weapon. "When falls the Colosseum . . ." The same group appeared at the Palatine Hill and in the Forum, which they described as "a cute bunch of rocks." This made me think I should head off and have some lunch before I said something that would make me a marked man in senior centers all over America.

I headed up via Cavour, dived into a trattoria I recognized from my Internet research, and ordered half a liter of house red wine even before my backside had hit the leatherette seat.

Like all Italians, Romans are obsessive about food. Every city and region have their own specialties. In particular, they like their pizza, and pizzerias dot the city, from the corner store selling it by weight from square blocks with different toppings, to the smartest restaurants with wood-fired ovens and the freshest high-end ingredients. As you know from my visit to New York, pizza is normally something I avoid, but when in Rome, et cetera. I ordered the Roman favorite, pizza Margherita, which—although it actually originated in Naples and is in theory the most simple of all to make, with little more than tomato and basil—is a source of constant discussion among Romans.

While that was being prepared, I fortified myself with another Roman favorite, *bucatini all' Amatriciana*, a dish of tubular, hollow pasta with a sauce made from pork jowl, pancetta, and tomatoes. This was much more to my taste, with a slight kick from a hot chili used in the cooking and the zest from the addition of lemon juice before serving. I was famished and attacked the bowl in a way that brought admiring glances from other tables and the staff, who quickly brought me another bowl of bread when I finished one sopping up the sauce.

The pizza arrived. It looked as I imagine a good pizza should, the toppings bubbling and glistening under a sheen of juices and a drizzle of olive oil, the base crispy and cracking under the pressure from my knife. It was a good example of the genre, but I just don't like the genre, and even this would not change my mind. I nibbled at a crust and ate a bit from the center, but my mind wanted to dwell on the meaty, rich pasta dish. In the end, I pushed the plate away, contents half-eaten, indicating that it was fullness not disgust, that had caused me to fail.

Much more energized the next day, I was out and raring to go at seven in the morning.

Stopping only for the requisite Italian pastry on the way, I found my way to Vatican City, and was the second person in line when the doors opened to St. Peter's Basilica, and was able to stand in awe before Michelangelo's *Pietà* for twenty minutes before another soul appeared. I was not so lucky when I headed out to the Vatican Museum where vast lines had formed.

It seemed silly to have gone all the way around the world and not be able to see one of the truly great pieces of art on my last stop. It was a hateful experience; since tour groups ruled, the solo tourist is the lowest on the pecking order, and I had to push my way through crowds with considerable force until I found myself staring up at the ceiling of the Sistine Chapel, its majesty shining through, despite the pushing and shoving of tourists and guides alike.

I got out of there and took a cab to the Piazza San Salvatore for my last lunch in Rome.

My mind was set on two other Roman specialities, the first, one of the most misunderstood of all pasta dishes, *spaghetti carbonara*, all too often a bowl of limp pasta swamped with cheese and cream, often from a jar. At its best, however, it is a beautiful mix of sautéed onions, crispy Italian bacon, large amounts of pecorino and beaten eggs that cook in the residual heat of the pasta.

To follow, it was just the time of year to order *abbacchio*, a dish of beautifully tender, slow-cooked spring lamb seasoned heavily with lots of garlic, sage, and rosemary and spiced with the anchovies just before serving. It was a simple yet glorious meal, and I lingered over it for a couple of hours, treating myself to a bottle of Brunello, the smooth, subtle wine from Tuscany, some gelato for dessert, and an unfeasibly large grappa to send me on my way, this time more with a slight sway than a hobble.

I had done a bit of sightseeing and had at least one excellent meal, but I had scarcely done Rome justice. Whatever my excuses, I could not say *"Veni, vidi, vici,"* but rather, "I came, I saw, I conked out."

Chapter 42
THE END OF THE ROAD

After a global journey that had involved so many long-distance trips, my final flight was only a short hop from Bilbao, where I had finished a final week's touring Spain's La Rioja with the Great Salami to celebrate the end of the trip.

I arrived at our London apartment shortly before midnight, and threw Big Red on the floor. As it hit the marble surface, air was squeezed out of a small hole on the side that had appeared in the last two weeks. It sounded like a sigh, which I thought fair enough for a companion who had done as many miles as I had done, and had traveled in considerably less comfort.

Like me, Big Red had endured nearly one hundred flights to and through more than thirty countries and had seen the inside of countless hotel rooms, my constant companion, often my only companion. Airlines had tried to lose it and crooks had tried to steal it, but together, in our very British way, we had muddled through somehow.

I peeled off my walking boots and tossed them to one side, promising myself and my painful and swollen foot that I would not wear them again for a little while, if ever. I made myself a large mug of strong tea and sat down to check my e-mail. A handful said, "Well done," but otherwise, the end of my journey seemed to have gone as little remarked upon as the day I quit my job. Not even a mention on the TV news, which seemed so desperate for stories they were talking to a woman who claimed to see the face of Jesus in a piece of toast.

Had it been worthwhile? Had I actually achieved anything after all that time, effort, and money?

Glancing up from my cup of steaming tea, into which I was dunking my second chocolate digestive biscuit, I saw an envelope propped up on the small dining room table. I opened it and a read the note inside. It was from Baba.

"Congratulations on finishing your round-the-world trip. Mum would have been very proud."

Then it all made sense to me. Of course, it had been worthwhile. I may have spent every penny I had in the bank and a little bit more, but it had been worth every last cent. I had made a journey that most people only dream of but few will ever embark upon. In fact, just about everybody I have met before, during, and after the trip and well over a thousand who e-mailed me told me that it is a journey that they want to make some day.

I may not have fulfilled my avowed aim to go everywhere, eat everything, but I had a good stab at it. I may not be the first person to eat rat in China, elk in Finland, barbecue in Texas, crickets in Manila, or cod sperm sushi in Kyoto, but there are not too many people out there who can claim to have done so in a little over a year.

For sure, I am the only Simon Majumdar to do it and that is good enough for me.

What about Simon Majumdar, where does it leave him? Well, apparently it leaves him talking about himself in the third person, which, at the very least, sees him getting a slap sometime soon if he keeps it up. It leaves me (that's better) broke but incredibly rich in experience. It leaves me with memories and more than twelve thousand photographs on my computer, mostly of all the different things I ate in all those countries. When I look at the pictures, I can still summon up the pleasing tastes and smells and the circumstances in which I ate them.

Most of all, it leaves me with hundreds of new people around this globe whom I can call "friend" and mean it. People who, because they shared the same passion for food that I have, opened up their lives and often their houses and homes for me.

A cynical man before I set out, my trip restored my faith in the intrinsic goodness of people. That, on its own, is an accomplishment and I suspect it would have been enough to make Gwen Majumdar proud, too. I am not sure I need, deserve, or want any other accolade apart from knowing that my father is, and my mother would have been, proud of me.

So, what now? Perhaps I should figure out a way to keep doing exactly what I have been doing for the past year, to keep finding ways to travel around this rapidly changing world of ours in search of the best food and the highest generosity of spirit, which makes it taste so good.

The offers and invitations are flooding in, even more so than when I first set out on the trip. There are still a hell of a lot of countries whose stamps I would love in my passport and, of course, there is so much good food out there still to try.

Perhaps, Big Red and I aren't finished quite yet.

Any ideas?

APPENDIX A

Simon's Shallow Search for the Perfect Martini

I like my martinis brutal and naked. I still hold with the first piece of advice given to me at the American Bar at the Savoy Hotel when I asked how much vermouth I should add to my drink and the bartender replied, "Sir, it is enough that the man delivering the gin once had a mother who drank vermouth."

The classic, however, is a little less uncompromising.

Four 1½-ounce shots good gin (Beefeater or Plymouth are my preferences)
One 1½-ounce shot dry vermouth (Noilly Prat)
1-inch strip of peel from an unwaxed lemon

Chill your shaker and glass. When cold, add ice to the shaker, and measure in the required amounts of gin and vermouth. Shake or stir as required. I prefer stirring as shaking can lead to shards of ice making its way into the final drink. Strain into your chilled glass and twist the lemon peel until it leaves a spritz of lemon oil on the surface of the cocktail.

Serve holding by the stem.

For people with more savory taste, use an olive instead of a twist.
If you want to use vodka, that's fine. Just don't call it a martini; it isn't.

APPENDIX B

Simon's Recipe for Life-Saving Dahl

1 cup red lentils

2 tablespoons vegetable oil

1 cardamom pod

2 cloves

1 cinnamon stick

1 chopped onion

1 chopped clove garlic

1 teaspoon ground turmeric

1 teaspoon ginger

1 teaspoon salt

1 chopped fresh green chili

1 unwaxed lemon chopped in quarters

1 bag spinach, washed

Dry-toast the lentils until they begin to release a nutty aroma. Add vegetable oil to a hot pan and add the cardamom, cloves, and cinnamon stick. Cook for 1 minute on low heat until the release their flavor. Add the onion and garlic and cook until they begin to soften. Add the ground spices, salt, and chili; mix well with the onion-garlic mixture, and cook for 2 minutes until the spices lose their rawness. If the mixture begins to stick, add a little water. Add the lentils to the pan and mix well so that all the lentils are covered with the mixture. Add 1 pint of water and the lemon and simmer for 25 minutes, until the lentils are soft. If the lentils start to go dry, add more water as necessary.

Add the spinach and allow to wilt.

I serve this with simple vegetable or fish curries or even just over a hard-boiled egg.

APPENDIX C

Simon's Top Twenty Tastes of *Eat My Globe*

(Of course, if you ask me this tomorrow, you may get a totally different answer.)

In no particular order:

1. Thiebou Djenne cooked for me by my friend Bath's sisters in Ruffisque, Senegal.
2. Tandoori Chicken at Bhukara, New Delhi.
3. Yakitori at the bars of Ueno, Tokyo.
4. Sichuan Hotpot in Chengdu, China.
5. Boiled new potatoes prepared by the Prinsessa, Finland.
6. Breakfast ribs at the American Royal, Kansas City, Missouri.
7. Seafood Kare Kare prepared for me by Claude Tayyag in Angeles, Philippines.
8. Souvlaki at Lamb on Chapel, Melbourne.
9. Pho on the streets of Hanoi.
10. Braai prepared by Emil Den Dulk, Stellenbosch, South Africa.
11. Shrimp Cocktail, Guadalajara.
12. Roast Chicken with my friend, Tana, in Santa Cruz.
13. Mee Krob, Chote Chitr, Bangkok.
14. Mutton Kebab Rolls, Bade Miyan, Mumbai.

15. Mrs King's Pork Pie, Melton Mowbray, England.
16. Jamón Ibérico with a glass of Tío Pepe, Jerez, Spain.
17. Pani Ca Meusa, Palermo.
18. Balik Ekmek, Istanbul.
19. Smoked Omul and Sig on the shores of Lake Baikal, Russia.
20. Roti Canai, Penang, Malaysia.

APPENDIX D

Simon's Top Ten Worst Tastes of *Eat My Globe*

It wasn't all good eating as I headed around the world; there was plenty of challenging and plain odd food too. I ate it so you don't have to.

1. Braised dog in Yangshuo, China.
2. Stir fried rat in Yangshuo, China.
3. Cod sperm sushi, Kyoto, Japan.
4. Mystery meat, Maputo, Mozambique.
5. Fermented mare's milk, Mongolia.
6. Harkl, rotten shark meat, Reykjavik, Iceland.
7. Deep-fried, breaded banana, Castletownbere, Ireland.
8. Arcaraje fried in dênde oil, Salvador, Brazil.
9. Dim sim in Melbourne, Australia.
10. Camel meat, Casablanca, Morocco.

APPENDIX E

Simon's Top Ten Snacks and Stuff Between Bread

1. Juanbing, a pancake filled with dried chicken, fried dough, chili, egg and sesame seeds in Beijing.
2. Mutton kebabs at Bademia Mumbai.
3. Boerwors in Cape Town.
4. Hot dog at Hot Doug's, Chicago.
5. Weisswurst in Munich.
6. Mrs King's Pork Pie, Melton Mowbray, England.
7. Pani Ca Meusa, the lung and spleen sandwich of Palermo.
8. Balik Ekmek, the mackerel sandwich served under The Galata Bridge, Istanbul.
9. Roti Canai, the breakfast snack in Penang, Malaysia.
10. Tripe taco in Guadalajara.

APPENDIX F

Simon's Top Ten Travel Tips

1. Invest in a good rucksack. Big Red was so much more than a suitcase. It was a seat, a self-defense weapon, and, on more than one occasion, a rudimentary bed.
2. Likewise, make sure you have strong walking boots. Even if all you are doing is sightseeing, the miles soon add up, and normal shoes or sneakers just don't hack it.
3. There is no need to travel with a library full of guidebooks. Most airports have at least one decent bookstore to buy a guide to your next destination. Always leave your guidebooks behind for someone else to benefit from. I picked up at least one extra guide in every hostel and bed-and-breakfast I stayed in and always left mine behind.
4. Pack smartly. Just because you are in Senegal, doesn't mean you can't buy toothpaste. However, decent razors are very hard to find, so take plenty of blades with you.
5. Don't be afraid of restaurants, stalls, and bars in foreign lands just because you don't know the system for ordering or understand the menu. Not once on the whole journey did anyone jab me with an electrical cattle prod saying, "Get out of my restaurant." If in doubt, point at something interesting someone else is eating and motion for the same. The worst that can happen is that you end up eating cod sperm sushi, like I did in Kyoto.

6. Crime is a genuine problem, particularly in countries where poverty is rife. However, if you let fear stop you from interacting with locals you will miss out on some of the great experiences of travel. Be sensible, don't carry more money or valuables than you have to, and seek local advice on areas to avoid.

7. Street food isn't always the best food, and just because the locals can eat from a stall without apparent fear does not mean that you can do the same without expecting a bout of furious vomiting. Look for stalls that are busy and are cooking fresh to order and take your food in paper rather than on plates, which are invariably washed in the same water all day.

8. Always carry at least two photocopies of your passport with you (including any visas). In most developing countries, the local police can demand to see it at any time and, if they get their hands on your real passport, you will have to pay a huge fine just to get it back, even if you have done nothing wrong. They may complain when you hand them the copy, but there is nothing they can do about it.

9. Always reconfirm your onward and return flights. In developing countries, flights are subject to regular changes and, while these may often only be a few hours, sometimes they can involve an extra overnight stay.

10. Always ask permission before taking photographs; people are leading ordinary lives, not working in a theme park. However, once they can see your enthusiasm for them, their food, and their country is genuine, then you will find it will be reciprocated. Some of my most memorable experiences happened when I made the effort to meet the locals.

ACKNOWLEDGMENTS

If I were to thank everyone who was of help before, during, and after my journey, this section would be longer than the book itself, so I hope that those mentioned in these pages will accept that as my sincere appreciation of all they did to make *Eat My Globe* such a special experience. It would not have happened without them

In the United Kingdom, I would like to thank my agent, Euan Thorneycroft and all at AM Heath for helping to turn an idea from a proposal into a book, and all at John Murray for their support and enthusiasm.

In the United States, I would like to offer much appreciation to my publishers, The Free Press, and particularly to Leslie Meredith and Donna Loffredo, whose pictures should both appear in the dictionary under the word *professional*. The value of their support along the way cannot be overestimated. Any factual errors in these pages are mine, not theirs.

Many people have provided support along the way. I would like to offer particular thanks to Anthony Bourdain for a supportive quote and Jay Rayner for offering the sage advice that only someone with his level of success can give. Sybil Villanueva was the first person I trusted to read the manuscript, and all her suggestions were spot on. Sarah Giles and Kirsty Jones all kept my spirits high with regular e-mails, and Paul Smith brought me back down to earth and reintroduced me to the fine phrase "mardy old sod," which I plan to use regularly from now on.

Finally, and, if the others will forgive me, most important of all, my thanks go out to the clan Majumdar, to Baba, Robin, and Jeremy, to Auriel and Matt, and to Evan Arthur and Biba Florence, who are already proving that the apples have not fallen very far from the tree.

ABOUT THE AUTHOR

Originally from the North of England, the product of a fiery Welsh nurse mother and distinguished Bengali physician father, who instilled in him and his siblings their own obsessiveness with food, Simon Majumdar moved to London in 1982, where he immediately became enthralled by the burgeoning restaurant scene which was sweeping the capital. From that day to this, he has been spending all his money on meals in London and around the world, which probably explains why he is single and has no children.

His food Web site, Dos Hermanos (www.doshermanos .co.uk), written with his older brother, Robin, rapidly became one of the most widely read food Web sites in the United Kingdom and was deemed, in 2007, by the *Independent* newspaper, number ten in their top fifty world food Web sites. His blog of his travels, eatmyglobe.blogspot .com, is also enormously popular. *Eat My Globe* has interest from UK television. He is also a regular contributor to the The Times Online, The Guardian Word of Mouth, the Lifestyle Channel of www.tiscali.co.uk, one of the largest broadband providers in the United Kingdom, and www .AskMen.com. In 2008, he was named one of the thousand most influential people in London by the *London Evening Standard*.